Your Towns and Cities

Tunbridge Wells
in the Great War

'A shell up-rooted a tree, which pinned three or four of my comrades to the bottom of the trench. Before any of us could get to their assistance a second shell burst, completely burying the unfortunate men in mud. Any attempt to extricate them was hopeless and they died a dreadful death."

Private Horace Le Breton – March 1915

Your Towns and Cities in the Great War

Tunbridge Wells
in the Great War

Stephen Wynn

Pen & Sword
MILITARY

First published in Great Britain in 2016 by
PEN & SWORD MILITARY
an imprint of
Pen and Sword Books Ltd
47 Church Street
Barnsley
South Yorkshire S70 2AS

ISBN 978 1 47383 364 7

Printed and bound in England
by CPI Group (UK) Ltd, Croydon, CR0 4YY

Typeset in Times New Roman by Chic Graphics

Pen & Sword Books Ltd incorporates the imprints of
Pen & Sword Archaeology, Atlas, Aviation, Battleground, Discovery,
Family History, History, Maritime, Military, Naval, Politics, Railways,
Select, Social History, Transport, True Crime, Claymore Press,
Frontline Books, Leo Cooper, Praetorian Press, Remember When,
Seaforth Publishing and Wharncliffe.

For a complete list of Pen and Sword titles please contact
Pen and Sword Books Limited
47 Church Street, Barnsley, South Yorkshire, S70 2AS, England
E-mail: enquiries@pen-and-sword.co.uk
Website: www.pen-and-sword.co.uk

Contents

About the Author

Stephen is a happily retired police officer having served with Essex Police as a constable for thirty years between 1983 and 2013. He is married to Tanya. His two sons, Luke and Ross, were members of the armed forces, collectively having served five tours of Afghanistan between 2008 and 2013. Both of them were injured on their first tours which led to the publication of his first book; *Two Sons in a Warzone – Afghanistan: The True Story of a Father's Conflict*, which was published in October 2010 by Clairview Books. His teenage daughter, Aimee, is still at school. Both of his grandfathers survived the First World War, one with the Royal Irish Rifles, the other in the Mercantile Navy.

Stephen co-wrote a book published in August 2012, entitled *German POW Camp 266 – Langdon Hills* (UKUnpublished Ltd) and has co-written three crime thrillers which were published between 2010 and 2012. He has also written other books for Pen & Sword Books, many of which are part of the Towns and Cities collection, which commemorate the sacrifices made by young men during the First World War.

Acknowledgements

Researching a book of this nature would not have been possible without the assistance of certain individuals and organisations. I would like to express my appreciation to the following: Andrew Pratley, for his research on Kent men who served in the Australian Army; Susan Featherstone and Susan Schibli for their photographs of Tunbridge Wells-related monuments; St Matthews Church for the photograph of the Memorial Tablet to those lost on HMS *Hythe*; St John's Church for the photograph of their Roll of Honour. I would also like to thank my wife Tanya, for her continued support, help and consideration.

Every effort has been made to identify and acknowledge the copyright holders of the photographs and documents that have been used.

Prologue
Pre-War Tunbridge Wells

Tunbridge Wells, given the prefix 'Royal' by King Edward Vll in 1909 dates back to Roman times. In 1606, Dudley, 3rd Baron North, discovered the chalybeate spring waters at The Pantiles which would ultimately make both him and the town famous. The town grew in popularity mainly due to the wells. People were drawn to the area to wonder at the claimed medicinal qualities of the spa's waters. Everybody came, including members of the Royal Family. With such

Grove Road, Tunbridge Wells. Pre-war photograph. (Unknown photograper)

Soldiers marching through Tunbridge Wells. (Unknown photographer)

distinguished patronage it was decided that the town needed a church, so the Church of King Charles the Martyr was built in 1676, becoming the first permanent brick built structure in the town. Services at the Church were reliant on visiting ministers until 1709.

Around 1750 Dr Richard Russell wrote a paper on the benefits of bathing in and drinking sea water as a possible cure for enlarged lymphatic glands. Then, in the early 1830s, the Church was visited by Princess Victoria and her mother, the Duchess of Kent. By now the town was the place to be for the more well off members of society and not just for a holiday or daytrip; they were making Tunbridge Wells their home.

In 1842 a new bus service meant the town could be reached from London within two hours. Three years later the railway followed, making it an even more accessible location. The town's affluence and population kept on growing and in 1889 Tunbridge Wells became a Borough.

During the First World War Tunbridge Wells had a significant military presence which continued throughout the war, with numerous regiments stationed in the town before going off to fight on the Western Front.

Tunbridge Wells would pay a high price in the number of its own young men that it lost during the war. Out of the nearly 3,000 who went off to fight, 801 would never return.

During the early years of the twentieth century, it was only the more affluent members of society who had the opportunity or money to go away on holiday to any destination, let alone one in a foreign country. On Saturday 1 August 1914, just three days before the outbreak of the First World War, Dr Claude Wilson, of Church Road, Tunbridge Wells, along with his wife and a female friend of theirs, found themselves in Lucerne, Switzerland.

Although the possibility of war had been hanging in the air for weeks, people were still holidaying in locations all over Europe as if oblivious to the potential danger they were in. Dr Wilson thankfully was not such an individual. He acquired train tickets to take them from Lucerne to Basle, with the intention of travelling on to Boulogne, which would have resulted in their arriving in Folkestone the same evening. The train arrived in Basle on time but that was when their problems began. Even though Britain had yet to declare war on Germany, and would not do so for another three days, the German army was already making its way through Belgium to get to France. Having arrived in Basle, Dr Wilson discovered that both the French and German borders were closed, which blocked his route to the Channel ports.

Basle was packed with many travellers who had found themselves in a similar situation and were unable to find a bed for the night, such was the unexpected influx of people. Confusion reigned as to how they could continue their journey. Eventually they managed to get a train bound for Paris; one of its stops was at Delle, on the French side of the border with Switzerland. The train arrived there at two o'clock in the afternoon of Saturday 1 August 1914, but rather than being just a scheduled stop on the journey to Paris, it was to be the end of the line and all the passengers had to leave the train. Another train arrived, but en route it was diverted to Nancy for military reasons (this was where the first big battle of the war was originally expected to take place). The journey to Nancy was long with numerous delays along the way, the train finally pulling in at twenty to eleven that evening. Once again, it was to be the end of the line.

Nancy was to prove somewhat of a nightmare. The station was

packed with French soldiers waiting to go to war with their German foes. Hotels, food and restaurants had been commandeered by the French military, making them unavailable to tired and weary civilians, who wanted nothing more than to return to the safety of their own homes as quickly as possible. It would have been a traumatic and stressful enough journey to have undertaken on his own, but Wilson had to worry about the ladies and their luggage. Just as it seemed all hope had gone and they were to be stuck in Nancy indefinitely, a train arrived which was going to Chalons and as it was closer to the coast they decided to get on it. It was packed solid, mainly with military personnel, most of whom got off at Toul, where there was a fortress. The journey between Nancy and Chalons usually took no longer than two and a half hours, but on this occasion it took nearly ten as the train was either travelling at a snail's pace or stopping completely, to allow troop-carrying trains through to the Front.

Along the track there were soldiers with bayonets fixed, every fifty yards or so and even more when the train crossed over a bridge. Every station was crowded with soldiers waiting to catch a train. The Wilsons finally arrived at Chalons at eight o'clock on Sunday morning. There were some sixty locomotives there on four sets of lines waiting to be coupled up to trains, full of troops. Initially the Wilsons were told to get off the train when it arrived but no sooner had they done so than they were told to get back on, as the train was now going to Paris. Having lost their previous seats they had to make do with what they could get, which was to be their suitcases in one of the crowded corridors. The train arrived in Paris at twelve noon on Sunday, the end of a journey which would, under normal conditions, have taken no more than twelve hours; on this occasion it had taken more than twenty-six.

The journey from Paris to Boulogne was a fairly uneventful one, but getting on the boat to England was not as straightforward. Its capacity was 500 passengers, but, given the circumstances, the crew managed to cram 1,100 people on board. To accommodate such an increase in numbers, no luggage was allowed other than what individuals could sensibly carry. What they could not had to be left behind. Somebody in France must have made a lot of money from all of those suitcases and their contents. To make matters worse, the journey was not the smoothest of crossings, which on a greatly overloaded ship, must have had its moments.

The Wilsons arrived at Folkestone at nine o'clock on Sunday evening, only to find that there were no trains running and no available accommodation; not ideal after a journey that had lasted for nearly two days, with little food or water and no opportunity to wash or change their clothes. Not to be beaten, Dr Wilson managed to acquire a car so that he could drive the three of them back home to Tunbridge Wells, where they finally arrived, tired, hungry and cold, at two o'clock on Monday morning, their epic adventure finally and thankfully at an end.

CHAPTER 1

1914
Eager for a Fight

Between 4 August and 31 December 1914, there were, according to figures compiled by the Commonwealth War Graves Commission, a total of 36,934 British and Commonwealth servicemen killed. Before we start looking at the events and the men who helped shape Tunbridge Wells' involvement in the First World War, it is useful to take a brief chronological look at some of the events which took place immediately before the outbreak of the war as well as those from the early months of the fighting:

28 June – The assassination of Archduke Franz Ferdinand, by Serbian activists, takes place in Sarajevo. This is the trigger for the outbreak of the First World War.

28 July – In response to Archduke Franz Ferdinand's assassination, Austria-Hungary declare war on Serbia.

1 August – Germany declares war on Russia and demands France's neutrality. France refuses and mobilizes her troops.

3 August – Germany declares war on France, an ally of Russia.

4 August – Germany invades Belgium to attack

Arch Duke Franz Ferdinand. (Unknown photographer)

France as part of the Schlieffen Plan. When Germany refuses to remove her troops from Belgian soil, Britain declares war on Germany.

5-12 September – The first battle of the Marne, with the British and French pitted against German forces. The battle is in effect made up of three smaller battles at Ourcq, Deux Morins and Saint-Gond Marshes. Even though it is known that some two million men collectively fight in the battle, casualty figures vary. One estimate suggests a total of 500,000 casualties with both sides losing approximately 250,000 men.

12-15 September – The first battle of the Aisne is an Allied offensive against the German First and Second Armies as they retreat after the first battle of the Marne.

15 September – Trenches first appear on the Western Front during fighting in the vicinity of Chemin des Dames in France, after British and German troops reach somewhat of an impasse when both refuse to retreat from the positions they hold.

19 October–22 November – The first battle of Ypres involves French, Belgian, and British troops fighting the might of the German Army.

8 December – The battle of the Falkland Islands, a victory by the British Royal Navy over the German Imperial Navy.

21 December – First German air raid on London.

25 December – Christmas Day truce in No Man's Land.

Newspapers are an invaluable source of information for the First World War; they tend to be broadsheets consisting of a dozen or so pages. Filling them took a lot of articles which made them very detailed and extremely helpful to future generations. Rumours would have been rife about what was going on, especially with the Defence of the Realm Act restricting certain aspects of the war from being reported

With the war only three days old, the *Kent & Sussex Courier* for Friday 7 August, not surprisingly carried numerous articles about it.

Movements of Local Territorials
Civic Farewell to the Rifles

'The 4th Battalion (Infantry Rifles) of the Royal West Kent Regiment were due to arrive back from Aldershot on Tuesday at 9am, but so great was the pressure of railway traffic, owing to the war, that it was 6am on Wednesday before they set foot in Tunbridge Wells. They arrived tired and dusty, after several hours waiting. Others didn't return for years and when they did, they weren't the same. The war had changed them forever, with the horrors of what they had witnessed haunting them for the rest of their lives.

'They were dismissed on reaching the Drill Hall in Victoria Road, and ordered to re-assemble at noon for orders and the civic farewell. They paraded at full strength, 274 strong, under Captain Cheale, Captain Kelsey and Lieutenants Stone, Pardington and Bourne.

'A dense crowd filled Victoria Road in the vicinity of the Drill Hall, chiefly composed of relatives and friends who had come to bid the "Terriers" "God speed," and many affecting farewells were seen outside the fateful red brick building. The crowds extended all up Camden Road to the cross roads, for it was fully expected that the Rifles would march to the station at once.

'Inside all was bustle and preparation. Kits had to be inspected, rifles and other accoutrements cleaned, while most of the men had little luxuries, such as bananas and sandwiches, brought by fond relatives, to pack away in their kit bags.'

The 4th West Kents finally left Tunbridge Wells at 9pm on the Wednesday evening, en route for Dartford. The battalion remained in England until 30 October 1914 when they were moved to India, where they remained for the rest of the war. On arriving in Bombay they became part of the Jubbulpore Brigade which was part of the 5th (Mhow) Division of the Indian Army. Twenty-three of them unfortunately never returned.

The call to the Scouts

'General Sir Baden Powell has asked the County Commissioner for Kent whether the county would supply one thousand Boy Scouts if required to guard culverts and telegraphs against spies, to run despatches, and carry out other suitable duties.

'The response from the Scouts of the county has been

unanimous, and the members of the various troops are keeping in touch with the authorities by reporting themselves at frequent intervals. The Tunbridge Wells Scouts are reporting themselves twice a day at their various headquarters.'

55 Horses Entrained

'This morning at 2am 55 horses were entrained at the South Eastern Station for Shorncliffe. They had been obtained for the Expeditionary Force by Mr Rupert Nevill and Lord Henry Nevill, who are the purchasing officers on behalf of the War Office for Area No. 7, which includes this district. Twenty-five were subsidised horses belonging to Mr Cundell. The remainder included some valuable horses patriotically parted with by their owners at low prices, one of them was Georgina, the well-known racer, formerly owned by Mr Wild of Hungershall Park.'

Local men's adventures in France
An anxious time

'Two Tunbridge Wells men, Messrs J Jefferies and A Blakeman had a rather exciting and anxious time on the continent during the weekend. They left Tunbridge Wells on Saturday for Paris, having no misgivings as to the international war peril, but on arrival in "The Gay City", the irony of that term now, found themselves in a somewhat awkward fix. They put in their appearance at a hotel kept by a German, where they had engaged rooms. The proprietor had to hurriedly leave the hotel, owing to the outbreak of war, and it is stated that the premises were searched. On Monday morning the voyagers, after experiencing some difficulty in obtaining permission to get their luggage from the hotel, managed to find seats in a military train, and to get away from the excited city. They arrived in Dieppe some hours later, and there joined several hundred other English tourists. The last boat had left the port absolutely crowded, but the British Consul cabled to Newhaven for another boat. In due course a steamer arrived, and it was quickly packed with English holiday makers, and others anxious to speedily renew acquaintance with the Homeland. The journey of about three hours across the Channel was made in perfect safety, but the boat was held up for a few minutes outside Newhaven, after searchlights had been directed upon it for some time, while inquiries were made.'

Why either man would have wanted to go to Paris on holiday at such a time, just three days before the outbreak of a war, when its imminence would have been blatantly apparent, is unclear, but it was certainly going to be a holiday that neither man would forget.

The *Kent & Sussex Courier* for Friday 14 August contained quite a few articles to do with the war.

Red Cross Preparations

'The various Tunbridge Wells and District Voluntary Aid Detachments of the British Red Cross Society are rallying with all that alacrity and enthusiasm which has always characterised the work of the Society in this district. Depots have been established for all districts, and the residents are splendidly supporting the movement with offers of hospital accommodation if needed. All the equipment necessary is being collected, and there is no doubt that should the need arise the various VAD's of this district will be ready to play their part "to the last letter".'

Red Cross VAD nurses. (Unknown photographer)

'The various Commandants would be glad to have the names of trained nurses who would give their services if required, and also the names of ladies willing to act as cooks at the various hospitals when established.

'The Tunbridge Wells Borough Detachments, on receipt of the orders to prepare for mobilization, immediately took steps to cope with all situations that are likely to arise. It is fortunate that the crisis has found these two detachments in a high state of efficiency.'

Being so close to the south coast where wounded troops returning from France could be landed anywhere from Dover to Portsmouth, potentially in very large numbers, preparation on such a scale was all-important, especially with Tunbridge Wells being one of the main line railway stations. It was clear that most people wanted to do their bit. Large empty houses were being offered by their owners to be used as hospitals. Car and van owners who were happy to supply their vehicles for use in medical emergencies or for transporting wounded servicemen, were being encouraged to register their names with their local VAD. Doctors in the town were more than happy to offer their services to the detachment as well.

This was one of the postcards that were available in the town for soldiers who were stationed there, to send to their loved ones. The sending and receiving of letters was an integral part of the war for most people. A soldier sitting in his trench, cold, wet, hungry and tired, would be re-invigorated through the simplicity of holding and reading a letter from his loved one back home. For those left at home who could only hope and pray that their husband, son, brother, uncle or nephew, would stay safe and one day soon return, receiving a letter or

A postcard of the day.

I'm sending you a P. C. for your collection from TUNBRIDGE WELLS postcard from the Front was a palpable relief. When a man went off to fight it was not just for six months at a time; there were no telephone facilities allowing soldiers to phone home In some cases men simply never came back.

There was an interesting article in the *Kent & Sussex Courier* on Friday 21 August about the proposed forming of a local military corps for Tunbridge Wells. The interest was such that Colonel Sydney Sladen wrote a letter to the Secretary of State for War dated Thursday 13 August 1914, offering to form a local corps consisting of gentlemen, tradesmen and their assistants, who because of business commitments, being over age or physical incapacitation were unable to enlist in either the Regular Army or Territorial Units. The forming of a home based corps would no doubt have provided a feeling of well-being in the knowledge that by being a member of such a corps, they were still doing their bit for their King and country as well as the war effort in general. The reply from the War Office was as follows;

'Sir,
With reference to your letter of the 13th inst. proposing to form a local corps, I am commanded by the Army Council to express their sincere thanks for your generous and patriotic proposal. The Army Council are however of the opinion that all the energies of the country should at present be directed to the raising of the New Army of 100,000 men, and they regret that until this has been accomplished they are unable to avail themselves of the proposal.
B B Cubitt.'

One of the problems with raising such forms of civil corps was that they were not officially recognised militarily across Europe. This meant that as they were not soldiers, any actions which they took which resulted in the wounding or death of foreign troops could technically have been classed as attempted murder or murder. Armed civilians subsequently captured by the Germans would not have been afforded the same rights as captured soldiers; instead they would no doubt have been shot. There was also the issue that the War Office strongly discouraged any unofficial organisations from drilling, especially in the case of men under the age of thirty-five, who it felt should be enlisting in either the Regular Army or the Territorial Force. There was a desire amongst some of the town's men to form a 'Town Guard' and with this in mind they assembled at the town's Drill Hall in Victoria Road on Wednesday 19 August. There they were met by Colour Sergeant Instructor Callaghan to be informed that he had received a message from the Army Authorities that they would not be allowed to use the Hall for either drill practice or shooting.

This particular letter was not sent from the Front, but 'just down the road' in Canterbury. It was sent by Captain A R Cheale of the 4th Battalion, Royal West Kent Regiment and was sent to the *Kent & Sussex Courier* and was printed in their edition of Friday 28 August.

'The Kings School
Canterbury, Aug. 24th, 1914.
To the Editor
Dear Sir,
I shall be grateful if you will allow me, through the medium of your columns, to thank the many inhabitants of Tunbridge Wells who have been kind enough to forward me parcels of underclothing, soap, towels, fruit, vegetables, etc. for distribution among the men of the two Companies of the 4th Batt. The Queens Own (Royal West Kent Regiment) associated with the town.

'I assure you sir that the thoughtfulness of our townsfolk is deeply appreciated by all concerned, and by no one more than Captain Kelsey and myself. A large consignment, including nearly a hundred pairs of woollen socks, flannel shirts, fruit, vegetables, etc, was brought down to us by ex-Colour Sergeant Callaghan, who has worked so assiduously on behalf of the men since our departure from Tunbridge Wells on Saturday, while other parcels have been forwarded direct to me at Canterbury.

'While I am extremely grateful for the many gifts that have been sent, I shall be glad if you will allow me to point out to your readers that at the present moment one of the men's most pressing needs is green vegetables, owing to the fact that for the past four weeks they have had to be content with a diet from which fresh vegetables have been entirely absent.

'Again expressing my appreciation of the kindness of our many friends in Tunbridge Wells.

I remain Yours faithfully

A R Cheale (Captain)

4th R W Kent Regiment.'

Gunner Walter William Marchant of the 35th Battery, Royal Garrison Artillery, had been in the army for many years before the war began and at the outbreak of hostilities was still on the Army Reserve list. At the time of his death he was 26 years of age, a married man with four children. He was born and grew up in Tunbridge Wells, attending King Charles School. His parents, Mr and Mrs Marchant, lived at Little Mount Sion, Tunbridge Wells.

A good friend and colleague of Walter's was Lance Corporal Copsey, who was with him when he was killed. On his return to England he wrote a letter to the *Kent & Sussex Courier* which was published in their edition of Friday 20 November.

'Lance Corporal Copsey of St John's, Tunbridge Wells writes;
'I am still keeping A1. Really it is the mercy of Providence that I am able to sit and write this letter because since I last wrote I have seen a sight that I hope never to see again. It was like this. The headquarters were billeted at a large Chateau, which was used as a reporting centre for everybody. We had been there all morning, but things got so hot that at 12 o'clock we had orders to move. We were on the point of going when two awful "coal-boxes" dropped right among us. After pulling myself together I looked around and what met my eyes I cannot describe. Poor Wally Marchant, my chum. It really broke my heart. I had not left him two minutes when it happened. Poor old Wally was buried in the chateau. He was a favourite with everyone. I am still among the "coal-boxes" and "Jack Johnsons", but hope to be among the Germans before long.'

Private Selwyn Smith, who was the grandson of the late Reverend J Smith, the first Pastor of the Baptist Tabernacle Church in Tunbridge

Wells, had been taken prisoner by the Germans.. He wrote the following letter to his parents on 16 October, but which they didn't receive until 9 November.

'My Darling Mother & Father,
'Have been captured by the Germans in Antwerp, and have been sent here near Berlin. We are being treated well, only have nothing left except what we stand up in, so that anything in underclothing, washing and wearing apparel, will be very welcome. You can send anything absolutely free, and also write as often as you like, but do not mention the war. I am quite well, and came through the siege without a scratch, although we lost a lot of men. Was in the firing line the whole while. Please write as often as you possibly can as we have nothing to read. Don't know how long we shall be here, but in any case don't worry, as I am quite alright. Please also send some cigarettes and tobacco. Don't forget you can send everything quite free. Don't forget the warm underclothing, gloves etc. as it is very cold here, and will be much colder. Have not had a wash or shave since we left England, the day you came to Canterbury. Do hope you have not worried about me too much and don't forget I am always thinking about you.'

The following article appeared in the *Kent & Sussex Courier* dated Friday 20 November and came from the brother of a man serving at the front.

'Mr Blundell, of Tunbridge Wells, has now received a letter from his brother, Private B Blundell, of the Royal Sussex Regiment, confirming the news that he has been wounded again. He was first wounded eleven weeks ago at the Battle of the Aisne and on being discharged from the Base Hospital re-joined his regiment, and was in the fighting at Ypres. The appearance of his name in the casualty list, was the first intimation his relatives had, and it was thought a mistake. It is now confirmed that he is again wounded, and is in hospital at Boulogne, from whence he writes very cheerfully, and hopes that he will soon be among the Germans again. He adds that at the Front they want to know when more men are coming from England to help them.'

Tunbridge Wells VAD

'The Tunbridge Wells (Kent 94) Detachment have established their headquarters at the Calverley Terrace, where Mr E Vaughan Gower has placed at their disposal an office room, a telephone, and a typewriter. Miss V M Moore (Commandant) and Miss Barratt (Acting Quartermaster) are in charge of the arrangements. Hospital accommodation has been placed at the disposal of Kent 94, and also an empty house has been offered them to turn into a convalescent home if needed. Lord Amherst has placed 'Hillside' at the disposal of the Tunbridge Wells members, and Miss Sawle has offered the Torrington House Nursing Home fully equipped.'

There were also other nearby VADs. There was the Eridge and Broadwater Down Detachment (Sussex 92), which had number 9

Postcard of a VAD nurse and patient.

Broadwater Down as their headquarters, lent to them by the owner, Mr F Bomert. The Detachment's Commandant was Mrs Stune, with Mrs Cleeve as the Quartermaster.

The Pembury, Matfield and Brenchley VAD (Kent 18) had Dr Crawford as their Commandant. It was truly amazing just how quickly all of the local VADs had pulled together in an extremely professional and proficient manner and also had mobilized so quickly after the outbreak of war.

A postcard was a nice way of letting VAD nurses know just how much their efforts were appreciated by all concerned, especially the wounded soldiers who they looked after and cared for.

The *Kent & Sussex Courier* newspaper dated Friday 21 August carried an article about the extremely low numbers of young men from Tunbridge Wells who had responded to Lord Kitchener's appeal to enlist in the Army.

Tunbridge Wells War Items

'The response of the manhood of Tunbridge Wells to Lord Kitchener's appeal is up to the present, very disappointing. At eight o'clock last evening, only two men who were not already soldiers had applied for enlistment in Lord Kitchener's force. The second of these only gave in his name last night, and has not yet passed the medical examination. Those who have enlisted in the Territorials have not volunteered for service at the front, and therefore do not share in the response of the country to Lord Kitchener's appeal. The disappointing local response to the appeal is somewhat mitigated by the fact that 42 time expired soldiers in Tunbridge Wells have joined Kitchener's Army, while since the local

An early recruiting poster.

Territorials departed, 88 more local men have signed for this branch of the service, thus leaving only half a dozen vacancies to be filled. The Cyclists and Yeomanry are already up to full strength. It is not the Territorials that now urgently need recruits, but Lord Kitchener's Army, and now that this point is clear we trust that the young men of Tunbridge Wells will redeem the credit of the town by a fair proportion of recruits for that branch of the service in which men are most needed.'

Although the young men of Tunbridge Wells would not have known this at the time, they were urgently needed in Kitchener's New Army, as during the first two weeks of the war Britain had already lost 20,000 men

With the war just two days old, the Royal Navy lost one of her light cruisers, HMS *Amphion*, on 6 August, when it struck a mine in the North Sea and sunk, with the loss of 149 of its crew. Mercifully, 160 of them survived.

HMS Amphion.

The following article appeared in the same edition of the newspaper.

'The full story of the loss of HMS *Amphion*, published yesterday, will thrill all British hearts. We are proud in Tunbridge Wells that a local man represented us among those who in perfect courage and discipline paraded calmly on the deck of their sinking ship. They will be remembered with the heroes of the *Birkenhead*. And to the eternal disgrace of Germans, it will be remembered that the mines which sunk the *Amphion* were laid before the declaration of war.'

The same day, the newspaper carried the following article.

Proposed Tunbridge Wells Town Corps

'Efforts have recently been made, in accordance with the request of many residents in Tunbridge Wells, to form a local military corps. Colonel Sydney Sladen, Colonel L A White, and Colonel A T Simpson, on the receipt of over 20 signatures for enrolment in such a corps, if formed, held a consultation, as the result of which a letter signed by Colonel Sladen was sent to the Secretary of State for War on August 13th (Thursday of last week). The letter concerned the formation of a local corps consisting of gentlemen, tradesmen and their assistants, who from ties of business, over age or incapacity for prolonged exertion, are unable to undertake obligatory duties (the majority of these are ineligible to enter Classes 1 or 2 of the National Reserve). The letter went on to state that "This application is made on the understanding that there will be no cost to the government, but in the event of the corps being unable to obtain rifles and belts, the Government would be asked to help the Corps to obtain these or grant the loan of the same. I enclose a list of the names of a few of those now ready and desirous of at once joining, and I am sure I could obtain another two hundred names.'

The expenses of the corps, if formed, were to be covered by subscriptions. The reply from the War Office was as appended;

'Sir, With reference to your letter of the 13th inst. proposing to form a local corps, I am commanded by the Army Council to express their sincere thanks for your generous and patriotic proposal. The Army Council are, however, of the opinion that all the energies of the country should at present be directed to the raising of the New Army of 100,000 men, and they regret that until this has been accomplished they are unable to avail themselves of the proposal.

'The war office is discouraging the formation of town guards or any new military corps whatever, at all events, until Lord Kitchener's new Army has been raised to its full establishment.

'The War Office has no objection to the formation of clubs

for rifle practice, or any similar organisations, but the objections to all forms of civil corps is that they are recognised in modern European warfare. Any steps they might take would be technically regarded as murder or attempted murder, and all armed civilians, whether organised or not, would if captured by the Germans, be summarily shot.'

What actual purpose such a proposed corps would have had was unclear. Some would say it was simply a patriotic gesture by some of those who, through age, commitments or infirmity, were unable to enlist in either the Territorials or the Regular Army, but still wanted to feel that they had done their bit for their King and country. Others would say that for the ones who carried with them no incapacitating ailments or were too aged, then it was no more than a subtle attempt at having a local corps officially recognised by the War Office, so that they could avoid having to enlist in either the Territorial or regular Armies but after the war was over, still claim that they had done their bit.

The *Kent & Sussex Courier* dated Friday 28 August contained an article about Special Constables.

Special Constables

'The Tonbridge Rural Parish Council have appointed 41 men to act as Special Constables, for the purposes of watching the railway and the telegraph wires in the parish which extends from Hawkenbury, Tunbridge Wells, to Hayesden, Tonbridge.

'Estate owners have acted patriotically in allowing their men to act as Special Constables, and agreeing to pay their wages while so engaged. Among those who have assisted in this way are Mr Love, of Pembury Grange; Mr Smith of Colebrook; and Mr O E d'Avigdor-Goldsmid, of Somerhill.'

The Special Constables would have been looked after and trained by experienced Police officers such as Sergeant Luck.

Sergeant Walter Luck –
Tunbridge Wells Police.
(Postcard)

'Mr W J Gane, who is the Chairman of the Parish Council, is the head of the Committee which has been appointed to superintend the movements of the Special Constables.'

The *Kent & Sussex Courier* dated Friday 4 September 1914 contained an article about the towns Voluntary Service Bureau.

The Voluntary Service Bureau

'This bureau, which is working at 2 Calverley Parade, Tunbridge Wells, in conjunction with the War Office, has now been running for over a fortnight in charge of Colonel Macpherson and Mr N P Edwards. During this time much useful work has been accomplished. A large number of offers of help of all kinds have been received and sorted off to the most likely quarters where such help can be best utilised to the public advantage. All day there has been a steady stream of callers; one man wants information about joining Kitchener's Army; the next, as a special constable; while the next offers money to pay for the expense of meetings to assist recruiting, or for Belgian relief. Then there are ladies who call with offers of hospitality to Belgian refugees; to make shirts for the wounded, or to act as nurses or teach invalid cooking. While the bureau does not profess to be a living encyclopaedia, a very considerable amount of information has been got together which callers would find a difficulty in obtaining through any other medium. Already a large number of recruits have been obtained for Kitchener's Army, and the bureau is being made in to a centre for the organisation of meetings for assisting recruiting throughout the country, as it has a large number of trained speakers working in conjunction with it.'

The initial surprise at men from Tunbridge Wells being slow to enlist in to Kitchener's Army, had apparently dissipated somewhat within a month of the outbreak of war, with the *Kent & Sussex Courier* of 11 September reporting the following.

Tunbridge Wells lads For Kitchener's Army
Enthusiastic Farewell Scenes
Address by the Mayor

'Tunbridge Wells gave a fitting send off on Wednesday to 78 of her brave sons who have volunteered for Kitchener's new Army. They formed the bulk of a local company for professional and business men, clerks, shop-assistants, etc. destined to be attached to the 7th Battalion of the Royal West Kent Regiment, the new service unit to be composed entirely of Kitchener's recruits.

The genius who holds the reins at the War Office had very thoughtfully ordained that if friends enlisted en masse, and expressed their desire to serve together, matters would be arranged so that they could do so. This local company was originated, with this idea in view by Mr H E Lunn, who has worked most untiringly and unselfishly to ensure the success of the project. The result has been very gratifying.'

What was being described here was in effect what became known during the First World War as 'Pals' Battalions, so called because they came from the same communities, friends, work colleagues and neighbours, men who knew each other very well. As the war continued, 'Pals' Battalions were discontinued, because what this 'genius who holds the reins at the War Office' had totally over looked was that when men went off to fight in a war together they usually died together as well. The ferocity and horror of war had changed so much, the first day of the battle of the Somme being a prime example, where in some cases entire battalions were wiped out in a matter of seconds. When this happened it also meant that large numbers of the adult male population of the same community back home had also been wiped out, which was absolutely devastating for the post war population. The article continued.

'Men of just the right stamp came forward rapidly, and at the time of departure on Wednesday Mr Lunn said that he was absolutely certain of bringing the strength of the company up to a hundred within a day or two. The 78 included 15 Corporation employees, ten from the Town Hall and five from the Electricity Department. The town bade farewell to this fine body of men outside the Town Hall. The Mayor, Councillor Emson, ably expressed the town's pride at their response to the county's call.'

There was a very interesting article in the *Kent & Sussex Courier* on Friday 16 October, which highlighted how attitudes have changed over the years.

'The suggestion to the Tunbridge Wells Town Council that female Police constables should be appointed during the sojourn of the military here has been capped by a still more remarkable proposal, which came before the Sevenoaks District Council on Tuesday in the shape of a resolution from the Church of England Men's Society, that steps should be taken to keep females indoors after 8.30pm during the presence of Territorials in Sevenoaks. The General Purposes Committee reported that they had considered the resolution, and recommended that no action be taken, to which the Council agreed.'

During the early days of the First World War, which involved German troops making their way across Belgium, hundreds of thousands of Belgians fled their country, rather than wait and see what their fate would be. Britain felt a responsibility towards Belgium, especially as Britain had declared war on Germany in defence of Belgium's sovereignty. During the course of the war a quarter of a million Belgian refugees sought and were given a safe haven in Britain. In the first few weeks of the war alone, more than 60,000 arrived in Kent at Folkestone. Some of these ended up in Tunbridge Wells, which had already set up its own Belgium Refugee Committee, so that the expected influx of Belgians coming in to the town could be dealt with more smoothly. Most of those who sat on the Committee, also happened to be prominent members of the local suffragette movement.

There was an article in the *Kent & Sussex Courier* dated Friday 16 October concerning Belgian Refugees.

Mayor's Appeal for Belgian Refugees
Tunbridge Wells Fund Opened

'The Mayor of Tunbridge Well, Mr Chas Emson, has decided to open a local fund for Belgian Refugees and has issued the following appeal: Owing to the fall of Antwerp the influx of Belgian Refugees has enormously increased during the last few days, and on Saturday evening, the 10th inst. the following telegram was received from the London War Refugees Committee:

'Many Belgian Refugees arriving; further offers of hospitality welcomed. Communicate War Refugees Committee, General Buildings, Aldwych, London. Enquiries made in Folkestone on the same date show that from 10,000 to 12,000 immigrants have to be dealt with and that many of the cases were of a most pitiable description. The need of assistance is most urgent. Offers of accommodation have already been received, but it is impossible for me to avail myself of these offers unless money supplied for the purpose, and I feel confident that an appeal to Tunbridge Wells and neighbourhood for monetary help will not be in vain. May I add that in addition to larger sums which I hope to obtain in response to my appeal, I shall be very glad to receive from any not in a position to give so freely, promises of 1s a week and upwards towards the maintenance of the families of these unfortunate people. By this means many others can extend practical sympathy to these Belgians who have been so cruelly deprived of their homes.'

The way people from Tunbridge Wells took the Belgian people to their hearts and homes and gave so readily to help their plight was a remarkable show of true human kindness. Food, money clothes and places of accommodation for the refugees were readily provided.

During the First World War, 5,242 members of the Royal Marine Light Infantry lost their lives. The first sixteen of them died when the Royal Navy ship they were on board, HMS *Amphion*, struck a mine on her way back to Harwich on 6 August. One of those who died was a 28-year-old single man, Private William Starks Vidler, who lived at home with his parents at 55 Nelson Road, Tunbridge Wells, making him the first man from the town to be killed during the war.

HMS *Amphion* was an Active-class scout cruiser that was launched on 4 December 1911 and commissioned into the Royal Navy in March 1913, becoming part of the 3rd Destroyer Flotilla with the Harwich Force which was in place to defend the eastern approaches of the

English Channel from ships of the Imperial German Navy. On 5 August 1914 ships from the 3rd Flotilla were undertaking a general patrol of their sector, specifically looking for German naval vessels. A British trawler, fishing in the vicinity, informed the Flotilla that she had earlier seen an unidentified ship 'throwing things overboard'. The trawler gave the direction in which she had seen the ship travelling and the Flotilla, led by *Amphion*, set off after the vessel. A short while later they came across the SS *Königin Luise*, which as it turned out, was a German mine-laying vessel. Before the war she had been a holiday ferry, carrying passengers from Hamburg to Holland, but with the outbreak of war she had been converted into a mine laying vessel by the Germans.

On the evening of 4 August 1914, the very day that Britain had declared war on Germany, the *Königin Luise* left her home base at Emden and set course for the North Sea, with her final destination being the Thames Estuary where she would lay her deadly cargo of mines. She was in disguise, not in the usual battleship grey that immediately indicated a naval vessel, but painted in black, buff and yellow which was synonymous with that of the Great Western Railway Company which traversed the North Sea from Harwich to the Hook of Holland. At first the true identity of the vessel or her intentions were not obvious to the Flotilla, but once she inexplicably attempted to flee from the advancing ships they had a pretty good idea that it was not anything right and proper. They gave chase and less than an hour later, the *Königin Luise* had been sunk and fifty-four of her crew of one hundred were killed. Ships of the Flotilla picked up survivors of the *Königin Luise* from the icy cold waters of the North Sea including eighteen who were taken on board the *Amphion*. The patrol carried on until the early hours of the following morning before the 3rd Flotilla started to make its way back to Harwich. On route, and just after 0630 hours, the *Amphion* unfortunately struck one of the mines that the *Königin Luise* had earlier laid. Other ships nearby took off the surviving crew members as well as the German crew who had earlier survived the sinking of the *Königin Luise*. Fortune intervened to prevent further loss of life, as just minutes after the last boatload of survivors were taken off the *Amphion,* she struck more mines and sank. As a result of the sinking, the total British losses were in the region of 150 officers and Other Ranks.

William Starks Vidler had joined the Royal Marines in 1907 when he was only seventeen years of age, so by the outbreak of war, he was already a seasoned professional, having been on board one of the British naval battleships that visited both Canada and America a few years prior to his death. He had also been part of the British Fleet, which after the Hull fishing fleet incident, followed the Russian Fleet into the Mediterranean. Sadly his life came to an end in tragic circumstances.

The Battle of Mons was notable as it was the first major action of the First World War which involved the British Expeditionary Force. They had arrived at Mons on 22 August and waited for an expected German attack. They did not have long to wait as the Germans arrived the very next day. The British were doing their best at holding their defensive positions at the Mons-Conde Canal against a numerically superior German First Army, but were eventually forced to retreat, a retreat which lasted for some two weeks, before a counter attack, with the aid of the French Fifth Army, was initiated at the outskirts of Paris, at what became the Battle of the Marne.

One of the British casualties from the Battle of Mons was Sergeant Arthur J Hitchman from Tunbridge Wells, who was serving in the 2nd Battalion, Royal Sussex Regiment, in which he had enlisted in 1902. He was shot through the right thigh during the fighting. He returned to Britain to have his wounds treated and after his operation, he was staying in barracks at Chichester whilst he recovered. Recuperating, he even did his bit at the town's recruiting office, encouraging young men to enlist. He was wounded very early on in the fighting which did not please him any as he wanted to do his bit and be able to look after the young men, most of them no more than boys. No sooner had he returned to Britain than he discovered that one of his brothers had enlisted and had become a member of 'C' Company, 4th Battalion, Royal West Kent Regiment.

When Sergeant Hitchman and his men arrived at Mons they discovered that the trenches that had already been prepared for them by their Belgian counterparts had already been overrun by the rapidly advancing German soldiers, so they began to dig their own trenches. This was proving to take too long in a rapidly changing military environment, with the enemy at close quarters. The reality for Sergeant

Hitchman and his colleagues, quickly became apparent that they would have to leave the trenches and beat a hasty retreat or risk being wiped out. Whilst the infantry on both sides were doing their best to kill each other, the French and German artillery units were trying to do the same. The Germans employed spotter planes to assist their artillery to be as accurate as possible with their shelling, but it was the French artillery that won the day. Sergeant Hitchman was impressed with the speed at which the Germans moved forward and in doing so prevented the British from re-organising themselves and from taking up defensive rear guard positions, let alone being able to conduct any kind of counter offensive. Intentionally or otherwise, it was an extremely effective tactic, but it was not just the sheer speed of the Germans that made it so effective; it was also their overwhelming numbers of men.

His parents lived at 2 Dale Street, Tunbridge Wells. A check on the 1911 Census shows parents William and Elizabeth Hitchman living at that address with Arthur and their other five sons: William, who was twenty-five years of age; Harry, twenty-three; Percy, twenty; Cyril, seventeen; Sidney, thirteen and daughter, Helen, who was eighteen.

Although almost every community throughout the entire country was affected by the First World War through losing family members, relatives or friends, it was questionable as to whether the enormity of the war was something which was ever fully appreciated. A telegram from the War Office informing a family about the death of a loved one, the booming sound of artillery bombardments from just across the English Channel, or the sight of a German Zeppelin gliding majestically yet menacingly overhead, were about as real as the war ever became for most people. Although the pain, sadness and trauma of losing a loved one in the war can only be guessed at, the gore and horror of what actually went on, was thankfully an experience that the civilian population of Britain never had to endure.

When a community woke up one morning to discover it had been taken over by the army and was now a military headquarters, with soldiers, vehicles, horses and large pieces of artillery in their midst, then it felt somewhat different. This is exactly what happened to the residents of Tunbridge Wells in September 1914, when the war very suddenly became very real. The town became the headquarters of the Territorial Army which saw the arrival of some 5,000 troops from different parts of the country for an unspecified period of time. A large camp appeared at nearby Crowborough whilst two signal companies sprang up on the local common to assist with communications between all the different units that had arrived. Headquarters was to be at the eminently suited Pavilion at Mount Ephraim which was home to the man in charge, Lieutenant General Sir Frederick Stopford, KCMG, KCVO, CB, along with the rest of his staff. The reason that Tunbridge Wells was selected to be a military headquarters was due to a combination of factors. It was in a central and commanding position. It was in close proximity to most of the major ports along the south coast and there were good rail links to and from the town. There were even rumours circulating at the time that the real reason for the sudden large military presence was because of an imminent German invasion, which was quickly squashed by the military authorities as being totally unfounded.

The added bonus for the town was that the army intended to purchase, where possible, all that they needed from local businesses, which would prove to be extremely beneficial for the local economy, although the actual feeding of all of these men was to be catered for by staff from the Army Service Corps. Tented army camps also sprang up at nearby Crowborough, Camp Hill, Maresfield and St Johns as well as the Lower Cricket Ground which had become a particular centre of interest to the local population, especially on a Sunday afternoon. It was not uncommon to see women carrying baskets of apples to feed to the fine looking horses that were either tethered to the railings which surrounded the field, or being exercised by the fit young men. Having soldiers working and living in their midst was an unfamiliar yet interesting sight for the local townsfolk.

It was not uncommon on one of these leisurely Sunday afternoons to have a group of socialists just outside the curtilage of the camp holding a meeting, the theme of which was anti-war. The discussions and debate which followed never ended in bad language, aggressive behaviour or violent conflict between those with differing views on the topic.

Despite all the tented camps, there was still a need to billet some officers and men in private homes throughout the area, which potentially presented a major problem for the relevant authorities to find a sufficient quantity of premises. Fortunately, the Chief Constable of Kent, Mr Prior, who also happened to be the county's billeting officer, was aware of the matter, and in conjunction with his military counterpart, had already made the relevant arrangements. He had been able to commandeer numerous large public halls, as well as a large number of empty privately owned houses. These locations included Culverden Castle, which housed thirty officers and thirty-five men along with twelve horses. The Crabb Memorial Institute housed a further 225 men. Byng Hall at St John's was home for a further 160 men, and the Great Hall was the new home for 250 more. Some of the private houses that were used were so large that they could comfortably accommodate 100 men. Local residents were in the main glad that nearly all of the soldiers had either been put up in camps or billeted in other accommodation, as this meant that no troops had to be billeted by local householders. The relief was due to the War Office having reduced the rate of pay they would provide for each soldier's board and lodging from 3s 4d per day to 1s 9d, suddenly making it not such an attractive proposition.

The Defence of the Realm (Consolidation) Act 1914 contained wide ranging powers for the government to be able to use as and when they saw fit. Saturday 24 October saw the departure from Tunbridge Wells by train, of twenty-four of the town's alien residents. The Defence of the Realm Act determined that as they were people of German origin they would now have to be interned at a secure location for the duration of the war. The individuals concerned were escorted by armed police officers, each carrying a loaded rifle, an unusual sight even in wartime Britain. The aliens were kept overnight at the town's police station. Although not a widely publicised event, word of their leaving had still permeated amongst some segments of the local community. In an attempt to avoid any ugly scenes, the police had arranged a large car for their journey to the town's railway station. On arrival they were taken to the far end of the Up platform so that they could board their train with a minimum of fuss. Their friends and relatives had been allowed to see them off. Besides one or two individuals hurling abuse at the party of Police officers and aliens, there were no other incidents. At the allotted time the aliens, along with their escort of armed police officers, took their seats in reserved compartments on board the 11.48 am train. Their eventual destination was not allowed to be reported in the press of the day for security purposes.

The *Kent & Sussex Courier* from Friday 20 November tells the tale of one very lucky soldier.

'Private A J Groombridge, of the Royal Sussex Regiment, who was wounded in the Battle of the Aisne, is spending a few days in Tunbridge Wells on furlough. It was while using a pair of field glasses about 900 yards from the German trenches, and giving his comrades the range, that Private Groombridge was wounded. A bullet struck the field glasses, which slightly deflected its course and it then passed through his hand and forearm, finding an exit near the elbow of his coat. Wounded a few hours after sunrise, Private Groombridge had to remain in the trenches all day, as owing to the persistent shell fire from the enemy's position the ambulance men could not get near him until dark.

'Private Groombridge is returning to his regimental depot next Tuesday, and expects to be sent back in to the firing line shortly afterwards.'

It would appear that Private Groombridge was targeted by a German sniper rather than one of the enemy simply taking a chance pot shot at him; if that was the case then luck most definitely played a big part in ensuring that Private Groombridge survived.

In times of war heroes come in all shapes and sizes and sometimes in the most unexpected ways. In the aftermath of war it tends to be those who died, the ones who paid the ultimate price, who are the ones remembered and eulogised on war memorials. Those who served their country and returned to carry on as they had done before the war, or those who received life changing wounds, history tends not to remember so passionately. In some cases they are completely forgotten, remaining only as a picture, letter or medal tucked away in an old suitcase in somebody's loft. This chapter could have filled up the entire book with the numbers of heroes Tunbridge Wells managed to produce during the First World War, so a few individuals have been chosen at random who are intended to be representative of them. For every story included there are tens of others which were just as worthy of a mention.

Private John Edward Wickenden (10151) of B Company, 1st

Battalion, Queen's Own (Royal West Kent Regiment) who was known to his friends as 'Jack', was killed in action on 12 October 1914 in France. His brother, Lewis Wickenden, a Private (784) in the 14 Field Ambulance, Royal Army Medical Corps, whose home address was 81 Goods Station Road, wrote a letter to his wife:

> 'Jack was only slightly wounded in the first place, but before they could get him out of the trenches he was absolutely riddled with bullets, as were his chums who were fighting near him.'

John Wickenden had originally enlisted at Maidstone on 9 June 1913 aged eighteen and arrived in France on 14 August 1914 as part of the British Expeditionary Force; by the time of his death he had already been involved in several of the war's early battles. He is buried at the Philosophe British Cemetery in Mazingarbe which is situated in the Pas de Calais region of France. As the cemetery was not begun until August 1915, John was initially buried elsewhere and his remains were moved to their current resting place later. There are the remains of 1,996 Commonwealth servicemen buried in the cemetery, 277 of which remain unidentified.

James Wickenden, another brother, had emigrated to Australia some years earlier, but when the war broke out he enlisted in the Australian Infantry and served during the First World War. Both Lewis and James survived the war.

Petty Officer (175521) Herbert Joseph Harris was thirty-eight years of age. He was based at Portsmouth working as a Navy diver. He was attached the His Majesty's Submarine *E3* when he was killed in action on 18 October 1914 in the North Sea. He left behind a widow, Violet May Harris and two young children, the youngest, only three months old, who he had only seen once.

HMS *E3* has the distinction of being the first submarine to be sunk by another submarine, when it was struck by a torpedo fired by the German U-Boat, U27. All twenty-eight members of the crew were killed, including Petty Officer Harris.

Private Ernest Baker of the 1st Battalion, the Rifle Brigade, who was

HMS E3. *(Unknown photographer)*

the son of Mr and Mrs Alfred Baker of 15 Vernon Road, Tunbridge Wells, was wounded whilst serving in France, during October 1914. He was twenty-one years of age and had already served with his regiment for three years. Ernest had already been on duty in the trenches for ten days without a break, before he was shot in the left arm by a bullet fired from a German machine gun. He then had to wait a further three hours before the fighting died down sufficiently enough for him to be moved, when he then had to endure a walk of more than five miles before he was able to receive medical treatment for his wounds.

Private C Twort of the 12th Battalion, Lancers, was taken prisoner by the Germans in October 1914 and spent the rest of the war in captivity in Gefangenen Lager, Doeberits, Germany. He was an officer's servant, and the officer who Private Twort looked after was wounded during the Battle of Mons.

Tunbridge Wells set up its own Belgian Refugees Committee which was chaired by the Mayor. The town did not only do its bit by putting up Belgian refugees during the war, but by treating and looking after some of its wounded soldiers, who were sent to Britain for convalescence. In total some 25,000 wounded Belgian soldiers were brought to Britain to have their wounds treated; once again, Kent played its part. On top of this there were another 150,000 Belgian troops waiting and training in England before returning to the Western Front to defend and ultimately free their country from the tyranny of German occupation. Even before the first Belgian Refugee had arrived in Tunbridge Wells, the townspeople already had an understanding of their plight This came in the shape of a letter sent from Francis, Count Rivarola, who was living at Bradshows, Tunbridge Wells, to the editor of the *Kent & Sussex Courier* and which appeared in the newspaper on Friday 2 October 1914.

'Dear Sir,

I have just heard of a large convent near Bruges, who have opened their doors as a haven of refuge to some hundreds of homeless fugitives from Malines, Louvain and the surrounding towns and villages. These occupy two of the large buildings in the convent grounds, and a third one is being used for 900 volunteers in need of medical attendance, who are being nursed and cared for by the good nuns. The sisters have sufficient time and material to make clothing, but money is wanted to purchase food for this large number of brave people. It is also very sad to think of these good sisters deprived of the pensions of a large number of their Belgian people owing to the war.

'This convent is well known to me and has always had a great deal of English people of all religions, and I shall be pleased to receive donations in money at once, so that funds may be forthcoming for the support of this great army of people. All donations will be gratefully received and promptly acknowledged.'

As nobody knew how long the war was going to last, it was anybody's guess as to how long the Belgian refugees would be staying in the town. They needed accommodation, food, clothes and jobs. This in part led to a relief fund being set up to help cater for the town's new long term visitors. Within just three weeks, the fund had already raised £2,423 3s 7d, which was a truly staggering sum of money when most working men did not even earn £1 a week at the time. Some of the more affluent members of the local community had donated sums of up to £100. The National Union Women's Suffrage Societies (NUWSS) were extremely helpful in the support of the Belgian Refugees, and it was interesting to note how, in a time of war, everybody pulled together for the common cause, and left their political and social differences at the front door.

On Friday 16 October, a group of thirty-five Belgian refugees, mostly from Brussels, arrived in Tunbridge Wells. They were met by a party of women from the town's Belgian Refugees Committee and then taken to addresses at Dudley Road, Southborough, 11 Linden Park and 47 Upper Grosvenor Road. The latter address was such a large property that it could comfortably cater for them all. For most it was smiles all round, smiles which had no doubt not been present when they began their journey of escape. Others were tearful, not out of sadness or fear, but out of surprise for the genuine warmth of their reception from people who spoke a different language and who were total strangers to them.

There were already twenty-nine wounded Belgian soldiers being treated at the town's General Hospital when the second group of wounded arrived the next day. Originally, they were due to arrive at eleven o'clock on Friday evening, but due to unforeseen difficulties at Folkestone, the train did not arrive until nearly six o'clock on the Saturday morning. The delay had resulted in an uncomfortable wait for the eight members of the Tunbridge Wells Detachment of the St John's Ambulance Corps who were waiting patiently at the station, on what was a particularly chilly evening. Their only protection from the cold were their uniforms and a few cups of piping hot Bovril. When the train finally arrived there were a total of twenty wounded on board, all of whom had fought so bravely against the Germans during the siege of Antwerp. On hand to translate between the Belgian soldiers and the St John's Ambulance personnel, was Miss Prior, the daughter of the Chief Constable of Kent, who just happened to have been educated in Belgium. The wounded were then conveyed to different hospitals throughout the town, including the Homoeopathic Hospital, the West Hall in Chilston Road as well as the Kent Nursing Institution at Jerningham House, Mount Sion. The men had a variety of ailments. Some were suffering from shrapnel wounds, others from bullet wounds and one had pneumonia.

During the war years, approximately 300 Belgian refugees were looked after in Tunbridge Wells; there was even a Belgian shop in the High Street. An entire ward at the General Hospital was set aside to treat wounded Belgian soldiers as well as civilians. The ward was awash with Belgian flags to give it a more homely feeling as the staff did their best to create a feeling of wellbeing amongst their patients.

Sunday 25 October saw the arrival of a further forty wounded Belgian soldiers at the town's railway station. Such was the respect shown to them that they were met by the area's Chief Constable; the Chief Officer of the district's St John's Ambulance Brigade, Mr Hickmott; Surgeon-Major Gunter of the local Army Territorials and Dr Wilson, a local GP. The medical men were in attendance so that they could quickly examine the arriving Belgians to confirm they were fit enough to continue their journey in the transport provided. Thirty of them had been allocated to go to Bidborough Court, where the Speldhurst Voluntary Aid Detachment of the British Red Cross Society had established a hospital, the house having been loaned for the duration of the war by its owner. The remaining ten were despatched to the Royal Victoria Hall, Southborough, which was used as a hospital by the Southborough Red Cross, of which Lady Salomons was the Honorary Commandant. The General Hospital cared for both British and Belgian wounded soldiers, which threw up a slightly unusual scenario, which would have been difficult to foresee. The hospital authorities had to engage the services of a barber to shave the sixty men who were currently patients of the military ward, who for numerous different reasons were unable to carry out this function for themselves. Because of the cost, the hospital authorities had to put out a public appeal to cover the cost of the barber's wages. The effort to which local townsfolk from Tunbridge Wells went to support Belgian refugees was truly amazing. Besides the direct support which they gave to both the civilians and the soldiers, the local branch of the Women's Liberal Association sent clothes and blankets which had been made at their fortnightly sewing meetings, to Holland, where other Belgians were living as refugees.

On Wednesday 3 November, there was a concert, held at the Grand Hall in Tunbridge Wells in aid of the Belgian Repatriation Fund. All of the performers were musicians and singers from Belgium, including the celebrated soprano, Madame Marie Van Hee; cellist Monsieur

Lucien Cavaye and Monsieur Edouard Deru, a Belgian Court violinist. The main purpose of the fund was to provide temporary housing accommodation for Belgians in their own country after the war was over. It was not known at that stage that it would be another four years before any such plans could actually be put in place. It was estimated that in 1915 alone, somewhere in the region of half a million pounds a month was being raised by charitable donations throughout Britain for different Belgian causes, such was the feeling towards their war time plight. On Saturday 21 November, there was yet another fund raising event held at the Grand Hall, in aid of the 'Heroic Belgians'. The show began at 3 pm and included singing and a series of mini plays.

The First World War undoubtedly changed the world for ever. Industrially, politically, economically and socially, things would never quite be the same again. Nowhere was this felt more than by women. Before the war, opportunities in the work place for women were greatly restricted, mainly because they were still seen purely as wives, mothers and home makers while the men were seen as the hunter gatherers, the bread winners, the money earners whom society expected to be able to provide for their families, by putting food on the table, clothes on their backs and a roof over their heads. For those women who did work it was usually as either a teacher, shop assistant or as a domestic servant, and the pay they received was in most cases much lower than a man would earn for undertaking the exact same type of work. The role of a secretary, which today is more commonly a position for women, was yet another job men did in the years before the war. To make matters even worse, if that was actually possible, women in Britain did not even have the right to vote in a general election and would not fully earn the right until 1928 when all women over the age of twenty-one were given the franchise. Not all countries were the same in such matters. Certain States in America had given women the right to vote as far back as 1869. New Zealand was the first country to grant all its women who were over the age of twenty-one, the right to vote. It was also the same in certain parts of Australia, with women there actually allowed to stand for Parliament as early as 1895.

Tunbridge Wells was no different from every other town or village throughout Britain during the First World War, in that it willingly gave up its young men so that they could go to fight and in doing so serve their King and country. This did not just happen the once, it was a continual trickle over a four year period, which resulted in men being taken away from their jobs, in industry in particular. Factories up and down the country were working at full capacity in their efforts to support the war effort, both on the home front and abroad, but as the war continued so did the need for the goods which they produced. A vicious circle of greater demand for the goods meant the need for a larger and sustainable work force was an essential requirement.

Local women such as Miss Manser, Miss V M Moore and Mrs Faulkner all played their part as nurses in the Tunbridge Wells VAD. There were only three Miss Mansers living in the town before the outbreak of the war, two of these being sisters Mary Gertrude and Olive Martenridge Manser. Violet Menella Moore, who was the Commandant of the Tunbridge Wells VAD, had what appeared to be somewhat of a privileged upbringing, living at 45 Upper Grosvenor Road, with her parents George Osbourne Moore, who according to the 1911 Census, was a retired Commander in the Royal Navy and a Barrister, and her mother Menella Moore. The family were of sufficient means to be able to afford to employ four servants.

Within days of the outbreak of war the various Tunbridge Wells and the surrounding District's Voluntary Aid Detachments of the British Red Cross Society, had all rallied to the cause, collecting all the equipment they were likely to need when dealing with wounded soldiers who had returned home from the front. Owing to its position as a mainline railway station, Tunbridge Wells became somewhat of a distribution centre for wounded soldiers. Once they had arrived in the town they were then sent to be looked after by various local VADs that were set up in neighbouring locations. The Tunbridge Wells Detachment, which was officially known as 'Kent 94', had its headquarters at Calverley Terrace, where they had a room, telephone and typewriter at their disposal, which had been provided by Mr R Vaughan Gower. Other members of the community came forward with offers of premises for use by the VAD. Lord Amherst placed 'Hillside' at their disposal and Miss Sawle provided the Torrington House Nursing Home, fully equipped. Both offers were greatly accepted.

Similar displays of good will and assistance were shown at the neighbouring VADs of Eridge and Broadwater Down, which was 'Sussex 92', the section which covered Pembury, Matfield and Brenchley, ('Kent 18') and the British Red Cross Society detachment at Frant. Everybody was pulling together to do their bit. Houses, church halls, village schools, even the courthouse at Frant was provided.

The intention for VAD nurses was for them to carry out the more mundane aspects of nursing, such as making beds, cleaning and washing patients who were bed ridden, even to care for those soldiers who were in the convalescent stage of their recovery. This in turn allowed trained and qualified nurses to deal with the more important and urgent aspects of the profession. It was some of these very same nurses who saw the VADs as a potential threat to their own jobs after the war. One VAD section, Kent 202, managed to acquire 'Rusthall'. The house was ideal not only in size, being a spacious property which had enough room for around fifty beds, but because of the extensive grounds that came with it, which were ideal for soldiers who were recuperating from operations and wounds. It is worth mentioning that at the start of the war there were some 40,000 VADs working at 1800 sections around Britain, who were used in a variety of roles such as nursing assistants, ambulance drivers, chefs, cooks and clerks. By the end of the war there had been a total of 126,000 men and women who had been members of the VAD, although these were predominantly women. Although the vast majority of these individuals were based within Britain, there were some who were posted overseas to such locations as Gallipoli, Mesopotamia, Malta, France and Belgium. Some of these would pay the ultimate price as 243 of them were killed during the war. Their bravery and heroism did not stop there, as some of them were actually taken as prisoners of war by the Germans. An amazing 364 of them also received gallantry awards for their bravery and heroism and a further 1,005 were Mentioned in Despatches for their actions and dedication.

It would be fair to say that morals were quite different from today. It would not be common practice for instance to see a group of women out drinking together on a Friday or Saturday night. It was extremely rare for women to even be seen in pubs, and those who were, ran the risk of having their basic moral fibre brought in to question. With so many soldiers stationed in the Tunbridge Wells area there was an outbreak of what has been termed, 'khaki fever'. This was not some previously unheard of tropical disease which had suddenly appeared in the town, but rather a term which had been born out of the colour of the uniforms that soldiers wore. There was not suddenly a concern that soldiers would be stalking the streets of Tunbridge Wells and throwing themselves upon unsuspecting women they might happen upon, but it had to do with their very presence in the town. There were some in the community who were concerned that, because there were so many soldiers about, some of the town's young women were becoming over-excited by their presence and were at risk of having their personal morality questioned. Such was the concern that members of the local branch of the National Union of Women Workers requested the town's Watch Committee to appoint women police officers who would be used to patrol the streets, being both a physical deterrent against what were then classed as acts of moral indecency, as well as being a standard and a potential role model for adolescent young women, out and about late at night.

The following article appeared in the *Kent & Sussex Courier* on Friday 9 October.

> The Watch Committee reported that a letter was received from Miss Scott, on behalf of the National Union of Women Workers, addressed to the Chairman of the Committee, on the subject of the appointment of two or three suitable women to work with the Police during the time the troops are quartered in the town, and to assist the Police in preventing our soldiers being pestered by bad women. It was decided that Miss Scott be informed that the Committee are not prepared to appoint women as special constables, but that nothing in this decision need prevent members of the National Union of Women Workers from exercising their moral influence.'

The request was refused. Not to be put off, the NUWW organised their own volunteers to carry out such patrols which would continue throughout the war years. Because moral standards were so different during the First World War, a woman out late at night talking to a man she did not know, unchaperoned, simply laughing and joking with him, was enough for her name and good character to be besmirched at a time when religion and the church played such a major part in everyday life. The Tunbridge Wells Watch Committee eventually changed their minds in May 1918 and hired three Policewomen, which did not stop the volunteers from the NUWW continuing with their patrols. Within a year, two of the three policewomen were given their notice, but purely for monetary reasons.

Balance this approach and attitude on moral issues with an article that appeared in the *Kent & Sussex Courier* on Friday 27 March 1914, with a somewhat different approach towards women's femininity.

Thin women can now develop their busts
Remarkable experience of lady reader

'Three weeks ago I read an article about a new food product which was claimed by the writer to possess the wonderful power or property of quickly improving the figure, and particularly the bust, without injury to the health, as is so frequently the case with drugs and appliances.

'As I had always been very thin, in fact never possessed any bust development worth mentioning, I decided to give this new scientific food, which the chemists call phormoid, a trial. I obtained from my chemist a small box of phormoid tablets (which my chemist advised as being the most convenient form) and took one before each meal. I really didn't have any faith in it, but much to my astonishment my bust measurement increased nearly one inch the first week, and now at the end of three weeks it has increased exactly three inches. I have gained five pounds in weight, and am feeling stronger and better than I felt for years, this, in spite of the fact that I am over forty years of age. Naturally I am delighted, and I trust you will publish this for the benefit of other thin undeveloped women.'

There was no mention of the woman's name or any explanation of what happened if one stopped taking the tablets.

Tunbridge Wells had its own branch of the Women's Emergency Corps, with its headquarters at 8 Monson Road and came in to being in October 1914. It was subsequently to also become the headquarters for the local Women's Volunteers in February 1915. The Tunbridge Wells branch had a list of seven reasons why women should support them. The first one was simply that their help was needed. There were a certain number of women who were really hard hit during the First World War, and it was their objective to help them. Some of those who were deprived of employment found it impracticable to qualify quickly for another. There was not a vast amount of distress or unemployment in the town but there was some.

Volunteers were also essential, as they visited all of the applicants who came to see them for work, so that they could see which of them were deserving and in most urgent need of their help.

Following these visits, they frequently put women in the way of obtaining permanent employment, after tiding them over a difficult time by providing them with temporary work. They had sent some of the unemployed dressmakers on their books to work at local drapers' shops who were in need of more dressmakers, thus obtaining employment for quite a number of women. They also sent a lot of their applicants to register at the local Labour Exchange.

They could help by giving temporary support; they did not give women monetary handouts, but they did some times help them by managing to find them temporary employment, such as sewing and knitting for those who needed some kind of work to tide them over until better times came along. They also taught some women, who were in ill health, the art of basket making which was also taught to wounded soldiers during their recuperation.

Soldiers and sailors would directly benefit, as some of the women who did sewing work, undertook work to make sandbags for the military, which were needed in ever increasing numbers on the Western Front. The quality of their work was checked by a lady named Miss Taylor, who was the London based agent for the War Office. Her job was to ensure that the sandbags continued to be made to an approved standard. Some women also undertook work for hospitals and soldiers by knitting woollen items, which were much in demand.

Other women who came to them and who were not experiencing financial difficulties, but who had some spare time on their hands, wanted to use that free time by being involved in 'war work', so that they could do their bit. The Women's Volunteer Reserve, whose office was at 49, Grosvenor Road provided many different classes, in such areas as first aid, nursing and even learning to drive, all of which went a long way to helping the overall war effort.

Those ladies who spoke French gave lessons to the soldiers about to be sent abroad. Many soldiers on their way to fight on the Western Front in France and Belgium, took the opportunity to learn French, making it an extremely popular course which continued to have a high take-up throughout the war.

CHAPTER 2

1915
Deepening Conflict

The first full year of the war saw a massive increase in the number of British and Commonwealth fatalities, with a total of 151,281 men killed. With this figure, those killed in 1914 that made a total of 188,215 men killed in seventeen months. These figures did not include those who had been wounded in the fighting.

As 1915 dawned, the war brought with it some frightening innovations:

19–20 January – The first German Zeppelin raids took place over England.

4 February – German U-Boats attack shipping from both Allied and neutral countries, in an effort to impose an effective blockade on Great Britain, who were reliant on their Allies for their overall survival.

22 April–25 May – First use of poison gas on the Western Front by the Germans, at the start of the 2nd Battle of Ypres. At about 5pm, German soldiers released chlorine gas over a five mile stretch of the Western Front near the Belgium Hamlet of Gravenstafel, during the Battle of Gravenstafel Ridge.

25 April – First Allied landings at Gallipoli.

7 May – The British Liner *Lusitania* was sunk by the German U-Boat, *SMU-20*. There are 128 American citizens amongst the

British soldiers blinded by tear gas.

The Lusitania *arrives in New York, 13 September 1907. (Library of Congress)*

dead. America didn't want to be dragged into the war, one of the reasons being that she had a large German immigrant population. Prior to America's entry into the war in 1917, the Justice Department prepared a list of all known German Aliens. The figure was estimated to be in the region of 480,000.

19 December – Sir Douglas Haig replaces Sir John French as the Commander of the British Expeditionary Force.

28 December – Allies begin the mass withdrawal of troops from Gallipoli. Turkey had sided with the Germans in October 1914 and closed the Dardanelle Straits and in doing so effectively cut

off the supply route to Russia, which greatly curtailed her ability to receive military aid from her Allies.

The *Kent & Sussex Courier* carried the following report on Friday 1 January, getting the New Year off to a less than hoped for beginning.

Fires at Tunbridge Wells

'At 9.35 o'clock on Monday night the Borough Fire Brigade received a call to a fire that had broken out in a stable at the back of the Greyhound Hotel in Upper Grosvenor Road. The match boarding covering a ceiling had caught alight, evidently as a result of a red hot cinder falling from the grate. Although the flames had secured a good hold, the outbreak was quickly conquered by the firemen. Several military horses were in the stable, and a number of soldiers held themselves in readiness to remove the animals, but it was not found necessary to do this.'

The following article was also in the same edition of the newspaper. It related to a letter which they had received. The letter had been sent to them from Driver Sydney Charles Westover, who was with the 7th Field Company, Pontoon Section, Royal Engineers. He at the time lived at 20 Woodbury Park Road in Tunbridge Wells with his parents, Charles and Keturah Westover and his two younger brothers, Herbert and Frederick. Sydney's letter included a description of his part in the retreat from Mons.

'After a short rest, we were preparing to move, when all of a sudden hell was let loose upon us. Under cover of darkness the enemy had approached to within 1,000 yards of us and opened fire with every gun and rifle they possessed. The noise was deafening. We happened to be quite ready to hook it, so we managed to get out all right. We were in the next field to "L" Battery, and only a short distance from the Queen's Bays. You have heard what happened to them. Their horses were galloping wildly past us, most of the riders having been killed. The enemy were driven off at one point later, and we captured several prisoners, while many others were done for.'

The picture of the mayhem created by Sydney's words, although detailed, most probably does not fully capture how brutal and scary that encounter must have been. With bullets flying and men dying all around him, he managed to prevail.

> 'We stopped at a large town, but not for long, as another attack was delivered, and soon afterwards the town was in flames. One morning some of us were having a wash in a stream. I was sitting on the bank sewing buttons on my uniform, when someone remarked, "Look at all those troops coming over the Hill! Wonder what mob they are?" We were soon to find out, for up galloped a Major, who shouted to us to clear off at once, as the enemy were upon us. The hills were alive with Germans. Three of our fellows were captured, but we got them back the same night with a number of Germans as interest.'

One moment he is describing a group of British soldiers simply relaxing and enjoying a much needed break from the fighting in a nearby stream, and in the very next instant the reality of war un-expectantly re-appears and he and his colleagues have to beat a hasty retreat to escape capture or possibly even death.

> 'One night when things cooled down a bit, a funny incident occurred near a wood. We had posted double guards, outposts, etc. but about midnight a breaking of boughs and heavy breathing was heard in the woods near us. Our sentry, getting no reply to his challenge, "let go" and soon we were blazing away into the wood. Still there was no answer, not a sound, so we had a look around and found a poor old cow with about 50 bullets in her. We were sorry for the cow, but it couldn't be helped, and we got a good laugh out of it.'

The ability to find humour at such stressful times is a classic example of how soldiers dealt with the fear of dying that is associated with war, where a soldier faces death on a daily basis and sometimes from the most unexpected of quarters, although admittedly the harbinger of death was unlikely to come in the form of a cow. Sydney made good his escape from Mons and eventually made his way back to England.

Later that year he married his sweetheart, Constance Bradley.

He had enlisted in the Army on 28 May 1906 at Eastbourne. And although he stated that the unit he wished to join was the Royal Engineers he was initially placed in the Army Service Corps as a Private (15590). Immediately prior to enlisting he was serving with a local militia. He served for two years and was then placed on the Army Reserve. On 5 August 1914 he was mobilized at Shorncliff Barracks in to the 7th Company, Royal Engineers. Having survived the war Sydney, was demobilized on 9 April 1919 and went on to live until he was eighty-one.

Sydney's brother, Herbert, also served during the war having enlisted on 13 May 1914 at Tunbridge Wells when he became a Private (972) in the Kent Cyclist Battalion. He arrived in France on 16 December 1916 and then later transferred to the 3rd Battalion, East Kent Regiment as a Private (15742) before moving on to the 6th Battalion of the same Regiment. On 28 March 1917 he reported sick at a Field Ambulance. What the sickness was has not been recorded on his Army Service Record, but it was bad enough to keep him in a hospital bed for eighteen days, before he returned to his unit on 15 April. On 30 November, Herbert was reported as being Missing in Action, but on 4 December, it was confirmed by the German authorities that Herbert was in fact being held by them as a prisoner of war in Munster. He was finally released from captivity on 1 December 1918. He was demobbed on 4 April 1919 and by November 1920, he had moved to 5 Cambridge Gardens, Hastings, Sussex. Herbert would eventually return to Tunbridge Wells, where he died, aged eighty-five.

Two weeks later the same newspaper carried a report of the sad death of 20 year old Lance-Corporal Albert West of 'E' Company, Kent Cyclist Battalion, whilst a patient at Canterbury Hospital. At the time of his death he was attached to the Army Service Corps as a motor transport driver in the Home Counties Division. He died not on the battlefields of the Western Front from a German bullet or bomb, but as the result of a tragic accident that took place in a tiny side street in Canterbury on 21 December 1914, where he was stationed at the time.

He was on foot at the time in the vicinity of the Cathedral, where the streets are particularly tight and narrow. As Albert was walking round the corner of Orange Street where it meets with Palace Street, he was pinned up against a shop window by a car which was being driven by Captain William Aneurin Thomas of the Army Service Corps, (West Lancashire Division). As a result of the accident he sustained a serious compound fracture to one of his legs and was taken to Canterbury Hospital. Doctors operated on him on Boxing Day to repair his leg, but his health declined and on New Year's Day, doctors had to amputate his damaged leg. Still his condition worsened and on Saturday 8 January 1915 he sadly passed away due to a combination of severe shock and exhaustion.

Interestingly enough, Albert's mother, Elizabeth West, who lived at 34 Bayhall Road, Tunbridge Wells, did not hear about her son's accident from the Army, but in a letter which she received on Wednesday 23 December from Mr Jarvis of 74 Castle Street, Canterbury, which is where Albert was billeted whilst stationed in Canterbury. The inquest in to his death took place on the afternoon of Tuesday 12 January at Canterbury Hospital, and was chaired by the City Coroner, John Plummer. At the time of the accident, Albert was with a friend and colleague, Lance Corporal Robert Emory. He gave evidence at the inquest that he estimated the speed of the car was between 12 to 15 miles per hour, which he considered to be too fast, considering the state of the roads. As the car came round the corner it mounted the pavement causing Albert and the witness to run, but unfortunately for Albert, the car struck him, pinning him up against a shop window. Other witnesses gave evidence that the car had been going at such a speed as to have to swerve to miss a hot chestnut barrow and then had to swerve again to miss striking an elderly lady who was crossing the road. Another witness claimed the vehicle was not being driven any faster than the speed a bicycle travels at and that the road was slippery and greasy. The inquest jury reached a verdict of 'Accidental Death'.

His funeral took place on Wednesday 13 January and Albert was buried at the Borough Cemetery in Tunbridge Wells with full military honours including three volleys of shots from a firing party whilst a bugler played the Last Post.

Friday 29 January saw the following article appear in the *Kent & Sussex Courier*.

'Mr Malin, of St Clair, Manor Road, Rusthall, has re-joined His Majesty's Forces. He served through the Boer War, in which he

was promoted to Sergeant, and was one of the first to leave
Tunbridge Wells and one of the last to return home. He has now
joined Kitchener's Army, and as a married man is setting a
splendid example to younger men. Mr Malin, since his return
from the Boer War, has been on the staff of Messrs. Carr, of
Calverley Road, and is very popular in the town. He is also well-
known as a soldier artist, and had the honour of submitting one
of the military pictures to the late Queen Victoria. Mr Malin
states that he feels so keenly the need for everyman who is able
to go to the Front should do so, that he has re-joined, although
he may claim to be a veteran. Mr Malin's many friends will
congratulate him, and hope that many others will follow his
example and that Mr Malin himself may come safely back after
adding to his South African War medals.'

Mr Malin was in fact Sidney Charles Malin of St Clair, 15 Manor View,
Rusthall, Tunbridge Wells. Messrs. Carr was a grocer's shop, and he
and his wife Jessie, had two children, Mary, who was born in 1909 and
Gordon who was born 1910. He survived the war and died on 10 July
1940.

On Tuesday 26 January the Chief Constable received an instruction
from the General Officer Commanding the Second Army, directing that
the Borough's lights should be extinguished between the hours of 5pm
and 7.30am the following morning. All relevant paperwork was
completed in double quick time and with liaison between the Chief
Constable, the Borough's Electrical Engineer and the Gas Company,
all lights were extinguished the same evening, ensuring the order was
complied with. Local police officers had done their best to pass the
message on to the town's residents about the restrictions as best they
could, their combined efforts ensuring that even though the order was
almost rushed through, it was still adhered to by nearly everybody on
that first evening.

Friday 12 March saw an article in the *Kent & Sussex Courier*.

'Private (10620) Horace Le Breton of the Kings Own Yorkshire
Light Infantry, who is well known in Tunbridge Wells, has been
spending a few days of his furlough in the town, and has now
left to re-join his Regiment. Private Le Breton is a nephew of

Mrs Rendell of Tunbridge Wells, and went straight from India to the Front, where he was wounded on his first day in the trenches. In the course of a few minutes conversation, Private Le Breton gave a graphic description of the horror of modern trench warfare, with shrapnel shells continually bursting immediately overhead. He had not been many hours with his comrades in the firing line when a fragment of one of these shells struck him in the back, inflicting a nasty V shaped wound, from which he is however now recovering. Although his experience of helping to hold a trench against the German hordes was so brief, it was none the less terrible. Private Le Breton describes how a shell up rooted a tree, which pinned three or four of his comrades to the bottom of the trench. Before any of the other soldiers could get to their assistance a second shell burst completely buried the unfortunate men in mud. Any attempt to extricate them was hopeless and they died a dreadful death, in a form only too frequent among our gallant fellows at the front.'

According to the 1911 Census, Horace's parents, John and Elizabeth Le Breton, were living at 67 West Street, Charlton, Kent, with eight of their children, by which time Horace had already left home. He survived the war and married at Woolwich in 1930.

On Friday, 7 May 1915 there was an article entitled,

Letters from the Front

Private T Canfield wrote a letter to the *Kent & Sussex Courier* about the taking of Hill 60, which appeared in their newspaper on Friday 27 August;

'I am writing this letter in my little dugout, which my mate and I call 'Sunnydale'.

'On April 17th my Company was chosen to do the charge with ———— Company in support and a company of ———— — called the KOSB, who dug trenches for us while we kept the German's back. I shall never forget that night. It was a grand sight and yet a sad one, and makes one shake to think of it. I was glad when we were relieved, about five in the morning, after beating back three counter attacks , in which the German's were ten to our one. Still, we had not finished, but were called out again and had a bad time of it with hand-to-hand fighting; but we drove them off, they being glad to retire,, and captured some of them. One I took, and he turned round and said; "Me no German; me Saxon; you Anglo Saxon; me no want to fight. "Well I had a laugh over it. Then we went back for three day's rest, and then to battle again with the Canadians at St ——. We had a very rough time of it with shells and gases, but I don't remember much of this as I was wounded on the second day, and went down country to hospital. I was very glad, being in need of a rest, and it was such a treat to be in bed for a bit. I believe I slept like a top, and when the Sister came to dress my wound she had to wake me up, and I believe I heard her say something like, "Sleeping Beauty".'

As can be seen from Private Canfield's letter, the official military censor clearly examined his letter very carefully, and removed parts with which they were not happy, especially when it came to the names of towns or villages or the details of particular Allied military units. Despite the censor's handy work, the essence of Private Canfield's letter hadn't been lost in translation.

The following article appeared in the *Kent & Essex Courier* on Friday 8 January, concerning the death of a Belgian refugee.

'The death occurred on Saturday (2nd) of Madam Euthalie Amelie van Vaerenberg, an Antwerp lady, who took refuge in England, and has been living at 3 Woodbury Park Road, Tunbridge Wells. She was 79 years of age and was well known to the local Belgian community, by whom she was greatly revered and respected.

'The funeral took place on Tuesday. Solemn Requiem Mass was celebrated at St Augustine's Catholic Church in the morning, and was attended by nearly all the Belgians resident in the town. Monsieur l'Abbe Lemmens, late of Malines, conducted the service, whilst the Rev. Cannon Keatinge assisted in the sanctuary, and gave absolutions after the mass.

'The Mass was sung by the Belgian nuns, who are now the guests of the Mayor of Tunbridge Wells, Mr C W Emson.'

Monday 10 May saw Bishop de Wachter, who was an official representative of both the Belgian Government as well as Cardinal Mercier, give a rousing speech to a large crowd at the Pump Room, Tunbridge Wells. He expressed the heartfelt thanks and gratitude of his king and country to the people of Tunbridge Wells for their collective kindness and consideration that they had extended to the Belgian refugees who had arrived in their midst since the start of the war, as well as the wounded soldiers they had treated and cared for in their hospitals. De Wachter had himself visited Belgian troops in their trenches on the Western Front, and had seen at first hand the conditions in which they lived and fought.

There was an article which appeared in the *Kent & Sussex Courier* dated Friday 23 July, which described Belgian refugees wanting to show their appreciation for how they had been accepted and treated by the Tunbridge Wells community. They had decided to have a life size bust made of the town's Mayor, and present it to the town as a permanent reminder of their gratitude of all that had been done for them. The work on the bust was being undertaken by the eminent Belgian sculptor, Monsieur Van Den Kerckhove. His work on the bust took place in one of the town's arts studios which had kindly been provided by Alexander Kirk, who had a well-equipped premises in Cumberland Walk. Mr Kerckhove was amongst the first groups of Belgians who had arrived in Tunbridge Wells, in October 1914. The bust was cast in bronze and the cost was met by the local Belgian community. The finished sculpture was unveiled in August 1916 at the Town Hall.

Tunbridge Wells man at Hill 60.

'Mr Francis of the High Street Dairy in Tunbridge Wells, has received a letter from a former employee, Private Ernest Wickins of the Royal West Kent, who writes:- While we were in the trenches we were told that Hill 60 was to be blown up, and that West Kent's had to make a charge. We saw the Hill go up in the air. It was a terrible scene. The charge of the West Kents was carried out with success, and we did not have many casualties. It was afterwards when the counter attack took place that we lost heavily, but thank God I got through it safely. When the Hill went up the Germans lost their heads and we took a lot of prisoners. We had an example of how Germans appreciate a good deed. A German officer was buried under earth after the explosion, and one of our fellows dug him out. When he saved him the German turned round and shot him through both legs. I am pleased to hear that more of your men are enlisting.'

The First World War, as is the case with every conflict, is about ordinary men who were plucked from their everyday life by the war, and who then went on to do their bit in a brave and honourable way, men who received just a few lines in the middle pages of a local newspaper for their efforts and what they had done. When the war was over they returned to their pre-war lives of obscurity and routine, content in the knowledge that when called upon, they had most definitely done their bit.

One such man was Private W H J Crouch who served with the Kings Own Yorkshire Regiment during the war even though his home was at 14 Francis Terrace, Victoria Road, Tunbridge Wells. By 15 April 15 1915, only nine months into the war, he had already been wounded three times. The first time was whilst he was involved in the British retreat from Mons, when he was shot in the neck. Amazingly, he survived the wound and after having been treated in England and fully recovered, he returned to France in January 1915. His second time of being wounded came about as a result of an exploding shell that went off close to him and a piece of shrapnel from the shell penetrated his back. Whilst his colleagues were removing him from the battlefield, he was shot in the head but, miraculously, once again he survived. He was sent back to England and was admitted to Reading General Hospital to have his wounds treated. He survived the war.

The *Kent & Sussex Courier* dated Friday 14 May carried the following article about the Paige brothers, Fred and Harry, who had both been wounded in France.

'Mrs F Paige of Berkshire Cottages, Tunbridge Wells, has received intimation that both her sons in the Royal West Kent Regiment, have been wounded. Pte. Harry Paige was in the recent severe fighting at Hills 60, and is now in a London

Hospital. Pte. Fred Paige has also been wounded, but is now recovered. Pte. Harry Paige was gallantly carried out of danger by a comrade when wounded and left in a dug out till the ambulance fetched him some hours later. Pte. Harry Paige is unfortunately more seriously wounded than his brother.'

According to the 1911 Census, Harry and Fanny Paige, actually lived at 7 Berkshire Cottages and had a total of eight children, six boys, including Harry and Fred, and two daughters.

There was an interesting article which appeared in the *Kent & Sussex Courier* dated Friday 1 October, which shows very clearly how the public's attitude had apparently changed towards returning soldiers. Not necessarily in a disrespectful manner, nor intentionally, but because people had seen so many returning wounded soldiers, it simply didn't grab their attention anymore in the way that it once had, it was almost like it was a sight that had simply become so common an event, it had lost its impact, and importance, in the eyes of the public.

'Wednesday 29 September 1915 was the anniversary of the arrival of the first wounded British soldiers at the Tunbridge Wells General Hospital. On that day there were very large crowds of people, who had been waiting for hours, outside the hospital to witness the arrival of that first group of twenty-four brave and wounded men. What a difference a year makes. This time some forty-two wounded soldiers arrived at the hospital, but there was no fanfare of trumpets, there were no crowds waiting anxiously outside the hospital for their arrival, in fact these wounded heroes arrived almost unnoticed. Despite this apparent apathy, sympathy, respect and admiration remained in abundance for their continued gallant actions in the face of the enemy and in the service of their King and country.'

The sinking of HMS *Hythe* took place at just after 8 o'clock, on the evening of 28 October in the Dardanelles Straits whilst en route to Cape Helles on the Gallipoli peninsula, when the ship collided with the much larger HMS *Sarnia*. Both vessels were adapted troop carriers, the *Sarnia* had already dropped off her contingent of troops and had left port whilst the *Hythe* was just about to enter. The *Hythe*, in line with

HMS Hythe *Roll of Honour. (Reproduced by kind permission of St Matthew's Church.)*

naval procedures, and so as not to be seen by the Turkish gun batteries in land, was sailing with her lights out for her own safety and that of the troops she was carrying as well as her own crew. As the two ships were passing each other they collided and the *Hythe* sunk in only ten minutes.

In the darkness, confusion reigned and out of the 275 men on board HMS *Hythe*, 154 of them, which included 11 members of the ship's crew, drowned in the cold waters of the Dardanelles. Of these, 129 were from the 1st/3rd Kent Field Company, Royal Engineers, who were from Tunbridge Wells and its surrounding towns and villages. HMS *Hythe* had set sail from Southampton on 11 October, stopping in Malta for two days for refuelling.

The names of all of the dead who were lost on HMS *Hythe*, are commemorated on the Helles Memorial in Turkey. The memorial commemorates the names of 20,879 identified men from the United Kingdom and India who lost their lives in operations throughout the Gallipoli Peninsula as well as those who either died or were buried at sea in the surrounding coastal waters.

Below are the names of the men from of Tunbridge Wells from 1st/3rd Kent Field Company, Royal Engineers who lost their lives when HMS *Hythe* was sunk:

Ashdown, Charles William, Sapper (904). His mother, Mrs Mary Ann Ashdown, lived at 120 Silverdale Road, Tunbridge Wells.

Banks, Hugh, Sapper (787). He was 21 years of age. His parents, Edward and Hannah Banks, lived at 6 Denbigh Road, Tunbridge Wells.

Benton, Percy, Driver (2241) was only 19 years of age. His parents, James Frederick and Emily Benton, lived at 26 Birling Road, Tunbridge Wells.

Betts, Sydney, Sapper (743). Sydney was a married man. His widow, Nellie, and their two young daughters, Violet and Dorothy, were living at 81 Silverdale Road, Tunbridge Wells, at the time of his death, although after the war they had moved on to 15 Hallbrook, Putney, London SW 15.

Bissell, William Henry, Driver (2052) was 42 years of age. His widow, Eliza Bissell, lived at 4 Holly Bank, Crescent Road, Tunbridge Wells.

Bone, Cecil John was a Sapper (854). His father, John Bone, lived at 1 Wolesley Road, High Brooms, Tunbridge Wells. The Commonwealth War Graves Commission website records Cecil's date of death as being 25 October 1915, which either means they have simply made an error, or he died at sea before the incident.

Brewer, Herbert Reginald, Sapper (1009). He was 20 years of age and the son of Mrs Amelia Brewer, who lived at 84 Auckland Road, Tunbridge Wells.

Brown, William Alfred, Driver (2024) was 19 years of age. His mother lived at 87 Silverdale Road, Tunbridge Wells.

Coppard, William Herbert, Driver (2089) was 33 years of age and a married man. His widow, Alice M Coppard, lived at 33 Cromwell Road, Tunbridge Wells.

Crittenden, Frederick, Sapper (890). He was 20 years of age and was married to Julia Elizabeth Esther Crittenden of 148 St James Road, Tunbridge Wells.

Ford, William Henry, Sapper (1039) was 19 years of age. His

parents, Henry and Rose Ford, lived at 18 St John Street, Tunbridge Wells.

Fuller, William Brookes, Sergeant (970). He was 31 years of age. His parents, Thomas and Caroline Fuller, lived at Calverley House, Calverley Road, Tunbridge Wells.

Funnell, Harry, Sapper (900). He enlisted on 31 March 1913 at Southborough, Tunbridge Wells. The Commonwealth War Graves website has his name as Harry and a Sapper whilst his military records clearly show his name as Henry and record the fact that he was a Driver, but it is definitely the same person number as they both quote the same service number.

His parents, Henry and Martha Funnell, lived at 224 St John's Road, Tunbridge Wells.

Funnell, William, Sapper (1633). He was 24 years of age when he enlisted at Gillingham on 4 January 1915. Prior to enlisting he had been a carpenter's mate, carrying out work for people in his local community. He left behind a widow, Agnes, and their two children, William who was nearly two years of age, and Amy who was only nine months old. According to William's military records, when he enlisted in the Army, the family lived at 21 Apsley Street, Rusthall, Tunbridge Wells, but after the war Agnes and the children were living at 29 High Street, Rusthall, Tunbridge Wells, whilst William's parents, Edwin and Rose Funnell, lived at 6 George Street, in the town.

Gilbert, John Robert, Driver (2240). He was 21 years of age. His parents, John and Annie Gilbert, lived at 6 Cemetery Road, Tunbridge Wells.

Godsmark, Thomas, Driver (2233). He was 21 years of age. His parents lived at 25 Gordon Road, High Brooms, Tunbridge Wells.

Gower, William, Sapper (1225) was a 41-year-old married man. His widow, Sarah, lived at 118 Silverdale Road, Tunbridge Wells.

Handley, Thomas Frederick James, Driver (2225). He was 19 years of age and his mother, Mrs Eliza Handley, lived at 19 Nursery Road, High Brooms, Tunbridge Wells.

Harmer, Frank, Sapper (892) was 20 years of age. His

parents, Edward and Sophie Harmer, lived at 95 St James Road, Tunbridge Wells.

Harmer, Frederick James, Sapper, (1354) was a 36-year-old married man and his widow, Mary Ann, lived at 57 Silverdale Road, Tunbridge Wells.

Harmer, William, Driver, (2252) was 20 years of age. His parents, Harry and Emma Harmer, lived at 89 Silverdale Road, Tunbridge Wells.

Hawkins, Clement, Second Corporal (741) was 34 years of age. His widow, Ada Mary Ann, lived at 19 Western Road, Southborough, Tunbridge Wells.

Heaseman, William, Sapper (786). His mother, Mrs Mary Ann Stringhill, lived at 32 Springfield, Southborough, Tunbridge Wells.

Hollamby, James, Sapper (2623) was 25 years of age. His parents lived at 7 Veermont Road, Rusthall, Tunbridge Wells, and his widow Flora was living at 2 Gladstone Road, Crowborough, Sussex, after the war.

Hughes, John Edward, sapper (1972) was a 29-year-old married man. His parents lived at The Laurels, Goodstation Road, Tunbridge Wells and his widow, Louisa, lived at 20 Auckland Road, Tunbridge Wells.

Jeffrey, Edwin, Sapper (939) was 23 years of age. His parents, George and Mary Jeffrey, lived at 96 Silverdale Road, Tunbridge Wells.

Manklow, Conrad Edwin, Driver (2028). He was 30 years of age at the time of his death. His parents, Edwin and Violet Manklow, lived at 18 Culverden Square, Tunbridge Wells, whilst his widow, Bertha, lived at 57 St John's Road, Tunbridge Wells.

Marriner, Percy Bertram, Sapper (2204) was a young man of 20 years of age. His parents, Alfred and Rose Marriner, lived at 6 Stone Street, Tunbridge Wells.

Parker, Harry, Lance Corporal (1990) was 29 years of age and his widow, Eva Agnes, lived at 68 Queens Road, Tunbridge Wells.

Martin, Frederick Thomas, Sapper (1966) was 34 years of age. His widow, Clara, who after the war had the surname of

Parsons, was living at 3 Gladstone Road, Rusthall, Tunbridge Wells.

Mepham, James, Sapper (1147) was born in Christchurch, Kent, in 1891. He had enlisted as a 19-year-old on the very first day of the war, on 4 August 1914 at Southborough. His home address that he provided when he enlisted was at 36 Grosvenor Park, Tunbridge Wells. It is also shown later on in his Army Service papers as being at 63 Grosvenor Park. He lived at home with his parents, James and Annie Mepham, his two sisters Annie and Caroline, as well as his five brothers, George, John, Herbert, Alfred and Ernest, of which only George and John would have been old enough to have served in the military during the war.

Miles, Sidney Isaac, Driver (2214). He was 24 years of age. His parents, Walter and Harriet Miles, lived at Blowers Hill, Speldhurst, Tunbridge Wells.

Neal, Frederick Arthur, Sapper (991) was only 19 years of age. His parents, Mr and Mrs J Neal, lived at 3 Denbigh Road, Tunbridge Wells.

Oxley, Ernest Edgar, Sapper (1150) was nearly 22 years of age when he enlisted on the very first day of the war on 4 August 1914 at Southborough. His home address at the time was shown as being 86 Auckland Road, Tunbridge Wells.

Peerless, Clarence Roland Walter, Sapper (1973), 21 years of age.

Peerless, Walter James, Sapper (1408). Louisa Peerless, who lived at 37 Common View, Rusthall, Tunbridge Wells, lost her son, Clarence, as well as her husband, Walter, in the sinking of the *Hyde* – a terrible thing for anyone to have to bear. Clarence enlisted on 14 April 1915 at Gillingham and had only just finished six months of basic training before he set sail for Gallipoli on what turned out to be a fateful voyage. Walter enlisted on 19 October 1914 at Southborough and at the time of his death he had been in the Army for one year and ten days. He had previously served in the 1st Battalion, Royal West Kent Volunteers.

Walter and Louisa had four other children, Lilian, Dorothy, Violet and Ernest although only the latter two were still living at home. Louisa received a pension for herself, Violet and Ernest of 23/6 a week commencing on 8 May 1916, some six months after Walter had been killed. There are lots of recorded incidents of brothers dying on the same day as each other during the First World War, but there can't be too many occasions where a father and son were killed on the same day as a result of the same incident. What makes their deaths even more tragic is that they did not come about as a result of enemy action but as a result of a tragic accident involving another Royal Navy vessel.

Roberson, Harry, Sapper (1564). The Commonwealth War Graves website and the British Army First World War Medals Roll Index Cards which cover the period 1914–1920, record the surname as Roberson, whilst the St Matthew's Church memorial records the name as being Robertson although they are clearly the same person.

The 1911 Census shows a 16-year-old Harry Roberson living at 10 Kirkdale Road, Tunbridge Wells, Kent, with his parents, Frank and Minnie Roberson, his elder brother William and his two younger sisters, Ivy and Dorothy.

Rogers, John, Sapper. He was 22 years of age and a Sapper (742). His parents, Richard and Sarah Rogers, lived at 19 Speldhurst Road, Southborough, Tunbridge Wells.

Salter, William Henry, Second Corporal (916) was twenty. His parents, William and Eliza Salter, lived at 9 Steward Road, High Brooms, Tunbridge Wells.

Saunders, William, Sapper (2092) was 28 years of age. His mother, Mrs Selina Saunders, lived at 2 Hayward's Cottages, St John's Road, Tunbridge Wells. After the war, his widow, Alice, was living at 96 Ealing Park Gardens, South Ealing, London.

Ticehurst, Edward, Sapper (848). He was 22 years of age and his parents, Mr and Mrs Robert Ticehurst, lived at 109 Silverdale Road, Tunbridge Wells.

Todman, Harry, Sapper (1411) was 28 years of age and his father, George Todman, lived at Ferrers Estate, Tunbridge Wells

Tutchener, Frank Leonard, Bugler (757) was 23 years of age. The 1911 Census shows the family home as being 44 Springfield Road, Southborough, Tunbridge Wells. Frank lived there with his parents, Henry and Mary Tutchener, his three brothers Henry,

Arthur and Hubert, who were all too young to have served during the war and his sister, Rose, who was five. By the end of the war his parents had moved the family to 3 The Retreat, London Road, Southborough, Tunbridge Wells.

Wood, Walter Edward, Sapper (1011) was born in 1897 in Speldhurst, Kent. The 1911 Census showed him living with his family at 2 Oak View, Tunbridge Wells. His parents, Albert and Francis Wood, had six other children besides Walter. Daughters Ether and Edith, along with four sons, Albert, Harold, William and Henry, who was only six years of age.

It would have been extremely painful for any community to have lost so many men from their midst and not feel the loss, but to have lost so many men on the same day and from the same incident, must have left the community scarred for ever more. One street, Silverdale Road, lost seven men. These are men and their families who would have known each other on a social setting, and in the ten minutes that it took HMS *Hyde* to sink, their lives were extinguished for eternity.

There is a memorial tablet in memory of the men of the 1st/3rd Kent Field Company, Royal Engineers who lost their lives when HMS *Hythe* was sunk, at St Matthew's Church, which is located at High Brooms Road, Tunbridge Wells. It has been there since 1969 and prior to that it had been hung on one of the walls at the old Southborough Drill Hall in the town.

On Saturday 31 October 2015, St Martin's Church held a special service to commemorate the centenary of HMS *Hythe*'s sinking. Surviving relatives of the men listed on the memorial were invited to attend. The names of the men are recorded on the tablet in four columns and the inscription reads as follows.

'This Memorial is erected to the memory of those of the 1st/3rd Kent Field Company, Royal Engineers, who volunteered to serve their King and country in the war of 1914 and lost their lives in Mudros, when upon HMS *Hythe*, which was sunk in a collision with HMS *Sarnia* on the night of October 28th 1915. The names of all those who perished in this catastrophe are inscribed below.'

The memorial tablet was unveiled on the date of the first anniversary of the disaster, on 28 October 1916 by Sir David Salomons, who was the father of Captain David Reginald Herman Phillip Salomons as well as being the individual whose idea it was to raise the 1st/3rd Kent (Fortress) Royal Engineers.

Mrs Tingley and her Seven Sons

Throughout the war there were many occasions when families had more than one of their sons who had enlisted in one of His Majesty's armed services, sometimes it was even fathers and sons. War memorials up and down the country record the names of cousins, uncles and nephews as well as brothers-in-law, all of whom lived and worked in the same community.

Mrs Fanny Tingley was a widow of Bough Beech in Edenbridge, who, since 1894 when her husband, Abraham, had died, had brought her seven sons up all on her own. By the time the First World War had started all of them had already been in the Army for many years, with some of them having also fought in the 2nd Boer War as well.

Seeing her sons go off and fight in a second war couldn't have been easy for her; they had all survived and come back to her safely once before, whether she was going to be so fortunate again, must have undoubtedly been playing on her mind.

An article about her receiving a letter from the King, who had been made aware of her circumstances, appeared in the *Kent & Surrey Courier*.

An Edenbridge Military Record
Seven Soldier Sons
Royal letter of Congratulation.

'In our last issue we gave details of the fine military record of the family of Mrs Tingley, of Bough Beech, Edenbridge, who has seven sons serving in His Majesty's Forces, and we have much pleasure in announcing that we have received from the Keeper of the Privy Purse the following gracious letter from His Majesty to be forwarded to Mrs Tingley:

'Privy Purse

Buckingham Palace 25th January 1915

'Madam,

'I have the honour to inform you that the King has heard with much interest that you have at the present moment seven sons in the Army.

'I am commanded to express to you the King's congratulations, and to assure you that His Majesty much appreciates the spirit of patriotism which promoted this example, in one family, of loyalty and devotion to their sovereign and Empire.

'I have the honour to be, madam, your obedient servant.

'F M Ponsonby

'Keeper of the Privy Purse'

Harry Tingley was the eldest of the brothers, having been born in 1872 He went on to become a Battery Sergeant in the Royal Field Artillery, serving in India for six years between 13 January 1896 and 21 April 1902, and serving for a total of twenty-one years, before finally being discharged on 26 November 1912 having served his time.

Harry re-enlisted in the Royal Field Artillery as a Battery Sergeant Major (149427) on 26 January 1915 at Aldershot, by which time he was already 42 years of age. He was finally demobbed on 26 April 1919 having served for a total of twenty-five years in the British army.

Tom Tingley had served as a gunner in the Royal Field Artillery for 12 years before the war, and had re-joined at the outbreak of hostilities when he became a private in the Queen's Own (Royal West Kent) Regiment. Tom's actual Christian name was Abraham, which was also his father's name. His brother Herbert was a gunner with the Royal Field Artillery, having enlisted in 1902, and was already serving in France by the beginning of 1915.

Norman was a gunner (20120) in the Royal Garrison Artillery and when the war began he was stationed at Ferozepore in India. He had originally enlisted in London on 18 May 1897, having just reached his nineteenth birthday, prior to which he had been a labourer. After the outbreak of war he remained in India with the 82nd Company, Royal Garrison Artillery, where he had served for eight years, until 9 June 1916 when an injury meant that he had to be sent back to England. He also served in France during the First World War between 20 November 1916 and 27 April 1918.

Norman was eventually discharged from the Army on 28 March 1919 after having served for nearly twenty-two years.

George was a Private in the Queens Own (Royal West Kent) Regiment and had already served all through the Second Boer War in South Africa, and afterwards took his discharge. His Army service record has not survived but we know that he re-joined the Army after the start of the First World War.

Stanley was a gunner in the Royal Garrison Artillery and had already served in the Army for eleven years by the outbreak of the war. He was stationed in Ceylon at the commencement of hostilities, but then returned to England where he was stationed at Portmouth, before setting off for France with his Regiment in January 1915.

Miles was a gunner (15262) in the Royal Field Artillery who had served twelve years with the regiment prior to the war; he re-enlisted on 19 September 1914 at the age of thirty-seven and was sent to their number 4 Depot Woolwich. Just over a month later, on 29 October 1914, he was promoted to the rank of Corporal and on 20 February 1915, he was promoted to the rank of Sergeant. He went out to France on 20 July but was only out there for two months before he returned to the UK on 24 September, where he would remain for the rest of his service. His Army Pension records do not explain why he only spent two months serving in France during the war, but as he left the Army on 20 September 1918, six weeks before the end of the war, it would be reasonable to believe he had been wounded whilst serving in France, returned to the UK to have his wounds treated and that eventually it was deemed that after three years, he was never again going to be fit enough for war service.

Albert Edward Allen was a Private (1559) with 'A' Company, 9th Battalion, The Kings (Liverpool Regiment) which was a Territorial Unit, when he died on 17 February 1915, just 18 years of age. Remarkably Albert had enlisted in the Army just two months after his fifteenth birthday on 3 December 1911, in Liverpool. His Army medical record shows that he was just over five feet one inch tall. Albert's death was a tragic accident, because he was accidentally shot by both a friend and colleague at 10 Queens Road, Tunbridge Wells, where along with other colleagues, he was billeted.

In the aftermath of the accident, reports were taken from nine of Albert's colleagues, one of these was from Albert's Sergeant in 'A' Company, C Jones.

'On the 17th February 1915 at about 1.30 I was sitting in my room at 10 Queens Road, when I heard a report (gunshot). I rushed into the room from whence the report appeared to come from and saw Pte Allen with his hands over his eyes leaning up against the wall. He said, "I have been shot, Sergeant", and repeated it. I asked him how and he made a statement in a faint voice which I understood to be, "By accident". Pte Wilson was at my back and he said, "By me, have I hurt him?" I then told one of the men to run for the doctor; in the meantime I examined Pte Allen and found he had been hurt in the thigh. I then asked Pte Wilson what he was doing. He explained to me that he had been trying to make a pencil case and handed me a bullet. He said he had removed the lead which he handed to me, but when he pulled the trigger he forgot the cordite was in. He was very anxious to know if he had done any real damage. By that time, Corporal Brown of the RAMC had arrived.

'I assisted Corporal Brown to dress the patient and when he had finished I told Corporal Brown that if the patient did not come round within an hour, I would send for him.

'Next Sergeant Clarke came into the room and questioned some of the men, then had a look at the patient and decided to send for the Doctor, Captain Mahoney, RAMC, who on arrival pronounced Private Allen to be dead.

'I found two cartridge cases, one bullet and several small pieces of lead near where Pte Allen was lying."

It would appear that it was the wadding from the empty cartridge that was still in the weapon when it was discharged, that caused the injury to Albert's left thigh. The cause of his death was officially recorded as a haemorrhage. The report does not include anything about what happened to Private Wilson or even an explanation as to how or why he came to pull the trigger on his Lee Enfield rifle.

All of the Voluntary Aid Detachment (VAD) hospitals played a vital role in the recuperation of wounded troops sent home from the fighting to have their wounds treated. Most were a place of peace and tranquillity, where both officers and men alike could find respite from the fighting whilst their wounds healed sufficiently for them to be sent back to the front.

VAD nurses and some of their patients. (Unknown photographer)

It was amazing that all of the work that the doctors and nurses did was voluntary and they relied heavily on people helping them in either a physical sense or by donating items for the hospital or in a monetary sense so that other items of need could be purchased.

Kent 154 represented the official reference to the VAD section at Rusthall, the Commandant of which was Miss Rachael Maud Ard, who according to the 1911 Census, was living at 5 Hungershall Park, Tunbridge Wells. The Quartermaster was Miss L Kemball.

On the evening of Monday 22 March 1915 a meeting was held at the Working Men's Institute in Rusthall, to let local people know the excellent work that was being carried out by Kent 154 VAD and what else was needed for the section's twenty bed hospital at Rusthall. It wasn't just nursing staff that the section required, they needed financial donations as well as specific items such as bed linen and furniture. They had women volunteers doing washing up, whilst male volunteers were working in the hospital's garden. A local woman who was a fully trained masseuse had provided her services free of charge to the hospital, which was of great help as massage was seen as an important factor in the healing process for injured soldiers.

Some of them had mentioned that after spending months in trenches on the Western Front, where they had been cold and wet whilst being continuously bombarded by German artillery, the comfort of the hospital and the kindness shown to them by the staff who were looking after them, had re-invigorated their spirits and given them the desire to return to the front so they could once again do their bit.

Rust Hall was located just off Langton Road and lay on the borders of Rusthall Common, in twelve acres of fields and woods with an orchard, bowling green, and lovingly tended lawns. Miss L Kemball, the VAD Quartermaster, had the luxury of using one of the cottages on the estate as her office. The house itself looked resplendent and notably had both the Union Jack and Red Cross flags flying from flag staffs at the front of the building, leaving nobody in two minds as to the work that went on there.

By April 1915, Rust Hall had twelve wounded British soldiers who were undergoing treatment, which had coincided with an influx of various donations. Members of the community had brought in flowers, vases, magazines, newspapers, eggs, apples, hymn books, cakes, cigarettes, bed socks, oranges, plants, pillow cases, dish cloths, a clock, and a hot water bottle.

Less than a month later the number of wounded soldiers had risen to forty, four of whom were Canadians. A new ward was built on the site, the cost of which had been met by a local resident, Mrs J J Barrow. New radiators as well as electricity were installed in every room, provided by Mrs Wrench. The hospital had two doctors/surgeons, two dentists and a list of individuals who were prepared to loan the hospital their motor vehicles for the conveyance of patients to and from the hospital.

The staff, seventy-one in total, were mostly local women thrown together to do their bit for the common cause, in the fight against Germany. Some were friends, some were sisters, and there was even the case of a mother and her two daughters all working together to help the best way that they could to serve. Some had money and a privileged life style, whilst others were just ordinary people, whose very existence was never going to be an easy one, but they all worked shoulder to shoulder, in an effort to make a difference.

The hospital's first patient, although totally unexpected, was a soldier who was stationed in Tunbridge Wells. He was on a route march on 5 April 1915 and was taken ill immediately opposite the main gates of the hospital. Between then and 31 December 1915, the number of soldiers being treated at the hospital at any one time varied between eleven and sixty-seven, whilst the total number of patients treated at the hospital had been 397. Of these, 230 suffered with gas poisoning, trench foot, gunshot or shrapnel wounds. No soldiers had died whilst being treated at the hospital, with 308 men staying for an average thirty-three days and on 31 December 1915, a total of 89 men were being treated at the hospital.

Because of Kent's geographical location close to the English Channel, it was always going to bear the brunt of having to provide medical facilities for the treatment of returning wounded soldiers to the shores of the United Kingdom. In total there were 2,500 women and 500 men volunteers who worked in the eighty-one VAD run hospitals dotted throughout Kent, which provided some 7,300 beds; in the first seventeen months of the war, approximately 25,000 patients had come through their doors.

Even though all of the VADs were doing excellent work, as was clearly shown with the efforts of those at the Rust Hall VAD Hospital, two years into the war there was an urgent need for more nurses as well as general service members. For a start the war had gone on for far longer than had been anticipated, coupled with the fact that the numbers of men who were being wounded was only surpassed by those who were being killed.

Rachel Ard, the Commandant, was awarded the OBE in August 1917 for the continuously outstanding work that had been undertaken at the hospital under her leadership. Rust Hall VAD Hospital was seen as one of, if not the, best run hospitals in the entire country, and Kent as a whole had three of the four best VAD hospitals in the country. Rust Hall had become so popular that it once again increased its capacity and added the nearby Rust Hall girls' school as part of its military hospital.

Such was the desire to do one's bit from all corners of society during the First World War, even the Suffragettes put their differences with the authorities to one side to help the war effort. They agreed to stop all propaganda and anti-establishment activities for the duration of the war. This included the Tunbridge Wells branch. The following notice was posted in the windows of their premises in Crescent Road.

An NUWSS banner. (Unknown photographer)

'All Political and Propaganda work is suspended. Members of this vast Union, at the request of their President, Mrs Henry Fawcett, bind themselves together for the purpose of rendering the greatest possible aid to their country at this momentous epoch.

'The committee of the Tunbridge Wells Branch has offered the use of its premises for the assistance of any scheme of relief which His Worship the Mayor's proposed Public Committee shall devise, and we call upon all our members and the friends of Women's Suffrage to volunteer to help in any capacity for which they are specifically fitted.

'Sarah Grand

'President.'

Their premises was also used as a War Relief Clothing Depot, where members of the public from the local community could bring in unwanted items of clothing, which were then used for the benefit of either British soldiers or the ever increasing number of Belgian refugees who had been relocated to Tunbridge Wells.

An article about the Tunbridge Wells branch of the Women's Emergency Corps appeared in the *Kent & Sussex Courier* on Friday 22 January 1915.

'Mrs J M Robertson presided at a meeting which was held at the Monson Hall, Tunbridge Wells, on Tuesday afternoon, for the purpose of forming a local branch of the Women's Emergency Corps. The Corps was formed soon after the outbreak of war for the purpose of gathering together and classifying all expert voluntary workers, and for securing the co-operation of societies of all grades of opinion, in one organisation, and to prevent overlapping and waste of time. One of the leading ideas was to safeguard the paid labour market by controlling volunteer help, and it was also decided to form an industrial centre for organising paid employment.

'The Chairman said they had to justify their existence. She was told that Tunbridge Wells was doing everything that could be done, and it certainly was doing a lot. Almost every Society was doing splendidly, but the one point where in they differed was that the Women's Emergency Corps wanted the voluntary workers to recognise that while they had to supply the brains of organisation, working women must be kept in employment.

'Mrs Kineton Parkes said the Women's Emergency Corps claimed more than anything else to have co-ordinated other societies. In London it was in touch with nearly every other society. It acted as a sort of clearing house and put workers in touch with voluntary helpers who had work to provide.'

CHAPTER 3

1916
The Realization

This was the third year of the war and the realization that it wasn't going to be 'over by Christmas' had long since passed. More and more men were leaving the comfort of their homes and families and going off to fight in the war, and more and more of them were being killed.

By the end of the year, another 235,927 British men would be dead as a direct result of the war, which meant that the running total of those killed had now reached 424,192 in just twenty-nine months, which meant on average 14,626 men had died for each month of the war.

The realization of just how bad things were going with the war was vividly put into perspective with the Military Services Act 1916 coming into effect, bringing with it as it did, conscription. Prior to this Britain had never before had a conscripted Army, those who had joined any branch of the British military, had up to this point in time, done so voluntarily. The need for conscription was a direct result of the alarming number of casualties Britain had sustained in the first twenty months of the war. To sustain their war effort and avoid defeat at the hands of Germany, Britain simply needed more men. Conscription was the mechanism by which the Government and senior military figures acquired the men that they needed to effectively continue with the war.

Here are just a few of the major military events of 1916.

21 February–18 December – The Battle of Verdun, which was fought between French and German forces, lasted for nine months, three weeks and six days. During that time, France had a total of 1,140,000 men involved in the battle, and of these over 500,000 became casualties, with more than half of these being killed. The German numbers involved were 1,250,000 men, of whom an estimated 400,000 were casualties. Of these some 143,000 were killed.

31 May–1 June – The Battle of Jutland took place between the British Royal Navy's Grand Fleet, which was under the control of Admiral Sir John Jellicoe, and the German Imperial Navy's High Seas Fleet, commanded by Vice Admiral Reinhard Scheer. The battle took place in the North Sea, near to the coast of Denmark's Jutland Peninsula. It was the biggest naval battle in history and the only one involving battleship against battleship. By the end of the two day battle the British had lost a total of fourteen vessels and just over 6,000 men who had been killed, whilst the Germans lost eleven vessels and 2,551 men. Despite the differences in losses, history has recorded the battle as being a strategic British victory.

1 July–18 November – The Battle of the Somme was one of the bloodiest battles of the First World War, with an estimated 50,000 Allied casualties on the very first day of the battle, of whom 20,000 were killed. By its end, in excess of 1,000,000 men on both sides had been either wounded or killed.

Those soldiers who made up the British Army at the Battle of the Somme were a mixture of what was left of the pre-war regular army, Territorial Units and Kitchener's New Army, the latter made up of Pals Battalions.

15 September – Tanks were used for the first time on the Western Front since the war had started, during the Battle of the Somme.

28 November – The first German air raid by an airplane as opposed to a Zeppelin, on Britain, took place over London.

6 December – David Lloyd George replaced Herbert Henry Asquith as the British Prime Minister. Prior to becoming Prime Minister he had also been the Minister of Munitions and the Secretary of State for War.

David Lloyd George.
(Library of Congress)

Tanks on the Western Front. (Library and Archives of Canada)

Herbert Asquith experienced the First World War on a very personal level. He was one of the hundreds of thousands of parents who had lost one of their children to the war. His son Raymond was a Lieutenant in the 3rd Battalion, Grenadier Guards, when he was killed in action on 15 September 1916.

Another example of how the war managed to take men's lives even though it had not happened in a war zone, but back in the relative safety of England was covered by the *Kent & Sussex Courier* on Friday 7 January.

Herbert Henry Asquith. (Library of Congress)

New Year's Day tragedy in Tunbridge Wells
Officer's Suicide in a Billet

'The officers' billet at The Dell, Ferndale, Tunbridge Wells, was the scene of a painful tragedy on New Year's Day. Private Finnigan went to the bedroom of his Master, Lieutenant and Quartermaster, Joseph William Lancaster, at about 7.30 am, and found him lying in a pool of blood with a severe wound in his throat. Life was extinct. The deceased officer, who belonged to the 2/7th Lancashire Fusiliers, and had been quartered in Tunbridge Wells since October, was 43 years of age. He had suffered with asthma for many years.

'Joseph had been in the Army before the war and having done his twelve year term of service had left, but re-joined the Army after the outbreak of war in April 1915.'

Private Finnigan had described the sight that had greeted him when he managed to gain entry into Lieutenant Lancaster's room, with lots of blood in different parts of the room. A bloodied razor was subsequently found on his bed and he had a four inch long wound to his throat.

A subsequent inquest found it to be a case of suicide brought about during temporary insanity, due to severe attacks of asthma, which had caused acute depression. How a jury quite came to such a detailed and in depth decision isn't clear, especially as nobody, friends, colleagues or doctors had ever noted any such behaviour that might possibly bring his sanity into question or suggest he had ever suffered from depression.

He was buried in the Tunbridge Wells Cemetery with full military honours. His coffin which was draped in the Union Jack, was conveyed to the cemetery on a gun carriage drawn by four horses.

A happier report appeared in the same paper on Friday 28 January with an article about a soldier from the town receiving a medal for gallantry.

DCM for Tunbridge Wells soldier

'Pte. G Jenner, of the Royal West Kent Regiment, who had been acting as a stretcher bearer, has been awarded the DCM for gallantry in rescuing an officer and a Private under heavy fire in front of the British lines in France. Pte. Jenner was able to get back to the British trench without being hit himself, and then rendered first aid to the wounded men. Pte. Jenner is a married man, whose home is at High Brooms, and was until he enlisted in Kitchener's Army, a greengrocer's assistant in Tunbridge Wells. He has been in France nine months.'

The citation for his award which appeared in the *London Gazette* on 11 March 1916 read as follows.

'For conspicuous gallantry. Sergeant Cresswell, under heavy fire, brought in an officer and a man of another regiment who were entangled in the wire. Later with Private Jenner, he went out three times to rescue the wounded. The enemy's trenches were about 70 yards away and they were firing heavily.'

Private (657) Jenner served with the 6th Battalion of the Queens Own (Royal West Kent Regiment).

The *Kent & Sussex Courier* of Friday 22 December carried an article about the Smith family of Tunbridge Wells.

'Mr and Mrs W E Smith of Medway Villa, 50 Quarry Road, Tunbridge Wells are to be congratulated upon their splendid family record, having three sons serving with the Colours, while the father, Sergt. Smith, until recently was also serving in the RFA, but is now on munition work. He first joined in 1884, went through the African War and the Boer War, and also served eight years in Egypt. Private George Smith, age 20, Royal West Kent Regiment, took part in the fighting at the Dardanelles, and is now in Egypt. He is an old St. James schoolboy, and served his apprenticeship with the late Mr Bishop, bootmaker, Crescent Road. Private Alec Smith, age 21, Royal West Kent Regiment, attached to the RAMC, joined at the commencement of the war. He has been at the Persian Gulf for some time, and is now in Mesopotamia. He was formerly employed at Messrs. Lipstone, and later at Sainsbury's. He is also a St. James' schoolboy. Private Billy Smith, age 22, Welsh Fusiliers, enlisted in 1914. He has been wounded once, and is now back in the firing line again. He was in the employ of Messrs. Lipton.'

Private (5602) (511912) Victor Sellers of the London Scottish Regiment and who lived at 2 St Luke's Road, Tunbridge Wells, was wounded, having received a gunshot wound to his left hand. He wrote a letter to his parents which they received on Thursday 6 July.

'I was slightly wounded in the left hand with a piece of high explosive shell. It is nothing much to worry about. I am very thankful indeed when I think how luckily I have escaped. We attacked the enemy's lines and achieved our objective. I was wounded while shooting at the Huns, who were retreating from their first line to their second. I am sorry about my chum, who was killed outright. He happened to be just behind me, poor chap. His name is W. Watson of Chiswick. I am currently at the No.2 Canadian General Hospital, suffering from my wound and slight shell shock.'

The War Diaries for the 2nd Canadian General Hospital, situated at

Le Treport, record that the officer in charge of the Unit was Lieutenant-Colonel K Cameron of the Canadian Army Medical Corps. The diaries show that on the very first morning of the Battle of the Somme, the weather consisted of bright sunshine, clear skies and that it was hot. There were 283 patients already being treated at the hospital. On Sunday 2 July it was still a nice day, it was a bright with clear blue skies and although the temperature had dropped slightly, it was still warm. At 1030 am that morning a convoy of 245 wounded along with 4 sick men arrived at the hospital and at 6.30pm that evening a further 381 wounded arrived. A large number of the men who arrived that day had sustained very serious wounds. On 5 July, 100 badly wounded soldiers were evacuated back to England for further treatment, followed by another 133 cases the following day, 6 July, of which Victor was one.

At 5.30pm on Friday 7 July, 144 wounded men were evacuated to England for further treatment. On the convoy that left the hospital with all of the casualties, the ambulances were driven by women, who had recently replaced the men who had previously carried out the role.

Victor had enlisted on 18 November 1915 at 69 Buckingham Gate, London, which was the headquarters of the 14th Battalion, London Regiment (London Scottish). He landed in France on 29 March 1916, returned to England on 7 July after he had been wounded, where he remained until he was eventually demobbed on 28 March 1919. His Army Service Record shows that he suffered a gunshot wound to his wrist and not a wound from an explosive shell to his hand. He was in hospital for 13 days having his gunshot wound treated, yet when he was admitted to the Roy Herbert Hospital in Woolwich for appendicitis on 13 August 1918, he remained there for a total of 63 days, finally being discharged on 14 October 1918.

Letters from the Front was a popular theme in most newspapers up and down the country, and Tunbridge Wells was no different. The edition of the *Kent & Sussex Courier* for Friday 3 March included a letter from a well-known local football player, Harry Hollamby, who was a Pioneer-Sergeant in the 17th Battalion, Middlesex Regiment, which he had sent to Mr & Mrs Molineux of 9 Calverley Road, Tunbridge Wells and was dated 21 February.

'Just a few lines to you, hoping you are all right and in the best of health, like myself. I have a chance to write now we are on a rest, having just come back from the line. It is quite a change from the noise of the guns and "whiz-bangs". I thank you very much for the parcels sent. We have been going on alright since we have been in France, but have plenty to do in seeing to all the sanitary arrangements for the troops. There are ten of us in our staff, and a fine lot of chaps too, they don't mind what they do or where they go. We have lost a lot of the "boys" lately in the trenches, but, on the whole, have been very lucky. This last time we only had three wounded, but, still, that is quite enough. We have been given very unthankful jobs sometimes, but soon get used to them. The weather is mild and the sun is lovely today. I hope it will not be long before the war is over, so that we can all come back to see the old folks again. Kindly remember me to all at the Wells.'

Harry Hollamby of 3 Albion Square, St Johns, Tunbridge Wells had enlisted on 1 March 1915 aged twenty-five, at Kingsway as a Private (922) in the Middlesex Regiment. He had previously served as a Territorial with the Queens Own (Royal West Kent Regiment) since 10 February 1913. Not only did he leave behind his beloved football when he went off to war, but also his lovely wife, Rose. They had married at Southborough Parish Church on 29 November 1908 when Harry was only eighteen. It would appear that Harry and Rose possibly had to get married as their first child, Harry James Arthur Hollamby was born on 16 March 1909, just four months after they were married. Their daughter Daisy May, was born on 18 April 1910.

Within only eight months of enlisting Harry had already been promoted to the rank of Sergeant, which was a remarkable feat. Despite being wounded in action twice, first on 1 August 1916 and latterly on 13 November 1916, as well as being Mentioned in Despatches for his actions on 9 April 1917, Harry survived the war, ending up as a Sergeant (26972) in the 13th Gun Battalion, West Riding Regiment, before finally being demobbed on 27 February 1919.

Sadly for Harry and his two children, his wife, Rose, wasn't so fortunate. She died on 13 October 1918 of 'Influenza and Pneumonia' at 89 St John's Road, Tunbridge Wells. Harry was still serving in France at the time of Rose's death and was given two weeks home leave to attend her funeral and spend time with his family, but he was back in France by 4 November 1918, where he stayed until 26 February 1919, finally returning to England for demobilization. He was awarded the 1914/15 Star as well as the British War and Victory Medals.

Private Edward Welsh of the London Scottish Regiment, and the eldest son of Mr and Mrs W S Welsh of Yew Tree Cottages, Eridge Green, wrote an interesting letter to his parents which described his experiences in the trenches. Private Welsh had previously attended King Charles School in Tunbridge Wells. He had enlisted in the Army on 11 December 1915 at Buckingham Gate in London, and had been in France for five months.

'I am back again in the trenches for 12 days after six days rest. The trenches are really a very curious mixture of War and Peace. Here less than 200 yards from the Germans, the trenches are fringed with cornflowers and scarlet poppies; not in little tufts, but in masses. Here and there one finds a cabbage which has run to seed, a few turnips, and today I saw quite a number of self-sown potatoes. Overhead one can hear the larks singing beautifully all day long, just as in dear old England.

'On the other hand at times one cannot hear one's self shout because of the crash and roar of guns and shells. When a strafe is on the place it is an absolute hell. And the hideous sights one sees! Only yesterday when one of our shells burst in the Hun's front line I saw a human leg go up in the air.

'Very curiously, the other day a very old number of "The Tatler" was handed to me, and the first thing I saw when opening it was the heading "Last Meet of the Eridge Hunt". An all-khaki gathering, and there were three snaps, one of the meet at the Gun Hotel, another of Lord Henry leading the field down "Washing Stool", and the other of the field at the Heavy Gate. The whole thing brought back memories of many jolly runs I've had behind the dear old pack.

'I am still well and fit, and am quite contented. Hope you are all ok.

'Your affectionate son.'

Edward William Sanderson Welsh was a Private (6263) (512446) in the

2nd/14th Battalion, London Regiment (London Scottish), which was a Territorial Unit. He served in both France and Egypt during the war and was demobbed on 6 April 1919 at the Shorncliffe Army Camp in Kent.

On Friday 10 March the *Kent and Sussex Courier* carried a column on page two and under the heading of 'Recruiting Appeals Tribunal' there were a couple of particularly interesting cases.

Doing Their Duty

'Mr Vidler a farmer, requested the tribunal to exempt his son L N L Vidler, a cowman. He stated that he had one son on active service, another on garrison duty, and another had been drowned on the *Amphion*.

The Mayor: "Your sons are doing their duty, no doubt."

Applicant: "Yes, one of them was the first sailor in Tunbridge Wells to be lost."

Exemption for one month (Equivalent to three) was granted.'

William Starkes Vidler was the son who had been lost with the sinking of HMS *Amphion*. There is no record of Leonard Vidler having ever served during the First World War, so it would appear that each time he went before a tribunal he was successful with his appeals. If this was in fact the case, it would appear that sympathy was being shown to the Vidler family because of their earlier loss.

Belgians Taking Englishmen's Jobs

'A J Tanner, bootmaker, employed by Mr Allen, was claimed as indispensable by his employer. Mr Allen, junr., said the man was making officers' boots. He admitted in reply to the Mayor that it was not a strong case.

'The Mayor: Could you not get a Belgian refugee? Many of them are being employed.

'Mr Saunders: When you refer to Belgian refugees Mr Mayor, I take it you refer to Belgians ineligible for military service?

'The Mayor: Their law is different, but more of them are being called up.

'Mr Saunders: However much we may be sympathetic with the Belgians, we are fighting to restore their country, and it is certainly a hardship for Englishmen to know they are being

called up and that able bodied Belgians are taking their places.
   'The appeal was rejected.'

In March 1916 the government brought in conscription for the first time, as the need for yet more and more fighting men grew. To make this piece of legislation even more effective they utilised women to replace soldiers who were employed in non-combatant roles, such as dispatch riders, telegraphists or clerks. Nearly all of these women came from the Women's Volunteer Reserve, a unit of which existed in Tunbridge Wells, which had grown out of the Women's Emergency Corps and had begun soon after the outbreak of the war in August 1914. To join the Women's Volunteer Reserve a member had to purchase their own uniform, which at a cost of £2 was a prohibitive sum of money for most women, but such was the determination to 'do their bit', most managed to find the money somehow.

   On Friday 2 June the *Kent & Sussex Courier* carried the following three reports that were certainly worthy of a mention. Firstly there was that of a wounded soldier under the heading of 'Tunbridge Wells Man Wounded'.

   'We recently recorded that Pte. Vic Rickwood, an old King Charles' boy, had been wounded. He has for some weeks past been in hospital in Malta, where he has undergone a further operation to remove some pieces of shrapnel which were not got out at Boulogne. He sends to a friend at Tunbridge Wells a photo of himself taken by one of the sisters in the hospital at Malta and states that he is now able to get about on crutches. He hopes to be quite on his own soon, and to get back to the fighting line in time for the big move.'

The second article was about a gallantry award for bravery and carried the heading, 'Military Cross for Tunbridge Wells Officer'.

   'Captain Leonard D Saunders, RAMC, of Tunbridge Wells, has been Mentioned in Despatches and awarded the Military Cross for conspicuous gallantry and devotion to duty. Captain Saunders had the honour of an audience with the King, as recorded in our last issue, when his Majesty conferred the decoration upon him. The deed of gallantry for which the Cross as awarded is thus described in the "London Gazette": Captain Saunders tended the wounded under heavy fire and finally got them away with great skill and care. His clothing was torn by fragments of shell, and he was at work for forty-eight hours without rest. This is the third time he has displayed great coolness and devotion to duty.'

The 1911 Census shows a thirty-five-year-old Leonard Douglas Saunders living at 24 Earls Road, Tunbridge Wells, with his elderly parents, John and Catherine Saunders, and his sister Gertrude. His father was a retired book seller, whilst Leonard was a doctor. He survived the war and, besides his Military Cross, he was awarded the 1915 Star, having arrived in France on14 July 1915, the British War Medal as well as the Victory Medal, for his war time services.

Lastly there was the remarkable story of a young man from Southborough who was awarded the Distinguished Service Medal. Eric Menhennitte Peacock was born in Billingshurst, Sussex on 30 January 1898. Before he became a Signal-Boy (J/24895) in the Royal Navy, he had lived with his parents, Philip and Helen Peacock, his younger brother, Philip and his three sisters, Winifred, Violet and Kathleen, at Nursery Cottage, 19 Vale Road, Southborough. He joined the Navy as a fourteen-year-old boy, and after completing his initial basic training, he joined HMS *Irresistible*, the ship he was with at the outbreak of the war. He was awarded his DSM for his service during the Gallipoli campaign whilst still only 17 years of age.

In February 1915 he was one of the men on board HMS *Irresistible* who was sent ashore to complete the destruction of the Turkish defensive Forts, which had already been heavily bombarded by British Navy guns. This was an extremely daunting prospect, as they had no way of knowing just how successful the artillery bombardment had been, and what they were going to be up against, enemy wise once they had landed.

When HMS *Irresistible* was sunk on 18 March, Eric was one of those on board, but he escaped uninjured. During the landings which took place at Gallipoli, after having volunteered for shore duty, Eric was attached to the Lancashire Fusiliers and landed on 'W' beach with them on 26 April. He was also one of the last men to leave when the decision was taken that all Allied forces were to be evacuated from the Peninsula on 10 January 1916, making him one of the first to land as well as being one of the last to leave.

When HMS *Hythe* was sinking, Eric didn't panic, as might be expected of a youngster of his tender years. Rather than look out for his own personal safety and abandon ship, he was the first person to fire distress signals from her decks. By June 1916, he had become part of the crew of HMS *Exmouth*. Not only did Eric survive the war, but he lived to the ripe old age of ninety-eight years, before he died in May 1996. At the time of his death he was living in Portsmouth, Hampshire.

The members of the Women's Legion, who were all volunteers, were formed in 1915 but it was eventually merged in to the Women's Army Auxiliary Corps, which had been set up quite late on in the war, in March 1917.

The *Kent & Sussex Courier* dated Friday 21 January 1916 included an article about the improvements which had been carried out at the hospital at Rust Hall.

New buildings opened by Lord Chilston.

'An extension block of new buildings has been erected in the grounds of the Rust Hall Red Cross VAD Hospital at Tunbridge Wells, two large wards having been added, which increase the accommodation of the hospital from 50 to 100 beds. The new block of buildings is substantially constructed of wood, and all the apartments, wards, recreation hall, nurses sitting room, kitchen, pantry, lavatories, bathrooms and linen store. All the rooms are well lit, have heating and are ventilated. At the end of each ward is a closed in veranda large enough to accommodate four beds, or eight altogether. Each veranda has removable glass panels, which can be adjusted to meet the varying conditions of wind and rain, and it is an ideal situation for the open-air treatment of special cases. The fact that the extension of the Hospital was carried out by the request of the authorities is in itself a sufficient tribute to the efficiency with which Miss Ard, the Commandant, and her staff, have performed the patriotic tasks to which they set their hands and hearts a year ago.

'The opening ceremony was performed by Lord Chilston, the county Director of the Red Cross Society.'

The cost of the extension came to £1,256. Lord Chilston, who officially opened the hospital extension, paid the following compliment to Mrs Ard and the VAD movement in general in his speech:

> 'The Surgeon-General had said to him, "I am sometimes told that we military men are jealous of your VAD hospitals, but all I can say is that we could not possibly have carried out this work without your aid. We had not the necessary number of beds, and nothing like the necessary number of nurses. You have saved the country from the disgrace of being unable to care for its wounded."'

Victor Andrew de Bier Everleigh McLaglen

Victor McLaglen. (Wikipedia)

Victor Andrew de Beir Everleigh McLaglen was born in Tunbridge Wells on 10 December 1886. He came from a large family. His parents, Andrew and Lily McLaglen, had nine children including him. He had a sister, Lily, and eight brothers; Clifford, Frederick, Lewis, Leopold, Arthur, Sydney, Cyril and Kenneth. Victor had an eventful life. His father, Andrew, was a bishop in the Free Protestant Episcopal Churchand who, in the mid-1890s, took his young family to South Africa. They didn't stay there for too long, however, as they had returned to England before April 1901. The census of that year shows the McLaglen family living at 23 East India Dock Road, Limehouse, London.

In the 1901 Census the family name was recorded as being spelled McLaglen, yet in the 1911 Census it is spelt as McLaglan, by which time they have moved on to 626 High Road, Chiswick. It was soon after this time that Victor left home; still only fourteen years of age, he hoped to join the British Army, so that he could fight in the Second Boer War in South Africa (1899–1902). He enlisted into the Life Guards but instead of fighting in South Africa he was stationed at Windsor Castle until his real age was discovered, which resulted in him having to leave the army.

He was a very fit and athletically built young man – strong as an ox – and at 6 feet 2 inches tall, appeared to be much older than his actual years. In his late teens he had moved to Canada where he took up wrestling and boxing, and because of his size he was able to fight in the heavyweight ranks.

On Wednesday, 10 March 1909, at the Vancouver Athletic Club, he fought a six-round exhibition match against the newly crowned heavyweight world boxing champion, Jack Johnson. Johnson had won the title when he defeated the reigning world champion, Tommy Burns, in Sydney, Australia, on Boxing Day 1908. His defeat to Johnson was one of only five he suffered in a sixty-eight fight career. When Burns, a Canadian, beat Marvin Hart on 23 February 1906, he became the first non-American to hold the prestigious heavyweight boxing title.

Between fights, McLaglen toured with a travelling circus where members of the audience were offered $25 if they could last three rounds with him. How many times the circus proprietor had to pay out is not recorded. On 26 September 1911 McLaglen fought Jess Willard in a four-round exhibition match in Springfield, Missouri. At the time, Willard was seen as the 'Great White Hope', and in 1915 he went on to beat the reigning world heavyweight boxing champion, Jack Johnson, who had held the title for nearly seven years.

In 1913 McLaglen returned to England and, when war broke out in 1914, he enlisted in the British Army and became an acting captain in the 10th Battalion, Duke of Cambridge's Own (Middlesex) Regiment.

Victor McLaglen and Jack Johnson, 10 March 1909, Vancouver, Canada.
(Unknown photographer)

He was sent out to Baghdad, in what was then known as Mesopotamia (now Iraq), where he arrived on 19 August 1916. In 1918 Victor became the British Army's heavyweight boxing champion. His brother, Leopold, had emigrated to Canada in 1902 and both Cyril and Kenneth were not old enough to have enlisted. Clifford, Arthur and Lewis all served with the Army Service Corps, although Clifford had also served with the 116th Heavy Battery, Royal Garrison Artillery, and Lewis had also served with the King's Royal Rifle Corps. Sydney had followed Victor into the Middlesex Regiment.

Frederick Carel Albertie McLaglen was a captain in the 13th Battalion, Lancashire Fusiliers. He was wounded while serving in France, returned to England and was having his wounds treated at St Georges Hospital in London when he contracted Blackwater Fever. He died on 26 May 1917 and was buried at the City of London and Tower Hamlets Cemetery.

Arthur was discharged from the Army on 4 June 1920 as he was deemed to be unfit for military service, having hurt one of his knees and being officially declared deaf.

Victor married Enid Lamont in 1919. Work wise, he began to take on acting parts in silent movies, and in 1920 he and Enid moved out to Hollywood. It was a move that was to prove extremely beneficial. Between 1920 and 1959, he appeared in 114 films as well as the TV programmes *Have Gun Will Travel* and *Rawhide*.

Four of Victor's brothers, Arthur, Clifford, Cyril and Kenneth, also became actors, but did not manage the same level of success that he did.

He was a popular character actor, often playing the part of a loveable drunk or an Irishman. So good was his acting that most people believed him to be Irish and not English.

Some of the films he appeared in were, *What Price Glory* (1926), *The Lost Patrol* (1934), *The Informer* (1935), a role he won an Oscar for as Best Actor, *Under Two Flags* (1936), *Gunga Din* (1939), *Fort Apache* (1948) and *The Quiet Man* (1952) where he starred alongside John Wayne, and was nominated for another Oscar for Best Supporting Actor. He was a favourite of renowned director, John Ford, and worked with other acting greats such as Cary Grant and Douglas Fairbanks Junior.

His first wife, Enid, who he had two children with, died in 1942. He remarried in 1943 to Suzanne M. Brueggeman. They were together until 1948, and in the same year he married for a third time to Margaret Pumphrey who he was with until his death in 1959.

The following are brief newspaper articles of Victor McLaglen and relate to him as a boxer. The first is from the *Evening Despatch* dated Saturday, 29 January 1916.

'Lieutenant Victor McLaglen, who leaves for the war in Mesopotamia in a few days, has seven brothers serving under the colours. Two stand 6ft. 6in, Victor himself stood 6ft. 3in, while his sister, who did good work selling programmes at the tournament at the NSC on Monday week for the wounded Allies, is 6ft. exactly.'

The *Sheffield Evening Telegraph* of Tuesday, 16 September 1919 contained an article about boxing and had got to the point where the topic of discussion was about heavyweight fighters.

'There has also been considerable discussion as to who should be asked to meet Beckett for the Lonsdale Belt, the most probable opponent appears to be Victor McLaglen, whose recent form in training is said to have given his supporters considerable hopes for his success; there are some who call McLaglen a second John Hopley. In all probability Beckett will have to wait for his chance for the belt until after he has met Carpenter, and if he wins, Dempsey also.'

How far up the ratings McLaglen was going to climb were possibly affected by his next outing, which was reported in the *Lancashire Evening Post* in the edition of Tuesday, 25 November 1919.

BOXING
Goddard's Easy Win

'At the National Sporting Club last night, the contest scheduled for 15 rounds between the heavyweight boxers Frank Goddard and Victor McLaglen came to a speedy termination. Goddard knocking his opponent out in the third round.

In the first round McLaglen landed well on Goddard's face, but the exchanges were very slow. In the second round Goddard became very assertive, and in some in-fighting he punished his opponent.

McLaglen became very weak and coming up for the third round, Goddard with a right to the jaw, settled the issue.'

Fast forward to 1935 and the British newspapers were constantly reporting the showings of McLaglen's films. There was even one article about a crash he had been involved in, whilst driving his car in Los Angeles, as reported in the *Sunderland Daily Echo and Shipping Gazette* on Saturday, 16 February 1935.

Claim Against Star

'It is learned that the claim for £2,200 against Victor McLaglen, the film star, for damages arising out of a motor accident, has been settled out of court on payment of £480, says Reuter from Los Angeles.

Mr Francis E. Donnelly, father of seven year old Edmund Donnelly, brought the action alleging that the boy had been injured and permanently scarred as the result of a collision between cars driven by Mr McLaglen and Mr Donnelly.'

Seeing the amount of money that the claim was eventually settled for, suggests that the original figure might just have been ever so slightly exaggerated because of McLaglen's status as a Hollywood actor, rather than the actual seriousness of the nature of the boy's injury.

Victor's son, Andrew, partly followed in his father's footsteps, not as an actor but as a film director. They worked together on one of Victor's later films, *The Abductors*, in 1957. Andrew was the director of the movie, whilst Victor had the lead role.

Victor passed away on 7 November 1959 in Newport Beach, California, at the age of seventy-two, from heart failure. He was laid to rest in Forest Lawn Memorial Park in Glendale, California. His life had seen him as a soldier, both as a man and a boy. He was a husband and a father. He was a boxer, a wrestler and finally an actor – a career that ultimately defined his life. Not forgetting that, he was possibly one of Tunbridge Wells' most famous, yet less remembered, individuals.

CHAPTER 4

1917
Seeing it Through

The war was now into its fourth year and still there was no end in sight. The excitement and anticipation which had been apparent during the early days of the war had long since been replaced with trepidation and a desire for the fighting to stop, once and for all. It was now just a case of 'seeing it through' till the end. Too heavy a price had already been paid in the loss of life and the numbers wounded, to stop now.

1917 was the worst year for British losses throughout the duration of the war. A total of 292,390 British service men were killed, bringing the total to 716,532, a number that would have been inconceivable at the outbreak of the war. 1917 was marked by the United States joining the war, but there were other events, in their own way just as momentous.

6 April – The United States of America entered the war against Germany, which would eventually add vast numbers of men in to the war on the Allied side and would have undoubtedly had a psychological effect in the minds of German troops.
9 April–16 May – The battles of Arras and Vimy Ridge, with British and Canadian Forces fighting in support of the French-led Nivelle Offensive.
3 May – A mutiny took place throughout the French Army, because their battle-wearied troops were physically and

emotionally exhausted. They had had enough of their commander's blasé tactics, which they saw as being somewhat suicidal in their execution. General Robert Nivelle favoured large scale frontal assaults, which unsurprisingly resulted in some extremely heavy French casualties. Nivelle was replaced with General Philipe Petain in an attempt at appeasing their troops and preventing further mutinies throughout the French Armies.

26 June – The first American troops arrived in France, under the leadership of General John Joseph "Black Jack" Pershing. By the end of the war some 3,700,000 American servicemen had served in France, this included 200,000 black Americans. Total American casualties would reach 306,000, of whom 50,000 were killed.

31 July–6 November – The Third Battle of Ypres. This differed from the previous two battles in so far as it was an Allied offensive whereas the First and Second Battles of Ypres had been German assaults on Allied positions. Controversy still remains to this day as to the use of the tactics employed by Haig during the battle, and whether his decision not to call off the offensive earlier than November, by which time some of the Allied objectives had been realised, resulted in the unnecessary deaths of thousands more Allied soldiers.

20 November–3 December – The third Battle of Cambrai was remembered in the main as the battle at which the British first deployed tanks in a mass capacity.

8 December – British Forces capture the ancient city of Jerusalem and in doing so end 673 years of continuous Turkish/Ottoman rule.

The *Kent & Sussex Courier* reported on Friday 5 January that a man from Tunbridge Wells, who was an officer in the Bedfordshire Regiment had been awarded the Military Cross for his bravery.

'Temporary Captain, Allan Oswald Rufus Beale, Bedfordshire Regiment, whose name appears in the list of officers awarded the Military Cross, is the son of Mr and Mrs Louis Beale, of "Linden," Linden Park, Tunbridge Wells.

Captured British tank at Cambrai. (German Federal Archive)

'Captain Beale, who is 25 years of age, was educated at Skinners School, Tunbridge Wells, University School, Hastings, and Tonbridge School. Soon after the outbreak of war he entered Sandhurst, which he left to take up a Commission in the Bedfordshire Regiment. In June 1915, the gallant young officer went over to France, so that he has seen over eighteen months of active service, and he was recently promoted to Captaincy. He was enabled to spend Christmas at home on leave, and the official announcement that the King had bestowed upon him the coveted award, was made just prior to his return to the Front.'

Captain Beale served with the 1st Battalion, Bedfordshire Regiment, first arriving in France on 27 June 1915. He was also awarded the 1915 Star, the British War Medal and the Victory Medal. It was an interesting article in so far as it didn't actually explain what the act of bravery was that had resulted in Beale being awarded the Military Cross.

Friday 19 January saw an article in the *Kent & Sussex Courier* about a soldier from Tunbridge Wells who had been taken prisoner of war.

Tunbridge Wells
Private H Snell

'Private Herbert Snell, of the West Kents, son of Mrs Snell of Church Road, was reported missing since November 18th, but Mrs Snell has now received a postcard from him stating that he is a prisoner of war in Germany. He had re-joined his Regiment in October, after being in Hospital at Rouen suffering from wounds sustained in the Trones Wood fighting. He is an old Victoria schoolboy, and was in the employ of Mr W Smith for five years before enlisting a few weeks after the outbreak of the war. Mrs Snell has two other sons in France and another in training in England.'

Herbert was a Private (1503) in the 7th Battalion, Queens Own (Royal West Kent) Regiment. It would appear that he subsequently died of his wounds whilst in captivity in Germany as he died on 27 November 1918 and is buried in the Berlin South-Western Cemetery. This was one of the four cemeteries in Germany where the bodies of Allied soldiers were moved to after the war, from what had previously been sixteen cemeteries all over Germany.

Berlin South-Western Cemetery. (Commonwealth War Graves Commission)

The *Kent & Sussex Courier* dated Friday 12 January carried the rather sad story of Gunner Harold A Huggett of the Royal Garrison Artillery.

Southborough Man in Hospital

'News had been received by Mr and Mrs Huggett, 4 Meadow Road, Southborough, Tunbridge Wells, that their youngest son, Gunner Harold A Huggett, 127th Battery, City of Bristol, Royal Garrison Artillery, is in hospital in Shrewsbury suffering from trench fever. He had been in hospital in France for more than a month before being sent to England, and had been very ill indeed. He says nobody would know him now, he has altered so since being ill. Gunner Huggett joined the Army soon after the outbreak of war, and he has been in France about nine months.'

This could actually relate to Harold G Huggett, who was a Gunner (195513) in the Royal Garrison Artillery. There were two hospitals at Shrewsbury that were used during the First World War for wounded soldiers. There was Quarry Place Auxiliary Military Hospital at Shrewsbury, which was more than likely a VAD/Red Cross Hospital, and then there was Berrington War Hospital which was attached to the Atcham Workhouse at Cross Houses.

Trench fever was a potentially a serious disease for a soldier to catch and was transmitted by body lice, which were rife in the trenches of the First World War. It has been estimated that as many as a third of all British troops who reported themselves as being ill, were suffering with trench fever, with similar numbers of German and Austrian forces suffering the same fate. The main symptoms of trench fever, which usually hit the sufferer suddenly, are a high fever with severe headaches and soreness of the muscles in the legs and back, with a full recovery sometimes taking more than a month.

From the same edition of the newspaper was an article about a conscientious objector.

Conscientious Objector Sentenced

'We are informed that Private Percy D Saunders, a conscientious objector, enrolled for military service from Tunbridge Wells, has been tried by court-martial at Winchester for disobedience to military orders, and sentenced to twelve months' imprisonment.'

Before the war Private (3498) Percy Douglas Saunders, of No.9 Eastern Region, Non Combatant Corps, had lived at 14 Dunstan Road, Tunbridge Wells and his Enrolment Paper showed that he was thirty-three years of age, it also included the following statement at the top of the page: 'For men deemed to be enlisted in HM Regular Forces for General Service with the Colours or in the Reserve for the period of the war, under the provisions of the Military Services Act 1916.' His Enrolment Form also stated that Percy was; 'Exempted from combatant service by West Kent Appeal Tribunal 14 April 1916.'

Percy was called up for service on 23 May 1916 and was ear marked for Garrison Service Abroad, but he failed to report to where he had been told to go, and was fined 45/- at Tunbridge Wells for being absent from 23 May 1916 to 19 December 1916, the latter date being when he finally enrolled. His Army Service Record showed that on 21 December 1916 he joined No.9 Region Non Combatant Corps but only after he had been arrested by Detective Sergeant Albert Edward Kingston of Tunbridge Wells Borough Police, who had stopped him in the street and then detained him in custody awaiting trial.

Between 22 December 1916 and 6 January 1917 he was tried and convicted by a District Court Martial at Pitt Corner, Winchester, for when on active service, disobeying a lawful command given by his senior officer. Sentenced to one year's imprisonment with hard labour and sent to a civil prison to serve his sentence.

Remarkably, when soldiers who had deserted were apprehended, an award was given to the person who had detained them. The amount could differ depending on the specific details of each case, for example, whether the deserter was in plain clothes or uniform and how far away he was away from his barracks when apprehended, but could range from five to twenty shillings. If he handed himself over of his own free will then no award was provided for the person who detained him.

Sometimes it wasn't only the letters sent by men to their loved ones that were tinged with sadness and emotion, sometimes it was letters that were sent on their behalf. The *Kent & Sussex Courier* of Friday 23 March, contained such a letter. Mrs Arnold who lived at 10 Woodlands Road, Tunbridge Wells, had initially received a letter on 6 March from the sister at the hospital where her son was being treated, to tell her that he had been seriously wounded, which had resulted in his left leg being amputated. On 10 March, she received another letter, this time from the Army Chaplain, informing her that her son had sadly died and had been buried in France. She then received the following letter from Major Ralton about the death of her son.

'I regret to inform you that your son E Arnold, of Kent Field Company R E, was seriously wounded on the 2nd of this month, and has since died of his wounds while at the Casualty Clearing Station. He was one of a party who were carrying up stores for some work in the front line on the night of the 3rd. When they were not far from the line a "whizz-bang" suddenly caught the party, wounding five, your son among them. One of his legs was badly twisted and broken by the explosion, but it was hoped that he would recover from the wounds. He lies in the Soldiers' Cemetery not far from the Hospital where he died, and his grave will be registered. Sapper Arnold had been with the Company ever since its embarkation for Gallipoli, and I shall feel his loss personally as that of one of the small remnant which went with me through the *Hythe* catastrophe. He died, however, doing his duty, and may that thought and the sympathy felt for you and the rest of his folk at home, by the Company be some consolation to you in your bereavement."

Two other of those injured at the same time as Private Arnold also subsequently died of their wounds. They were all buried at the Grove Town Cemetery in the village of Meaulte. Sapper (1970) (541121) Edward Ian Arnold, who was born in Pembury, Tunbridge Wells in 1894, was serving with the 497th (Kent) Field Company.

The *Kent & Sussex Courier* dated Friday 27 April carried a report concerning the death of Corporal Nelson Colin Taylor, whose father and sister lived at 56 Edward Street, Southborough, Tunbridge Wells. Mr Taylor received the following letter from the Captain of his son's company.

'With feelings of sincere regret, I have to inform you that your son, of this company, was accidentally mortally burnt at about 7.15am on the 12th inst. I have a record of the place of burial, and will communicate it to you later. Corp. Taylor was most popular amongst the men and officers of the Company, and I offer my most sincere sympathy in your great loss.'

Reuben Charles Crowhurst was a Private (2033936) in the 7th Battalion, Middlesex Regiment, when he died on 26 August 1917, he was 37 years of age. When he enlisted at Eastbourne on 11 December 1915, he was already 35 years of age, but he had previously served in a local Militia for 6 years prior to that. He finally left for France via Southampton on 1 July 1916 with his records showing that he was initially with the 12th Battalion, London Regiment, but was diverted and joined the Middlesex Regiment. There is no explanation recorded as to why.

Part of Reuben's Army service Record included a 'Medical Report on an Invalid'. It was dated August 1917 and made for some extremely interesting reading. He is still shown as being with the 7th (Reserve) Battalion, Middlesex Regiment, but his service number has changed to 6615. Under the heading of *Statement of Case* are included points (9), (10), (11) and (12). Number (9) asks for the date of the origin of the disability which has initially been recorded as 3 August 1916. This has been crossed out and replaced with 'before enlistment'. Point number (10) asks for the place of origin of the disability, this was originally recorded as having taken place on the German counter, France. Somebody has subsequently crossed out these words and changed them to read, Eastbourne. Point number (11), which is the main facts of the matter, states the following.

> 'He states until this time he was in good health, but on this date he was compelled to report to his medical officer with pains in his feet and legs. He was treated for a week at a Field Ambulance and returned to his Unit for "Light Duty." He carried on until the end of August when he again had to report to his Medical Officer with severe pains in his feet and legs. He states he was then sent to Hospital suffering from "Trench Feet and Rheumatic Fever." Then sent to Rouen, there one week and sent to Lewes Crescent Hospital Brighton 2.6.16 with Rheumatic Fever and Trench Feet. Discharged end of November 1916 to VAD Hospital, East Chilterton. There till 17.1.17 and discharged to Furlough. Sent to Eastern Command Depot, Shoreham 19.2.17 with "Rheumatism and Trench Foot. Discharged 13.7.17. Classified.'

Point (12) (b) asks if the disability had been caused by active service, climate or ordinary military service. Originally the words, "Climatic Conditions" had been entered as the answer. Somebody has subsequently crossed this out and replaced with, "Not so caused," The hand writing of the two entries is different.

Another of the forms included in his Army Service Record is a Form B.2090; *Report of Death of a Soldier to be forwarded to the War Office immediately after the date of Death*. This form contained basic details about Reuben, such as date and place of birth. When and where he enlisted in the Army, and his profession before becoming a soldier. Under the heading 'Cause of Death', it said 'Suicide during temporary insanity. Rifle bullet through brain'. This sad incident took place at Bayhall Camp at Tunbridge Wells. The day before Reuben committed suicide he had sat before an Army Medical Board where it was decided that he was to be 'discharged from the service' as he was 'no longer physically fit for War Service'. His last day in the Army would have come in to effect two weeks later. What the actual reason was behind why Reuben took his own life is not explained in the pages that make up his Army Service Record.

Corporal (30393) Taylor was with the 17th Division, Signal Company, Royal Engineers and he was twenty-five years of age at the time of his death and he is buried at the Caberet-Rouge British Cemetery at the village of Souchez in the Pas de Calais region of France. He had first arrived in France on 30 July 1915.

Postcards can be especially poignant, such as this, written by a father to his son, and which had been sent from Boulogne in France to an address in Tunbridge Wells, Kent. The post card is dated 13 July 1917. It is addressed to Master Vyvyan Pedrick of number 28 Earls Road, Tunbridge Wells, Kent, who at the time was only five years of age. The card reads;

'Dear Vyvyan,
'Today I'm sending you a post card of a fishing fleet, these boats go out to catch fish for us, so now you will know how they eventually get on the table.
'Best of love
'XXX from Daddy Boy.'

Vyvyan's father was Percy Vivian Giles Pedrick, affectionately known as 'Fatty' by his close friends and loved ones. In July 1917 he was a Lieutenant in the Royal Army Medical Corps, serving in France. Before the outbreak of hostilities he was a civilian dentist, but as the war continued into its third year he decided that it was time for him to enlist for a year and put his skills and experience at the disposal of the British Army. During his year in the Royal Army Medical Corps, he was stationed at the No.2 General Hospital, in Etaples, France, which was a major base for the British Army. When he had completed his one year's service with the Royal Army Medical Corps he returned to England and was placed on the Army Reserve.

Over a period of time Percy had started suffering with very bad migraines, these became so bad that he had to sit before a National Services Medical Board in Maidstone on 18 July 1918, where he was diagnosed as being permanently and totally unfit for future military service, which resulted in him being removed from the Army Reserve list.

Picture postcard of Boulogne-on-Sea.

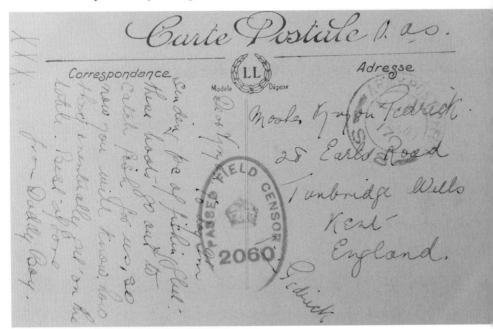

348 BOULOGNE-SUR-MER. — La Sortie des Barques de Pêche. — LL.

Percy Vivian Giles Pedrick's postcard to his beloved son.

The first photograph overleaf shows Percy wearing jodhpurs and riding boots, even down to the detail of spurs. The second photograph shows him wearing more traditional uniform bottoms with shoes. From the height of the bush on the right side of both of the photographs, it is clear that they were taken at the same time, possible minutes apart whilst Percy popped back to his tent to change his trousers and footwear.

A travel warrant allowed Percy to travel back to England on the completion of his year's contract in the ranks of the Royal Army Medical Corps. Note the unearthly start time of train journey which began at 0349 hours on 6 August 1917.

It is also interesting to note that rather than returning straight home on his arrival back in England, so enabling him to be with his family as soon as possible, he first had to attend a meeting at the War Office in London.

Percy in uniform at Etaples, France.   *Percy in the same location wearing different uniform trousers.*

Travel Warrant made out to Lieut. V G P Pedrick. (From family papers)

Copy for retention.

D.D.M.S.
No. 2 /117/17
ETAPLES.

O.C.,
        No.20. General Hospital.

        Herewith Warrant for Lieut. V.G.P. Pedrick,
R.A.M.C., to proceed to England and report to the War
Office on 5/8/1917, on termination of Contract.

H.Q., Etaples.   sd. J.A. TURNBULL.
4th August 1917.   Major, R.A.M.C.
                                  for D.D.M.S.,Etaples.

        -Order of Movement-
        -------cOo--------

        In accordance with the above instructions
Lieut.V.G.P.Pedrick,R.A.M.C.,will proceed for reporting
to the War Office on 5/8/'17.
        He will proceed by the train leaving Camiers
at 3.49,a,m.,6/8/'17.

Camiers,   Lieut-Colonel R.A.M.C.
5/8/'17.   Commanding No 20 General Hospital.

Certificate No. A 99483

M.N.S. Form R 2079

(WARNING.—If you lose this Certificate a duplicate cannot be issued.)

CERTIFICATE TO BE ISSUED TO A MAN IN THE ARMY RESERVE WHO HAS BEEN FOUND BY A NATIONAL SERVICE MEDICAL BOARD TO BE PERMANENTLY AND TOTALLY UNFIT FOR MILITARY SERVICE.

Region No._____

Full Christian Name and Surname *Vivian Percy Giles Federick*

of *28 Earls Road. Tunbridge Wells*
(Registered Address as on Registration Card.)

A member of the Army Reserve was on the *18th* day of *July*, 19*18*,

found by the National Service Medical Board at *Maidstone*

to be permanently and totally unfit for any form of Military Service and it is hereby certified that he is discharged from liability to be called up for Military Service.

Dated this *18th* day of *July* 19*18*

(Signed) *J. Vincent Jon*

Assistant Director of Recruiting.

For Minister of National Service.

Stamp of Area Recruiting Office.

*Description of the above-named man on the *18th* day of *July 1918*

Age *31 yrs 11 mths*

Height *5 ft 3* Weight *132 lbs*

Marks or Scars*.

Signature of above-named man *Vivian Federick*

* Should agree with particulars on the Medical History Sheet A.F.B. 178.

(1787) Wt.11702/427. 2500 Bks. 200 21-12-17. J.H.&C.

Exemption Certificate from future military service. (From family papers)

The *Kent & Sussex Courier* dated Friday 11 May included an article about 2nd Lieutenant H G Lanaway who had been wounded during fighting in France. The British Army Medal Rolls Index Cards for the First World War, record his name as H J Lanaway.

'2nd Lieutenant H G Lanaway, son of Mr H Lanaway of 66 Stephens Road, Tunbridge Wells, is in Hospital in London suffering from shell shock and injuries to his back, which compel him to keep his bed; but we are pleased to learn that he is progressing favourably.

'He joined the 4th Royal West Kents soon after the outbreak of war, and he saw service in Suvla Bay and was invalided home, and lay for a time in St Mary's VAD Hospital. After returning to duty he received his commission in November 1916 and left for France, where he served with the Royal West Kents. He took part in the advance on Lens, and while in a German dug-out was unfortunate enough to be buried with the remaining officers. After being in this perilous situation for five hours he was rescued and found to be the only one alive. He lay for a week in Hospital in France, and has now been brought to England.'

Initially he was a Private (TF/3647) in the Royal West Kents, before receiving a Commission on 21 November 1916 with the same Regiment, when he became a 2nd Lieutenant. He had first arrived in France on 9 August 1915, and despite his wounds and injuries, he survived the war. When he received his war time medals on 30 September 1920, the 1914-15 Star, British War Medal and the Victory Medal he was living at 14 Mountfield Place, Tunbridge Wells.

Friday 5 October saw an article appear in the *Kent & Sussex Courier* about E Fraser, a Wireless Operator on board an un-named Royal Navy vessel and how his good fortune saw him survive. This was in fact Edward William Fraser. The 1911 Census shows that Edward, who was twelve years of age at the time, was living with his parents, Alex and Sarah Fraser, his two sisters Elsie and Hilda and his older brother, Alexander, at 18 Mountfield Gardens, Tunbridge Wells. His family were especially pleased to see him again when he had returned home on leave, after he had been involved in two incidents at sea, either of which on another day could have well resulted in his death.

The article was sparse with the details of the name of the ship or where the vessel had sailed to and from, one would imagine for security reasons, but on its outward journey, it was in collision with another British vessel which thankfully did not result in loss of life on either of the ships. When the ship was returning to England it was torpedoed by a German submarine. To make matters worse, the surprise attack happened at midnight in total darkness. Anticipating that the ship was certain to sink, the crew took to the life boats but remained alongside their stricken 'lady'. After a period of time when they realised that she wasn't actually going to sink, they got back on board and managed to get her slowly and safely back to port. When the ship was torpedoed, Fraser was below decks in his wireless cabin. He would later describe that moment as a 'decidedly unpleasant experience', an understatement if ever there was one.

The following article appeared in the *Kent & Sussex Courier* on Friday 26 October 1917, under the heading of *War Notes*.

'In our last issue we recorded that the response in Tunbridge Wells to the appeal for the Women's Army Auxiliary Corps had been very disappointing, and we are glad to learn that there has been an improvement in this respect. Applications have been coming in more freely, and it is felt that when the women of Tunbridge Wells realise what is really required of them that there will be no further cause for complaint. The fact must be emphasised that the need of this Corps is really urgent, and that its claims take precedence over all other appeals for women's labour. At least 10,000 women volunteers are wanted at once. All information can be obtained from the Tunbridge Wells Labour Bureaux.'

Women's Army Auxiliary Corps
Women of Kent and Sussex are urgently required for
work with the above Corps

'A public meeting took place on Wednesday 31 October at the Pump Room in Tunbridge Wells, which was Chaired by Viscount Hardinge and had nine guest speakers ready to encourage women to enrol in the Women's Army Auxiliary Corps and be prepared to undertake work such as being cooks, waitresses, clerks, drivers, mechanics, as well as domestic workers. Members were wanted for work at both home and abroad. The Royal Flying Corps wanted 500 women to work as sail makers, to help make and repair aeroplane wings.'

CHAPTER 5

1918
The Final Blow

In what would be the final year of the war the steely determination of Britain and her Allies was being tested to its limit. Resources were nearly exhausted both in manpower and equipment. The cost of fighting the war had been an economic drain on the country, one that would take many years from which to fully recover. History would ultimately decide whether the price which had been paid in blood, sweat and tears was worth it, or whether it would ultimately prove to be no more than a Pyrrhic victory.

British and Commonwealth losses for 1918 were less than they had been in 1917, but not by much; a total of 281,303, which took the overall figures to 997,835.

Here are just a few of the major events of the war throughout the final year of war in 1918.

9–20 April – The battle of Lys took place, which in essence, was a German attack on Flanders.

15 July – The second battle of The Marne, which was a German offensive.

8 August – Both Australian and Canadian forces reached the Hindenburg Line. It was also the beginning of the Battle of Amiens as well as the start of the final one hundred day push to victory.

26 September – A massive Allied attack successfully broke through the Hindenburg Line.

9 November – Kaiser Wilhelm ll, who was the last Emperor of Germany, as well as the King of Prussia from 15 June 1888 to 9 November 1918, abdicated on this day. He was the eldest grandson of Britain's Queen Victoria as well as being related to other European Royal families.

11 November – The Armistice between Germany and the Allied nations was signed and the First World War was finally over.

Kaiser Wilhelm ll. (Bains News Service)

A frightening reminder of the war as if it was needed, took place not in the trenches of the Western Front, but on Rusthall Common, as reported in the *Kent & Sussex Courier* on Friday 15 February.

'Serious injuries were sustained by a 12-year-old boy named Frederick Gasson at Tunbridge Wells on Sunday as the result of a singular accident. It appears that the lad found a copper cylinder attached to a stick, presumably a rifle grenade or Verey light, on Rusthall Common. He took it to his home at High Street, Rusthall, and while endeavouring to remove the stick from the cylinder an explosion occurred, shattering the whole thing to pieces and blowing off the thumb and two fingers of the boy's left hand. Mrs Gasson, the mother was struck in the left ear by some pieces of metal. Both were taken to Rusthall VAD, and there received treatment, being afterwards conveyed in a taxicab to the Tunbridge Wells General Hospital, where the boy was detained. The mother, who has become deaf as consequence of the explosion, was able to return home later. Several pieces of thin copper were found by PC Grinter after the occurrence, and from these it may be possible to precisely ascertain the character of the cylinder found by Gasson.'

The following was taken from an article in the *Kent & Sussex Courier* dated 15 March.

'Mr and Mrs George Barshell, of 25 Monson Terrace, Tunbridge Wells, have received the welcome news that one of their adopted sons is taking up a commission in India, where he is now stationed. Private Cecil Shuell was an Old Victoria School boy, and on leaving was employed at Newn's Library, Grosvenor Road, the only situation that he held.

'Cecil joined up in September 1914, in a Battalion of the West Kents, and was soon despatched to India. He was in charge of the Orderly Room for some time at Jubbulpore, and becoming very popular with both officers and the rank and file, he was induced to take up a commission, and is now at Bangalore College, undergoing the necessary examinations. He is well educated, and just turned 21 years of age, and in every way fitted for the qualification.

'Mr and Mrs Barshell have also another adopted son in the Army, Private Walter Frank Shuell, serving in the ASC in France. He is brother to Private Cecil Shuell, and has been there for eighteen months. They were both brought up from babies by Mr and Mrs Barshell, who have an only son, Private George Barshell, also serving in the Army Service Corps in France, and a nephew, Private William Munn, of the Kent Cyclists, serving in India. He joined up in 1915, and previous to that was a groom at Nevill Court Mr and Mrs Barshell may well be proud of their patriotic family. Mr Barshell is a well-known tradesman in the town."

Thankfully all four men survived the war.

The *Kent & Sussex Courier* of Friday 12 July carried the following article about Thorold Ben Bendell of 79 Calverley Road in Tunbridge Wells.

'Friends of Thorold Ben Bendall, youngest son of Mr C Bendall, of Calverley Road, Tunbridge Wells, will be interested to learn that the French Government have awarded him the Croix de Guerre. The citation translated reads: Thorold B Bendall, as voluntary leader of ambulance work since 1916, was noticeable for his devotion, coolness and courage in Flanders, and especially on the Somme, May 30th 1918. He remained to the last with an advanced dressing post, and only retired after having seen the complete evacuation of the wounded.'

An award well deserved but one which begged the question why the British hadn't made a similar award to him for his actions as described in the French Government's citation.

Mrs Piper of 20 Weare Road, High Brooms had been informed by the War Office that her 19-year-old son, Private (27913) J Piper (Military Medal), of the 2nd Battalion, Hampshire Regiment, had been reported as missing. He had originally joined the Royal Field Artillery as a Gunner in November 1916, but later transferred to the Infantry. He first went to France in April 1917 and was awarded the Military Medal in November that year for his gallantry. In an attempt at obtaining clarification on the matter of her son's situation, Mrs Piper wrote to his Commanding Officer. The reply that she received was published in the *Kent & Sussex Courier* dated Friday 18 January.

'In answer to your letter of the 31st ultimo, I am sorry to say that your son has been missing since December 2nd. He was my platoon runner, and won his Military Medal while with me. He was attached to the Battalion Headquarters during the Cambrai battle, and as I was in command of another Company at the time, I did not hear of his fate until December 7th, and I have been longing and praying he might re-join his colleagues, his comrades, but in vain. He was carrying a note from Battalion Headquarters to a Company in the Front line, and after duly delivering that he was not again seen, but I am hoping he is a prisoner.'

Private Piper is officially recorded as having been killed on 30 November 1917 and is buried in the Flesquieres Hill British Cemetery, on the outskirts of the village, which is situated in the Nord region of France.

The *Kent & Sussex Courier* dated Friday 17 May carried an article about a soldier from Tunbridge Wells, Sergeant W Fermor of the Queens Own Royal West Kent Regiment, and his experiences as a prisoner of the Germans that he had written about in a letter he sent to a cousin who lived at Uckfield. He was captured in November 1914 and remained in captivity in Germany for three and a half years, until May 1918.

'It is a great relief to know we are free again. We had some jolly bad times in Germany, and are very lucky to have any health and strength. Of course many of our comrades have died for want of proper medical treatment. I can assure you that if relatives and others had not sent us the precious food parcels, very few would be in Holland today. The food they gave us was very often uneatable, and at the best of times was very poor. However there are others who have suffered worse than we; the Russians and Italians have been and are being very badly treated. Thousands have died of slow starvation, and many have been shot in cold blood. Unless you actually saw what was going on you would not think that a nation, which is supposed to be civilised, would treat human beings as they do. They used to tell us that England was a nation without a spark of honour left. Well, I guess they have got a great deal to answer for when the right time comes along. Many of our boys who were unluckily captured in the Somme offensive 1916, were kept behind the German lines and made to work until they dropped, exhausted, and then only the worse cases were sent to the camps. It was heart rending to see young boys nothing but living skeletons. We used to collect food for them and give them a jolly good feed when we had it. I wish it were possible to exchange all. Thank goodness I am not in that country!

'We always used to write and say we were all right to save our relatives worrying at home, and to make certain that our letters reached home safely. They asked all Sergeants to volunteer for work, and of course, we refused. Consequently we were all placed in close confinement for three months under the worst conditions.

'We were released on the day before the American Ambassador came, but of course we told him all about it. Finally they made us work on the land at the point of the bayonet. I might add that the crops are very bad. They are in a very bad way in Germany at present.

'Of course they can hang on for a long time yet, but the women and children are suffering terribly. They want peace badly. Some of their own soldiers even admit that they cannot possible win the war.

'We were warmly received here by the Dutch people, and when we crossed the frontier we cheered so much that many of us had to whisper for a few days afterwards. This is a lovely and very healthy place. We are billeted in very nice houses, with every convenience. At present we get 200 grams of bread per day.

'We must not grumble. We are contented at present to know we are free. We are allowed to go anywhere within a radius of seven miles without an escort. There are several places of amusement here and we are quite happy. (Some of the boys are courting already,) I hope they will soon send us home. They are trying to make arrangements on account of the food question here.

'Keep merry and bright, the dark cloud will soon be removed, and we shall win.'

Private (41403) Percival John Reader was with the 2nd/6th Battalion, North Staffordshire Regiment. He had joined the Army in 1917, having enlisted at Maidstone in Kent. His family lived at 35 Western Road, Tunbridge Wells. He was reported as missing in action in March 1918, but on Wednesday 6 November his mother, Mrs C A Reader was officially informed by the War Office that he had been killed in action on the same day as he was initially reported as missing, although his body was never found and he has no known grave.

His name is commemorated on the Arras Memorial which in total has the names of 35,000 men from the United Kingdom, South Africa and New Zealand, inscribed on it. All of these men were killed between April 1916 and 7 August 1918. The memorial was unveiled on 31 July 1932 by Lord Trenchard, Marshal of the Royal Air Force.

Private (34425) Frederick Odian Cassingham was thirty-five years of age and serving with the 5th Battalion, Gloucestershire Regiment when he was wounded whilst serving in France. He was admitted to hospital but sadly died four days later on 23 October 1918. Prior to serving in France he had seen action in Italy but had then returned with his Battalion in readiness for the final push to victory on the Western Front. He is buried at the Roisel Communal Cemetery which is located in the Somme region of France. It contains the graves of 878 servicemen who were killed in the fighting of the First World War, 120 of which remain as unidentified.

Arras War Memorial. (Commonwealth War Graves Commission)

There appears to have been another Frederick Odian Cassingham, who served in the First World War. He was a Pioneer (325730) in the Royal Engineers who enlisted at Redhill, Surrey on 10 December 1915, and was discharged at Chatham, Kent, on 18 January 1919.

The *Kent & Sussex Courier* of Friday 22 March carried an article about two acts of bravery where men from Tunbridge Wells were honoured for their actions.

Lieutenant O K Griffin

'Lieutenant O K Griffin, a nephew of Mr E C Jenkinson, of Mount Pleasant, who commenced his Army career in this town, has had the Order of Chevalier de la Couronne conferred upon him by the King of the Belgians. Lieutenant Griffin served through the Gallipoli campaign, and has been acting as Battalion Intelligence Officer in France.'

The Order de la Couranne, which in English means Order of the Crown is a Belgian award which may be bestowed on either Belgian nationals or foreigners who have distinguished themselves by artistic, literacy, scientific and military services.

Quartermaster J Chandler

'For gallantry in saving life in connection with the sinking of a transport in the Irish sea, Quartermaster J Chandler, who is a Tunbridge Wells man, has been awarded the Albert Gold Medal.'

The Albert Gold Medal was a British award to recognise the saving of life, although it was originally awarded purely for the saving of life at sea. It was first initiated on 7 March 1866, in memory of Queen Victoria's late husband, Prince Albert.

The *Kent & Sussex Courier* carried an article on Friday 12 April about the funeral of a soldier at Rusthall. He was a local man and had served with the Queens Own (Royal West Kent) Regiment.

The gold and bronze versions of the Albert Medal.

'The funeral of Private F S Holyer, the youngest son of Mrs Henry Holyer, of 21 Nevill Street, took place at Rusthall Churchyard on Saturday afternoon. The gallant young soldier died in hospital at Stockport from wounds sustained during the fighting in the neighbourhood of Oppy last July.

'After 10 months suffering, death came as a happy release on the anniversary of the day he took part with the West Kent Regiment in his first battle, the attack on Vimy Ridge in April 1917. Full military honours were accorded, the coffin being covered with the Union Jack and conveyed from the Pantiles to Rusthall on a gun carriage drawn by four horses, while the bugler and firing party which followed was composed of men of the Royal West Surrey Regiment. The service at the church and graveside was conducted by the Rev A W Oliver MA, Vicar of King Charles the Martyr Church, and the mortal remains of the gallant young soldier were laid to rest in the same grave as that of his grandparents and next to that of his father. A volley was fired over the grave and the "Last Post" was sounded.'

Every week local newspapers up and down the country were full of the latest casualty lists of local men, who had either been killed, wounded, were missing in action or who had been taken as prisoners of war. An article appeared in the *Kent & Sussex Courier* on Friday 5 April concerning Sydney Strange, who was a Private with the Royal Sussex Regiment. He was wounded during fighting on the Western Front on 20 March when he sustained three shrapnel wounds to the head, one of them being to his left eye. He had been serving in France for approximately two years. He was sent back to England where he was admitted to the 1st London Hospital in an extremely serious condition. Prior to enlisting, Sydney, a married man, whose home was at 12 Vernon Road, had been a postman in Tunbridge Wells and to those that knew him, was remembered for his cheery disposition.

When the war broke out in 1914, Sydney was already 37 years of age. It would appear that despite his injuries, Sydney survived the war.

Charles Frederick Bench was a 3rd Writer (M/19797) in the British Royal Navy, who was stationed at HMS *Victory*, a land base at Portsmouth. He died on 9 September 1918 aged twenty-eight of an unspecified illness. He was one of eight men, all from HMS *Victory*, who all died from illness on the same day. Possibly because of the date of Charles's death, it was as a result of the flu epidemic that was sweeping across Europe at the time. Charles' parents, Tom and Ellen Bench, lived at 24 St Peter's Street, Tunbridge Wells, whilst his widow, Maude Eveline Bench lived at 19 Bayhill Road, in the town.

William James Thomson McCall was a Corporal (11039) in the Royal Army Pay Corps when he died, aged thirty-five, on 12 November 1918, the day after the war had ended, a victim of the flu epidemic.

With the war now over and a new dawn fast approaching the social structure of society, there was much hope for a better tomorrow which hopefully would lead to a brighter future for everybody concerned. The

Kent & Sussex Courier dated Friday 22 November provided a sharp reminder of the high price that Britain had paid for peace.

'Owing to the departure of the Brigade stationed at Tunbridge Wells, St Marks Hospital will be closed at the end of the year. The hospital was organised in October 1914, by the members of Sussex 92, a detachment which had been undergoing training for the previous four years and was offered to General Sir Frederick Stopford for the reception of the casualties and sick of the troops connected with the Headquarters Staff, 2nd Army Central Force, then stationed in Tunbridge Wells. Since its opening on October 13th 1914, the hospital has not been closed for a single day, and has been attached in succession to every Brigade which has since been stationed in the town.

'During this period, 1,862 cases of sick, many of them very serious, have passed through its wards, and since the addition of an operating theatre in 1916, 325 operations have been performed.'

Humour can be found in the most unusual places and at the most unexpected of times. The following article appeared in the *Kent & Sussex Courier* on Friday 15 November.

'The following paragraph appeared in the "Daily Express" over the signature of "Beachcomber". The hilly ground above Tunbridge Wells has proved very trying to the feet of the recruits who have been training there since the beginning of the war. So the Mayor of the Wells very kindly put a room of his private residence at the men's disposal. He called it "The Soldiers' Foot Room," and here the men vaselined and bandaged their sore and bloodied feet. One day the Mayor looked into the room in a friendly way. A soldier hailed him: "Art tha' t' chap as cuts corns?"

On page 3 of the *Kent & Sussex Courier* for Friday 6 December under the heading of 'Prisoners of War Return' were the stories of four soldiers from Tunbridge Wells. This included Private Robin K F Yeoman of the 2nd/2nd London Regiment, who before the war had worked for the Tunbridge Wells Gas Company. He had been taken prisoner by the Germans on 24 April during fighting at Hangard Wood. Private R G Hunter of the 3rd Battalion, Coldstream Guards, returned to his home at 44 Tunnel Road, Tunbridge Wells, on Sunday 1 December, much to the surprise and shock of his parents. He had been a prisoner of the Germans since 13 April 1918, when he was captured near Merville.

Lance Corporal Crossland of 38 Mount Sion, Tunbridge Wells, had been captured by the Germans on 25 March 1918 and returned home to his widowed father, on Thursday 5 December. Unwittingly he set the tone of a generation by declining to speak of his wartime experiences and captivity, when asked to do so by a reporter from the *Kent & Sussex Courier*.

The fourth of those prisoners of war to return home was a very interesting character indeed. Here is how the *Courier* reported his homecoming.

'Private E J Smith, DCM, MM, 7th Royal West Kent Regiment, of Tunbridge Wells, has arrived in Hull, after having been a prisoner of war in the hands of the Germans since March last. He joined up at the announcement of war, and went to France early in 1915. It is understood he is the only man in Tunbridge Wells to receive these two decorations. He has on several occasions refused promotion, preferring to remain a Private. Prior to joining the Colours he was in the employ of Mr C E Westbrook, auctioneer and estate agent, Mondon Road.'

What the newspaper article didn't include, because it hadn't yet happened, was the fact that Private Smith was to later receive a Bar to his Distinguished Conduct Medal. Citations for both awards appeared in the *London Gazette.*

London Gazette 15 November 1918
'205707 Sjt. E J Smith, RW Kent R. (Willesden).
'For conspicuous gallantry and ability while acting as company serjeant-major during an attack. After his officers had become casualties he assumed command of the company and by his splendid example and leadership successfully accomplished

their share in the attack. Later, he led his company with great skill, securing the flank of the battalion, and eventually bringing his command out of action with a minimum of loss. He rendered most valuable service.'

London Gazette 10 January 1920

'205707 Sjt E J Smith, DCM, 1st Bn. RW Kent R. (Tottenham). 'For marked gallantry and good leadership near GOUZEAUCOURT on the 29th September 1918. When the officers and company sergeant-major had become casualties he led the company to the attack with conspicuous gallantry. He consolidated the line gained, and went through a heavy barrage to battalion headquarters to report, afterwards returning to his company. He showed a splendid example to all ranks.'

The newspaper article throws up some confusion as despite it reporting that Private Smith had turned down the offer of promotion on several occasions, both *London Gazette* articles clearly show him as being a Serjeant. The other point which is unclear are the dates in all of this. If it is accepted that the E J Smith, DCM, who is mentioned in the *Courier*'s report, is the same man who is mentioned in the London Gazette DCM citations, how can it be that he was captured in March 1918, but was then awarded a Bar to his DCM for actions he had taken part in on 25 September 1918, some six months after he had been taken prisoner.

Postscript
Aftermath of the War

The signing of the Armistice wasn't the end of the war's fatalities. Figures compiled by the Commonwealth War Graves Commission show that in the three years after the end of the war up to and including 1921, a further 61,953 Commonwealth service men would die from either their wounds, illness or disease. In 1919, the number of deaths were 36,908. In 1920, a total of 14,506 would die and in 1921 a further 10,529 would lose their lives. These figures would include those serving soldiers who died as a result of the influenza pandemic sweeping across Europe at the time.

Figures for military-related deaths in the First World War vary for different reasons and are broken down in to different categories. There are those killed in action, those who died of illness or disease, or those who died as a result of an accident, including whilst being held in captivity as a prisoner of war. One such figure for those who died from all of the nations involved in the war, is 10,000,000 combatants. This is broken down in to a total of 6,000,000 for Britain and her Allies along with 4,000,000 for Germany and her Allies. The figures for those wounded, is estimated to be twice as many as those who were killed or died.

It truly was a devastating war, with an estimated two and a quarter million civilians killed as a result of military action or who were murdered by enemy nations. A further estimated figure of five million civilians died as a result of disease and malnutrition. It brought about major social change in numerous countries across Europe. At the end of the war, four powerful pre-war Empires had fallen and were no more. New countries had been formed in both Europe and the Middle

East, and America had risen to prominence as an economic power on the world's stage.

18 January 1919 was the start of the Paris Peace Conference, which saw diplomats from thirty-two of the victorious Allied nations agreeing on the peace terms of the Armistice for the defeated nations of Germany and her Allies. The terms covered the areas of military arms, territory along with guilt and reparations which came to the massive total of £6.6 billion. The conference also saw the birth of the League of Nations, which had its headquarters in Geneva, Switzerland. The organisation would last for twenty years before being replaced by the United Nations on 20 April 1946.

In 21 June 1919, the German Fleet was scuttled at Scapa Flow on the orders of Rear Admiral Ludwig von Reuter, who was in charge of the fleet which consisted of fourteen capital ships, seven light cruisers and fifty torpedo boats.

On 28 June 1919, the Treaty of Versailles was signed by the Allied and German military authorities, which officially brought the First World War to an end. Its intention was to create a lasting peace for future generations, but due to what many saw as the harsh and unfair conditions of the treaty, it ultimately led to the outbreak of the Second World War.

Although everybody was glad and relieved that the war was over at last, pre-war normality was still a long way off. It was never going to be a straightforward case of one day the war would end and then the very next day, it would suddenly revert back to how it had been before the outbreak of the war. Now that the war was over British and other Allied soldiers who were still in France, Belgium, Germany and other similar theatres of war, simply wanted to get home to be with their loved ones, but that was neither possible nor realistic. For some it would be days, for others it would be weeks and for the really unlucky ones, it would be months before their turn came to return to their families.

Wednesday 23 July 1919 saw the wounded soldiers who were still patients at the Rusthall VAD Hospital, enjoy a day's entertainment as part the peace celebrations. The bulk of the day was taken up with varied sporting events. There was food and drink, the band of the Veterans' Association provided the music, hoopla, a fortune telling tent, Sergeant Temple did his Charlie Chaplin impersonation and Private

Crowcroft was presented with a Gallantry medal by Major-General E Owen Hay, CB, carrying out the duties of a Company Runner whilst serving in the trenches in France.

The sports included an inter-ward tug-of-war event, a slow bicycle race, a potato race, a wheelbarrow race, pillow fight, thread and needle race, a bed making competition, an obstacle race, blind boxing, hat trimming, blindfolded driving, a boat race, a crutch race, and observation competition, a general knowledge competition and musical chairs. Although an enjoyable day was had by all who were present, I am glad to report that none of these sports subsequently went on to gain official Olympic recognition.

Part of the Mayor's speech contained the following sentiments.

'The peace they had been celebrating, the Mayor continued, had been won by the gallantry of the men such as those in the Hospital and we could not do too much, not only for the wounded and disabled but also for the discharged and demobilised men. He hoped they would be treated as finely as they deserved to be. The town hoped shortly to recognise the services of all men who had served during the war. Some months back he had suggested this and had approached the leaders of the men's organisations on the matter. And was told that it would perhaps be better to wait until others returned home.'

In the months and years after the war time moved on and gradually normality, even if not exactly the same as it had been before the war, returned.

Rusthall VAD Hospital which had played such an important part in the lives of so many wounded soldiers, closed for business, with the culmination being a grand sale at the premises on 27 September 1919, when beds, bedding, cupboards, tables, wardrobes and other similar items were put up for sale, bringing to an end the building's use as a war time hospital.

The hospital had closed during the last week of August after a truly remarkable existence. It had begun life back in August 1914, soon after the outbreak of the war with sufficient accommodation to treat 40 wounded men. This rose to 60 and after the two large wards had been added in 1916, this figure rose to 103 beds. When in early 1917 the hospital's recreation room was turned into yet another ward, this increased the capacity to 137 beds. Finally in April 1917 when the nearby Rusthall Girls School became an annexe of the hospital, the number of available beds rose to 203 and in May 1918, when it was at its peak, the number of beds had risen to 250.

In April 1919 when the Rusthall Girls School annexe had to once again revert back to being a school, the number of beds that were then available fell to around the 200 mark. Throughout the war years the hospital had treated some 4,000 wounded soldiers, and remarkably 80 of the nurses who worked there had been with the hospital from the very beginning.

The *Kent & Sussex Courier* dated Friday 22 August included an article about ex-servicemen being welcomed home and a reception and banquet held in their honour.

Tunbridge Wells Welcome Home
Ex-Service Men Entertained
Reception, Banquet and Presentation

'Whilst on Sunday the inhabitants of Tunbridge Wells paid tribute on the Common to the fallen heroes of the Great War, they are entertaining in right royal fashion this week those who have been fortunate enough to survive the stress and trials of the prolonged conflict, and there has been every manifestation of the high appreciation and esteem in which the town holds those men who assisted to bring about the defeat of a ruthless enemy.'

So many ex-service men, nearly 1,800 in total, took up the offer to attend the festivities, that the event took place over four days, as the town's Pump Room couldn't cater for so many people all at the same time. On the Tuesday a staggering 400 men turned up to be met by a well decorated location, with flags and bunting and the walls adorned with messages in large letters to greet them. 'Welcome Home', 'To our Gallant Boys of Kent', 'To our Victorious Army' and 'God Bless our Navy.'

The food, which was served by women from some of the nearby VAD Hospitals as well as some from the YMCA, was impressive, including pressed beef, ham and tongue, game pie, salmon mayonnaise, Russian salad, fruit tart and custard, cheese and coffee.

At the end of the evening, proceedings were brought to an end by Colonel Herbert Henry Spender-Clay, who had served during the First Word War as well as the Second Boer War with the 2nd Battalion, Life Guards.

On the day of the unveiling of the Tunbridge Wells War Memorial, it was estimated that a crowd of well over 2,000 people, ex-service men and local residents turned out to pay their respects to their townsfolk who had fallen during the First World War. Colonel Spender-Clay commented that he felt it was only right and proper that those who had returned from the war to the community and the bosom of their family, had first paid their respects to the memories of their fallen comrades before celebrating their own return. Each of those who had returned home after the war would be presented with a framed certificate as a mark of respect of their war time service, which read as follows:

'The Mayor, Aldermen and inhabitants of the Royal Borough of Tunbridge Wells welcome you home after your service with His Majesty's Forces in the Great European War. It is due to the self-sacrifice and gallantry of you and your comrades in arms that the British Empire and its Allies have been victorious, and this memento is presented to you as a token of the appreciation and regard in which you are held by your fellow townsmen.'

The Mayor of Tunbridge Wells for the period 1918-19, was the newly appointed Knight of the Realm, Sir Robert Vaughan Gower, his award having been announced in the king's birthday honours list in August 1919. He was knighted for the support which he had given to a scheme for preserving businesses in the absence of those serving in the First World War. He was presented with his knighthood in a ceremony at Buckingham Palace on 18 August 1919. He had previously been awarded the Order of the British Empire (OBE). During the war he had tried to enlist, but he had been unsuccessful in his attempts as explained by Colonel Spender-Clay.

'He knew that during the war Sir Robert did all in his power to join the Forces. He went to see the speaker on the subject and left no stone unturned in this direction, and he realized full well the disappointment he felt that he was unable to join his fellow townsmen in the service of his country during the Great War.'

In the article about Tunbridge Wells welcoming home their ex-service men, which appeared in the *Kent & Sussex Courier* on Friday 23 August, was the following paragraph.

'Some of them had felt he (Sir Robert) was a slacker whilst they were away fighting his battles and those of their fellow townsmen, but he felt sure they would now agree that he could not have done more than he did under the circumstances (applause).'

Sir Robert was thirty-three years of age at the outbreak of the First World War. In 1924 he became the Member of Parliament (MP) for Hackney Central in the General Election of that year. In the 1929 General Election, he chose not to defend his seat at Hackney, but instead he was elected as the MP for Gillingham in Kent, a seat he held until he retired from the Commons at the 1945 general election.

In 1919 tanks were presented to towns all over Kent, including Ashford, Canterbury, Chatham, Deal, Farnborough, Faversham,

Postcard of the Tunbridge Wells tank.

Folkestone, Hythe, Maidstone, Rochester, Tonbridge and Tunbridge Wells. Some of the tanks had actually seen action on the Western Front in France during the war. Some believed that the tanks were presented to towns and intended to be war memorials to the young men they had lost during the war, but that was not the reason. After the war, towns that had been successful in persuading their residents to purchase War Saving Certificates were acknowledged for their efforts with the presentation of the tanks. It was another way for the government to raise money to help with the war effort, whilst for the individual it was a sound investment that they could collect on after the war was over. What would have happened to these investments if the war had been lost, isn't clear, but can be guessed at. The original idea was for a town to purchase a certain number of certificates, which would pay for the cost of a tank, which would then be sent out to the Western Front.

The town of Tunbridge Wells received its tank on 30 July 1919. After it had arrived in the town by train, it was driven to its final resting place on a grassed area outside of Vale Road Post Office.

Southborough War Memorial
In the early years after the end of the war, towns and villages up and down the country decided that the best way to commemorate their war dead was with a war memorial. Most of these were erected and unveiled in about 1921.

The Southborough war memorial. (Postcard)

The Southborough War Memorial is located on the village green and was unveiled three years after the war had finished on 13 February 1921. It commemorates the names of 207 local young men who gave their lives during the Great War. It also commemorates the names of a further 44 men who were killed during the Second World War. Most if not all of the names that are commemorated on the Southborough War Memorial are also recorded on the nearby one at Tunbridge Wells.

Judith Johnson has written a comprehensive book entitled *Southborough War Memorial* (Odd Dog Press) which was first published in 2009. It contains the details of all of the men from Southborough who served in His Majesty's Armed Services during the First World War and who were either killed in action or who subsequently died of their wounds.

Rusthall War Memorial
Rusthall is a village community which dates back to the 8th century and is now part of Tunbridge Wells. The Rusthall War Memorial is situated in the grounds of the villages St Paul's Church. Many of the 116 names that are commemorated on the memorial are also included on the one at nearby Tunbridge Wells. Most, if not all of the men who are named on the Rusthall Memorial would have no doubt known each other, some would have more than likely been neighbours or work colleagues.

The Memorial was unveiled on 23 July 1922, by whom, is sadly not recorded, although the memorial was created by Sir Giles Gilbert Scott. Besides commemorating the names of those young men from Rusthall who were killed or died during the bloody and often barbaric fighting of the First World War, it also contained the following inscription.

'In grateful memory of the men of Rusthall, who gave their lives in the Great War 1914-1918.'

Rusthall War Memorial.

There was no officially set criteria as to how it was decided whose name would be recorded on a particular War Memorial. It was down to those who raised the money for the individual memorials to decide. For some it was a case of those who were born in the parish, village or town. Other locations recorded the names of those who had been living in the immediate area at the start of the war, and in some cases it would include those families who had moved into the parish whilst the war was going on. Sometimes names would be spelt incorrectly. Some memorials would have the soldier's full name, rank and regiment, whilst others would simply have a surname and initial. There were even a few memorials around the country that had recorded the names of everybody from the village who had served during the war, regardless of whether they had been killed or subsequently returned home after the war. It was not unheard of for some men's names to have appeared on three or four different local war memorials. There were sadly also occasions where names were omitted from memorials because families

Postcard of Tunbridge Wells War Memorial.

The unveiling of the Tunbridge Wells War Memorial. (Postcard)

had moved during the war years and one village would assume that the man's name would be recorded on the memorial of the new village or town where his family had moved to. Sometimes it would take years for these oversights to be rectified and in some cases they no doubt never were.

The Tunbridge Wells War Memorial was unveiled by Colonel Viscount Hardringe, on 11 February 1921. This came about after the Tunbridge Wells Borough Council had decided that they would erect a Memorial to commemorate the names of those local men who had lost their lives whilst serving their King and country during the First World War.

The 4th Battalion, The Queen's Own (Royal West Kent) Regiment provided a guard of honour at the ceremony, looking resplendent in their uniforms, rifles resting gently on their shoulders as the cold steel of their polished bayonets glistened in the mid-day sun.

With all War Memorials, especially ones such as the one at Tunbridge Wells that have such a large number of names recorded on it, there is always the likelihood of one or two discrepancies, where either a surname has been spelt incorrectly or the wrong initial has been recorded. This is particularly confusing where individuals have the same surname and Christian name or initial. From the names recorded

Tunbridge Wells War Memorial. (Postcard)

on the memorial, the most represented Regiment is the Queens Own (Royal West Kent Regiment) followed by the 1st/3rd Kent Field Company, Royal Engineers.

Tunbridge Wells Cemetery

Tunbridge Wells Cemetery contains the graves of seventy-two British service men who lost their lives during or as a result of the First World War.

Tunbridge Wells Cemetery Cross.

It is a very old cemetery, with the first person having been buried there in 1873. It now covers a massive area of some twenty-eight acres and is situated in the Frant forest area of the district, close to the border with the neighbouring county of Sussex. The cemetery is owned and maintained by the local Corporation. The fact that these men are buried in Tunbridge Wells Cemetery, strongly indicates that they either died in one of the town's hospitals where they were having their wounds tended to after having been sent home, usually from the fighting on the Western Front, or that they died as a result of illness or disease.

During the First World War, servicemen who were killed, no matter what their rank was, never had their remains sent back to the United Kingdom for burial, it simply wasn't practical. Men were either buried close to where they died in battle or near to the hospital in which they died. That's why war memorials played such an important part in local communities, because for a lot of friends and relatives of those sons, uncles, fathers, brothers and husbands, a memorial was the only means they had of commemorating the people close to them who they had lost in the war, as most didn't have the financial means to be able to travel out to France to find where their loved ones were actually buried. It also has to be remembered that for tens of thousands of young men they had no grave as their bodies were never recovered; all they had was their name inscribed on a war memorial that was located in a far off field, somewhere across the Channel in either France or Belgium.

Pembury War Memorial
Forty-nine young men who died during the First World War are recorded on the Pembury War Memorial which is located immediately outside of St Peter's Upper Church. Their names are commemorated so that future generations may remember and never forget the sacrifice which they made. The Memorial was unveiled on Sunday 25 September 1921 by the Reverend H Sinclair Brooke, who had been the Vicar of Pembury during the First World War, and would have no doubt known most of the men named on the memorial personally

According to www.pembury.org, eight of the names that are commemorated on the Pembury War

Pembury War Memorial.

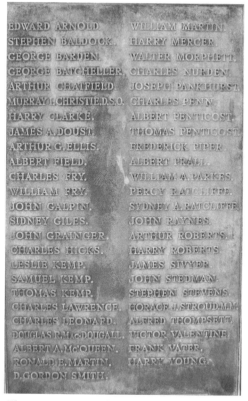

The names on Pembury War Memorial.

Memorial are misspelt. This wasn't such an unusual occurrence as it may at first appear. There were numerous occasions on War Memorials up and down the country, when men were recorded by their nicknames or a middle initial was incorrect, which then made future research much more complicated.

Speldhurst War Memorial

The Speldhurst War Memorial is located in the grounds of St Mary's Parish Church. There are forty names of young men from the village who died in the First World War and are commemorated on the Memorial. Over the years the memorial has had its battles with the elements, which resulted in it looking a shadow of its former self, but recent restoration work has seen it once again restored to its former

Speldhurst War Memorial.

glory. More detailed information about each of the men named on the Speldhurst War Memorial can be found on www.kentfallen.com.

Langton Green War Memorial
Langton Green is a Parish of Tunbridge Wells and its War Memorial is situated in the peaceful setting of the south-east corner of the All Saints Parish Church, in Langton Green. The Memorial was unveiled on Sunday 14 August 1921 by Colonel C Pulley. The memorial in the

shape of a cross, is eleven feet three inches tall and is made out of sandstone which was quarried in the parish and the base is made from Yorkshire Stone.

The Langton Green Memorial carries the following inscriptions;

'Cease not to praise God for these men who fell gloriously, 1914 -1918.'

'To the Glory of God and in the hallowed memory of Langton men who gave their all in defence of the honour of the Empire and in cause of common humanity.'

Langton Green War Memorial.

The hymns *Ten thousand times ten thousand*, and *The Saints of God! Their conflict past*, were sung at the unveiling with prayers being offered by the Vicar of Langton Green, the Reverend R H Douglas. After drawing aside the Union Jack which screened the base of the Memorial, Colonel Pulley made the following address to those present.

'My friends, we are met together today to unveil and dedicate to the glory of God this war memorial, which has been erected to perpetuate the memory of those of and connected with this parish who gave their lives for their King and their country in the Great War. It seems hardly necessary for me to dwell on the nature of the supreme sacrifice these gallant fellows made for you and me, and for the nation at large. I feel sometimes however, that we who watched and waited at home through those long anxious, weary years of the war have never probably fully realised what those lads had to face, the horrors they had to witness, the scene of wreckage and desolation, the earth and sky a sheet of flame, the continuous roar of the guns, and the nerve racking strain of being exposed day and night to constant shell fire, a veritable hell on earth. It is impossible we could realise it.

'I see amongst us a number of ex-servicemen, of whom we may well be proud. Remember these men, many of them sat in those long lines of trenches with bayonets fixed, in grim silence waiting for the signal to go over the top. They carried their lives in their hands, and death stared them in the face at every turn. There never has been such a war, and pray God, there never again may be. May he of his infinite mercy grant to the nations far and wide in the future, in the word of our church litany, unity, peace and concord.

'We are hopeful this Memorial will serve to remind us all, and especially to those who come after us, when the first sharp agony of this terrible ordeal will have passed away, of the example of magnificent courage and unselfish devotion to duty these our boys have set us. To those of you who are mourning your nearest and dearest, may I say grieve not; they are not dead, neither do they sleep, they are ever with you, present in our midst at this moment. Let us be thankful for that, eagerly look forward to re-union in that glorious after life that is before us, where regrets and sorrow, tears and partings, will have no place. In the meantime let us cherish in affectionate and proud memory these our dear ones who in England's hour of dire distress and peril, when the fate of the Empire hung in the balance, responded to the 'call to arms', and died as British soldiers know how to die, unflinching to the last.'

Colonel Pulley's own son, Major Charles Pulley, who was killed in the war, is also commemorated on the War Memorial, giving the Colonel's words more meaning and poignancy.

There are fifteen names actually recorded on the Memorial of men who fell during the First World War. The Kent Fallen website (www.kentfallen.com) has a section entitled Kent War Memorials Project. They record a total of twenty-nine names for the Langton Green War Memorial; this includes the names of the fifteen men who are actually commemorated on it as well as a further fourteen that have subsequently come to light since the Memorial was erected and unveiled in 1920.

Roll of Honour – Christ Church.

1914 -1918
IN PROUD AND LOVING MEMORY

Cpl.	Herbert Baker	Lond. Regt.	2/Lt.	Ralph Gale	R.E.	Rfn.	Arthur O'Sullivan	R.Ir.Rif.
L/Sgt.	John Ball	R.Ir.Fusiliers	Rfn.	Sydney Geoghegan	K.R.R.C.	2/Lt.	Leo Parsons	The Buffs
Pte.	Charles Beecher	R.Sc.Fusiliers	L/Cpl.	Harry Hayward	N.Z. Rif. Brig.	Capt.	Charles Paterson	S.Wales Bord.
L/Sgt.	George Chapman	11th Hussars	Tpr.	Eric Jarrett	Imp.Camel C.	CQMS	Thomas Ryan	R. Fusiliers
Pte.	Edward Colbear	R.A.M.C.	Pte.	William McDonald	R.W.Kent Regt.	2/Lt.	John Stevens	R.F.C.
Cpl.	George Eagles	A.S.C.	Spr.	John McNally	R.E.	Rfn.	Edward Wall	Lond. Regt.
Capt.	Hubert East	York & Lanc. Regt.	2/Lt.	Charles Morgan	King Edw.O.C.	Gnr.	J. Woodford	R.F.A.
Pte.	Patrick Edwards	21st Can. Inf.	Pte.	Edward Murphy	R.Suss.Regt.	Pte.	William Young	50th Can. Inf.
			Pte.	John Murphy	R.W.Kent Regt.			

REQUIESCANT IN PACE

GREATER LOVE HATH NO MAN THAN THIS,
THAT A MAN LAY DOWN HIS LIFE FOR HIS FRIENDS.

(John, 15:13)

Roll of Honour - St Augustine Church.

Roll of Honour - St Peter's Church.

Roll of Honour - St Mark's Church.

As in all towns and villages around the country there are an abundance of old Parish Churches in Tunbridge Wells that have memorials and rolls or honour adorning their walls to commemorate the names of the men who were once part of their community and congregation, but who sadly lost their lives during the bloody fighting of the First World War. Here are just a few of them.

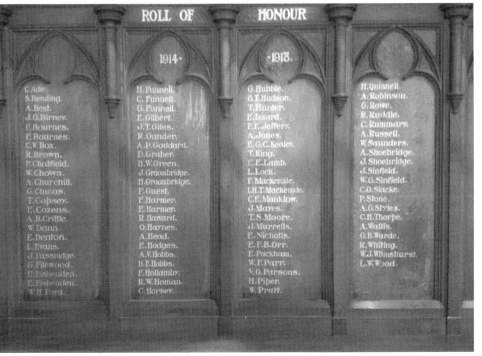

ROLL OF HONOUR

1914- -1918.

C.Adie.
S.Bending.
A.Best.
J.G.Birney.
F.Bournes.
F.Bournes.
C.W.Box.
R.Brown.
P.Chaffield.
W.Chown.
A.Churchill.
G.Clucas.
T.Copsey.
E.Cozens.
A.B.Criffle.
W.Dann.
E.Denton.
L.Evans.
J.Fassnidge.
G.Filewood.
H.Fishenden.
E.Fishenden.
W.H.Ford.

H.Punnell.
C.Funnell.
G.Punnell.
E.Gilbert.
J.T.Giles.
P.Gander.
A.P.Goddard.
D.Graber.
H.W.Green.
J.Groombridge.
H.Groombridge.
F.Guest.
F.Harmer.
E.Harmer.
R.Haward.
O.Haynes.
A.Head.
E.Hodges.
A.V.Hobbs.
B.F.Hobbs.
F.Hollamby.
R.W.Homan.
C.Horsey.

G.Hubble.
G.T.Hudson.
T.Hunter.
E.Izzard.
P.E.Jeffery.
A.Jones.
E.G.C.Keeley.
T.King.
E.E.Lamb.
L.Lock.
F.Mackenzie.
I.H.T.Mackenzie.
C.E.Manklow.
J.Mayes.
T.S.Moore.
J.Murrells.
E.Nicholls.
E.F.B.Orr.
E.Packham.
W.F.Parr.
V.G.Parsons.
H.Piper.
W.Pratt.

H.Quinnell.
A.Robinson.
G.Rowe.
R.Ruddle.
C.Rummary.
A.Russell.
W.Saunders.
A.Shoebridge.
J.Shoebridge.
J.Sinfield.
W.G.Sinfield.
C.O.Skicke.
P.Stone.
A.G.Styles.
C.H.Thorpe.
A.Wallis.
G.B.Warde.
R.Whiting.
W.J.Wilmshurst.
L.W.Wood.

Roll of Honour – St John's Church.

Most of the names which appear on Parish Church Memorials or Roll of Honours are usually included on the War Memorial of the main town that the parish sits in, which in this case is of course Tunbridge Wells.

At the time of the First World War religion played a major part in everyday parish life, where nearly everybody in the local community not only knew each other, but attended church together on a Sunday morning in their best clothes. Those who did not attend were noticeable by their absence.

Men from Tunbridge Wells not only joined regiments from all over Great Britain, but from other countries as well, such as South Africa, Canada and Australia. Quite a few of these men fought and died for their adopted countries with passion, pride and a belief that they were doing their duty, a duty that not only would have been expected of them but one which they would have expected of themselves.

Tunbridge Wells men in Australian Army. (Permission of Andrew Bratley)

Australian Imperial Force Cap Badge.

There were many more men who emigrated to Australia before the outbreak of the war and then subsequently enlisted in their adopted countries' armed forces, before going off to fight in a war, thousands of miles away from home.

When it was officially announced that the war was over at long last, celebrations broke out all over the country, in cities, towns and villages alike. After four years of bloody and destructive war, peace once again reigned, and the world took stock of the terrible price it had paid as well as the social changes that everybody knew were coming. There simply could be no going back to how life used to be for large sections of society. For them, a class system which condemned them to a life of servitude was no longer acceptable. They wanted and expected more out of life, especially after the price the working classes in the main had paid in blood and loss of life to secure peace.

The *Kent & Sussex Courier* of Friday 15 November described the celebrations in some detail. Here is some of what the article had to report.

Tunbridge Wells
The Scene in the Streets

'When the news was made known in Tunbridge Wells that the armistice had been signed, flags began to appear in all directions, and by noon there was quite a display of bunting in all the main thoroughfares, while many private houses also displayed flags of the Allies.

'Street sellers with rosettes of red, white and blue, and miniature flags, also appeared suddenly on the scene, apparently springing from nowhere, and did a brisk trade,

'A merry chime was rung in the afternoon from St Peter's belfry and the chimes of St Augustine's answered the bells of St Peter's. During the daytime there were no considerable outbursts of jubilation in the streets, but great interest was excited by the boys in blue from the VAD Hospitals organising a procession of their own.'

The next part of the article shows how markedly the English language has to some extent changed, where words of yesterday can have a totally different meaning today. The reporter concerned did not mean any offence by his words and remarks, but imagine the potential for public outcry if the following sentence appeared in a British newspaper today.

'A pathetic feature was the presence of disabled soldiers in their invalid chairs, who were drawn by more fortunate comrades in the procession, and fully shared the high spirits of their friends.'

Today, the word 'sad' would probably be a better choice than the word 'pathetic'.

> 'All sorts of vehicles from a motor car to a perambulator, displayed the red, white and blue, and the hospital ambulance cars and ASC lorries came in for a special reception in the streets as their occupants sported the colours. There was a good deal of flag waving and singing of popular choruses, which increased during the evening, as the rain did not damp the ardour of the demonstrators.
>
> 'The arc street lamps, regardless of the Fuel Controller, were once more lighted in the principal thoroughfares, which were patrolled by crowds of people wearing rosettes. Military discipline was relaxed, and the remaining soldiers billeted in the town indulged in patriotic demonstrations on their own, in which they were joined by the inevitable girl. From dancing a breakdown on the pavement to vociferating the favourite music hall refrain of the moment, Tommy Atkins, assisted by Thomasine, displayed his personal satisfaction with the armistice.'

One of the main streets in the town that saw a lot of the rejoicing was Calverley Road. Large crowds in a condensed area, letting off fireworks, and behaviour that was nothing more serious than good humoured horse play. These weren't football supporters celebrating their favourite team having just won the FA Cup or the Premier League title, these were people who had just lived through four years of death and destruction on an industrial scale which had resulted in millions of people having been killed or wounded with life changing injuries, rejoicing at the end of a war. The relief that it was finally over coupled with an element of sadness as individuals remembered friends and loved ones who had been victims of the war, must have been truly palpable.

> 'Bands of soldiers with flags, marching up and down the road singing popular choruses, and in other ways found vent for a pardonable exuberance of spirits, and the streets presented an animated appearance which they have not worn since the first year of the war.
>
> 'In other parts of the town, apart from Calverley Road and the vicinity, quiet prevailed, and the Pantiles which was not

included in the relaxed lighting regulations, remained in darkness, save for a bright spot at the YMCA Headquarters, and comparative solitude in contrast to the old Fifth of November scenes which in bygone years were centred on the Pantiles. The excitement now was completely transferred to Calverley Road, but there was fortunately nothing approaching "Mafficking".'

'The evening trains brought numerous soldiers into the town returning from week end leave, and there was a good deal of cheering as the trains drew into the station, and a certain amount of good humoured badinage. Large crowds assembled outside the "Courier" office during the day and until a late hour at night to read the armistice terms, which were telephoned down by the Central News to the "Courier" office as soon as the announcement was made in the House of Commons. The general attitude of the hundreds who read the terms set forth was not one of undue elation, but rather of grim regret that the wily German was escaping punishment for unspeakable outrages, and a fear that the Boche might also escape making full reparation for his crimes. But of the various expressions of opinion heard outside the "Courier" office, the most apt of all was perhaps on Sunday, when the British official was posted that the English Army was back at Mons. "It would be an insult to the Old Contemptibles to talk about an armistice before we were back at Mons," was the remark of a veteran who was reading the telegram. Certainly with the British back once more at Mons the wheel had come full circle.

'In the schools of the town, which have re-assembled after the epidemic of the "Flu", the enthusiasm of the youngsters was perhaps chiefly excited by the announcement of a day's holiday, and to their youthful minds the tragic side was happily absent."

There was a part in the article which said in essence that there was a common belief that the 'Boche' might escape making full reparation for their crimes, ironically a sentence that would turn out to be extremely prophetic. Germany subsequently saw the terms of the Treaty of Versailles as being extremely harsh against them, which to a large degree was responsible for the rise in National Socialism in Germany, this in turn led to the Nazi Party coming to power, which ultimately led to the outbreak of the Second World War.

The signing of the Armistice on 11 November 1918, saw an end to the actual fighting, but it took another six months of in depth negotiations at the Paris Peace Conference to conclude the treaty which forced Germany to disarm militarily, make certain territorial concessions and pay financial reparations to some of the Allied nations. By way of example she had to pay Britain £6.6 billion, which today (2015) would be the equivalent of a massive £284 billion.

The Mayor of Tunbridge Wells, Alderman Vaughan Gower MBE, had announced that Tuesday 12 November should be a general holiday for one and all and that the townsfolk should join together in a public thanksgiving service. There was a procession which wound its way slowly around the town which started at Calverley Road, carried on in to Mount Pleasant, through the High Street and then back round via the London Road ending up at the Lower Cricket Ground, where a temporary platform had been put in place.

The procession included wounded soldiers from the local Hospitals, VAD nurses, police officers as well as the Federation of Demobilised Sailors and Soldiers, all of whom received a rousing reception from the crowds of people who had lined the route of the procession. Members of the Fire Brigade and Ambulance Corps were in attendance. Also part of the procession were women from the Women's Army Auxiliary Corp's, the Women's Police Force, and the Land Girls. The Volunteer Battalion of the West Kent Regiment were represented, there was even an effigy of the German Kaiser who was being carried by a group of off duty soldiers and eventually burnt on the Common, much to everybody's amusement. There were also troops from other regiments who were still billeted in the town, who the Government censor had forbidden from been mentioned by their unit's name. There were a group of the Belgian refugees, who had lived in Tunbridge Wells throughout the entire war and who had arrived in the town within a matter of weeks of the outbreak of hostilities.

The accompanying musical entertainment was provided by the Band of the Royal West Kent Battalion, the Trumpet and Bugle Band of the Royal West Kent Regiment Cadet Corps and the Salvation Army Band, all trying their very best at outperforming each other. They played many different tunes including the National Anthem and Rule Britannia.

The same celebrations were going on all over the country as the War to End All Wars came to a close.

Bibliography

Commonwealth War Graves Commission. www.cwgc.org
Ancestry.co.uk. www.ancestry.co.uk
British Newspaper Archive. www.britishnewspaperarchive.co.uk
Inspiring Women. www.womenshistorykent.org
Kent History Forum. www.kenthistoryforum.co.uk
www.pembury.org
www.europeanhistory.about.com
Southborough War Memorial by Judith Johnson.

Index

Pearson's Canal Com[panion]

SEVERN & AVON

GLOUCESTER & SHARPNESS, COTSWOLD CANALS, UPPER THAMES

Published by Central Waterways Supplies of Rugby.
Tel/fax 01788 546692. email: sales@centralwaterways.co.uk
Copyright: Michael Pearson - All rights reserved.
Fifth edition 2003. ISBN 0 907864 99 6

C000257451

tillerman

Hello! This is the fifth edition of our guide to the rivers Severn and Avon and the connecting canals which form the popular Avon Ring cruising circuit. The River Avon and the Stratford-on-Avon Canal were at the cutting edge of the inland waterways revival that occurred in the wake of the formation of the Inland Waterways Association in 1946. The Lower Avon Navigation was restored by 1962, the Upper a dozen years later; whilst work on the Stratford Canal was completed in 1964. The vast majority of the work involved in revitalising these three waterways was undertaken by amateur volunteers with the help of the Army and parties of men detained at Her Majesty's pleasure. Their achievement is therefore all the more remarkable and everyone with an interest in the inland waterway network is in their eternal debt.

Canal restoration in the 21st century is an altogether different, corporate-led affair, and this new edition of our guide includes, for the first time, the Cotswold Canals, subject of a multi-million pound restoration scheme earmarked for completion in 2010. The mud-splattered stalwarts of the 1960s can only be astounded at such changes in official attitude. In their era canals were anathema, now - and in no little way due to their fortitude and foresight - they are widely seen as essential to the very fabric of commerce generally and tourism in particular.

Michael Pearson

River Severn, Worcester

river
AVON

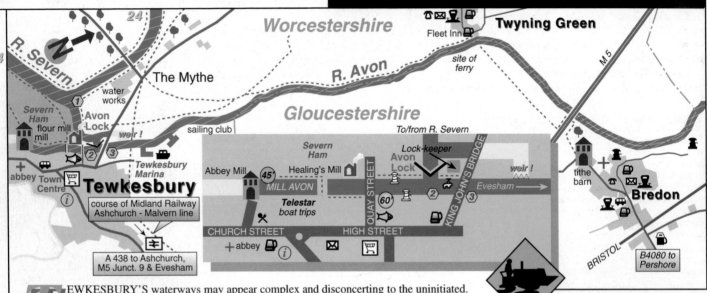

TEWKESBURY'S waterways may appear complex and disconcerting to the uninitiated. For instead of being content with one confluence with the Severn, the Avon branches into two channels. The main navigation passes through AVON LOCK and meets the Severn below Mythe Bridge, whilst the 'Mill Avon' flows between the back of the town and the open pastures of The Ham, being navigable as far as the ancient and picturesque Abbey Mill. However, for visiting boaters Avon Lock serves as the 'gateway to the river'. During working hours it is manned, and operated mechanically, by members of the Lower Avon Navigation Trust, who are normally prepared to dispense liberal quantities of local information and advice; they will certainly help you find a mooring (the best facilities being located on the Mill Avon between the lock and Healing's Mill) and may even try and sell you something from their range of souvenirs. LANT deserves your support, for without them there would be no navigable Avon.

1. Entering or leaving the Avon from or for the Severn it is important to avoid the sandbar. Give this a wide berth by keeping over towards the southern bank as you turn into the Avon, and by making sure that Mythe Bridge is in view before turning upstream into the Severn.
2. Travelling downstream you may have to wait until Avon Lock is free for your use. Try to avoid being taken past the lock entrance by the current.
3. Use the largest arch only at King John's Bridge.

Tewkesbury's waterfront is a delight. So many scenes catch the eye: the ancient arches of King John's Bridge; the quiet backwaters of the mill stream reflecting half-timbered houses and the town's towering abbey; and Healing's barges berthed against the dusty red-brick flour mill, vessels which sadly, look as if their sorties down to Sharpness for the collection of grain are increasingly rare. If you are not already afloat there are regular trip boats to catch or motor launches to hire.

Leaving Tewkesbury, however reluctantly, in your wake, you soon find yourself lost in a timeless landscape of lush watermeadows.

The M5 motorway intrudes briefly, and noisily, into the river's secret world, before disappearing as rapidly as it arrived. And how delightfully intimate and cosy the Avon seems if you have come off the mighty Severn. How elevated your view of things, now that there are no high banks to hide the outside world. The riverside villages of Twyning and Bredon, frustratingly difficult to visit by boat, are in different counties because this reach of the Avon forms the boundary between Gloucestershire and Worcestershire.

Tewkesbury *(Map 1)*

It is feasible to have fallen in love with Tewkesbury without ever having been there, for this is the fact behind the fictional 'Elmbury' of John Moore's *Brensham Trilogy*, those glorious post-war portraits of a Gloucestershire market town and its surrounding area. And, if you are familiar with these books, reality - even allowing for traffic pollution and redevelopment - lets you down gently, for this is an outstanding example of an English country town which, architecturally and atmospherically, would be hard to better. The radiant abbey of St Mary's looms maternally over the tumbling roofs of tight-knit streets, alleyways and courtyards which lead, at dizzy intervals, to tantalizing glimpses of boats moored on the Mill Avon.

BERKELEY ARMS - Church Street. Tel: 01684 293034. 16th century inn serving Wadworth, Badger and guest ales. Good food and a ghost!

NOTTINGHAM ARMS - High Street. Tel: 01684 292012. It's a long way from Southwold in Suffolk but the Adnams beer travels well to this quaint town centre pub.

ROYAL HOP POLE - Church Street. Tel: 01684 293236. Comfortable hotel (which Dickens booked

Mr Pickwick into) offering bar and restaurant food and customer moorings on the Mill Avon.

ABBEY MILL - Mill Street. Tel: 01684 292215. Coffees, lunches and teas in a mill mentioned in *John Halifax Gentleman*.

TUDOR HOUSE HOTEL - High Street. Tel: 01684 297755. Another hotel with a long garden going down to the riverbank and limited customer moorings - bar or restaurant food; lunchtime carvery.

OLDE BLACK BEAR - High Street. Tel: 01684 292202) Possibly the oldest inn in Gloucestershire: pleasant riverside garden. Also lots of ethnic restaurants & takeaways, plus two good fish & chip shops - Kingfisher by Healing's Mill and the nicely named Steamy Windows on Barton Street.

All the butchers, bakers and delicatessens that you would hope to find in a country market town plus some fine gift, antique and book shops. But if it's more mundane merchandise that you're seeking, a Somerfield supermarket lies at the back of the High Street. Market days are Wednesday and Saturday. There's a launderette by the Town Cross.

i TOURIST INFORMATION - Barton Street. Tel: 01684 295027. Small admission charge

for adjoining museum of local history.

JOHN MOORE COUNTRYSIDE MUSEUM - Church Street. Tel: 01684 297174. Admission charge. Open Tue-Sat plus Bank Holidays.

TEWKESBURY ABBEY - Church Street. Tel: 01684 273736. Open daily. The Visitors' Centre features displays, exhibitions and educational presentations, as well as a refectory that overlooks the Abbey grounds.

THE ROSES - Sun Street. Tel: 01684 295074. Wide choice of entertainment at this little theatre.

BOATING - motor boat hire and trips upriver to Twyning. Tel: 01684 294088.

BUSES - Service 71 links Tewkesbury with Gloucester hourly Mon-Sat, calling en route at Ashchurch railway station. Cheltenham, Malvern and Evesham are also served. Tel: 01452 425543.

TRAINS - Ashchurch (for Tewkesbury) station lies a mile east. Tel: 08457 484950.

Twyning Green & Bredon *(Map 1)*

Twin villages both devoid of public moorings. You can visit Twyning Green (complete with general stores and huge village green), however, by patronising the THE FLEET INN (Tel: 01684 274310) which has good moorings for customers.

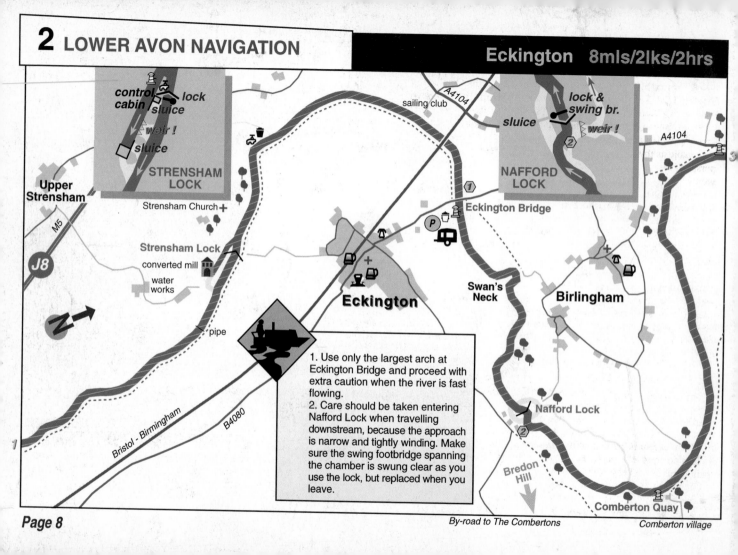

control cabin
lock
sluice
weir !
sluice
STRENSHAM LOCK
Strensham Church

Upper Strensham

M5

J8

Strensham Lock
converted mill
water works
pipe

sailing club

A4104

lock & swing br.
sluice
weir !
NAFFORD LOCK

A4104

Eckington Bridge

Eckington

Swan's Neck

Birlingham

1. Use only the largest arch at Eckington Bridge and proceed with extra caution when the river is fast flowing.
2. Care should be taken entering Nafford Lock when travelling downstream, because the approach is narrow and tightly winding. Make sure the swing footbridge spanning the chamber is swung clear as you use the lock, but replaced when you leave.

Bristol - Birmingham

B4080

Nafford Lock

Bredon Hill

Comberton Quay

By-road to The Combertons

Comberton village

THE Lower Avon seems infatuated by Bredon Hill, never letting it out of its sight, fascinated by the summit's constantly changing shape. Half wooded, half bare, like mottled baize, it forms an island between the Cotswold Edge and the distant serrated outline of the Malvern Hills. Because its peak falls short of a thousand feet, some 18th century eccentric built a folly on its top so that he could stand that high above sea level. But what are a few feet here or there in countryside as delectable as this? Each ravishing curve in the Avon reveals a new perspective, as if you are falling deeper and deeper in love with a woman who is going to mean an awful lot to you.

This Avon is second only to the Thames in the amount of writing it has inspired, and this stretch is particularly rich in literary associations. Every guidebook quotes A. E. Housman's poem *In Summertime on Bredon* (an odd geographical aberration for a set of poems entitled *A Shropshire Lad*), but a better poem was written by Sir Arthur Quiller-Couch about Eckington Bridge. 'Q' had canoed the river as a young man in 1890, and had been inspired to compose a magnificent ode to the bridge which speaks of 'eloquent grooves worn into the sandstone by labouring bargemen'. Quiller-Couch also employed the river in his adventurous tale *True Tilda*, dramatised by the BBC not so long ago, painting an especially evocative scene of the bustling barges and steam tugs at Tewkesbury. Following his own journey down the river in 1910, Temple Thurston used Nafford Mill as the setting for his Richard Furlong trilogy, now long-forgotten and out of print, but still wonderful reading if you can find them (as it is reasonably easy to do) second-hand. It is not difficult to see why such writers were moved to capture the spirit of this quintessentially English landscape. It would be one of life's missed opportunities, were you not to moor, at Comberton Quay or Eckington Bridge, make an ascent of Bredon Hill, and see for yourself Housman's 'coloured counties' and *your* river, meandering through this peerless panorama like a wandering minstrel.

Strensham Lock, like Avon Lock at Tewkesbury, is manned and automated. Being separated from the M5 by a church-topped hill, it could be a million miles from the service area that shares its name.

Either side of the lock the river roams attractively past shallow banks of reeds and lily-pads rutted by cattle intent on quenching their thirst. Downstream of Eckington's marvellously medieval bridge, in a reach plied by sailing craft from the Arden club, the busy Bristol-Derby railway crosses the river by way of a not ungraceful iron span resting on stone piers. It comes as something of a surprise to learn that Herbert Spencer, the great Victorian philosopher, was instrumental in its design during a youthful sojourn in the engineering offices of the Birmingham & Gloucester Railway Company.

The railway bridge at Eckington, River Avon

Summary of Facilities

Birlingham and Great Comberton, pleasant villages though they are, can boast just two telephone boxes and one quiet pub between them. Eckington, however, is a different kettle of Avon fish with two pubs and a general store.

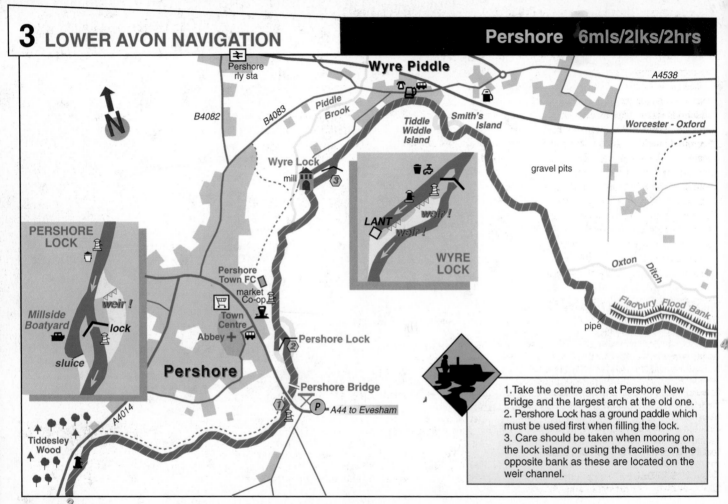

Wyre Piddle

A4538

Worcester - Oxford

Pershore rly sta

B4082

B4083

Piddle Brook

Tiddle Widdle Island

Smith's Island

gravel pits

Wyre Lock

mill

LANT

weir !

weir !

weir !

WYRE LOCK

Oxton Ditch

Fladbury Flood Bank

pipe

PERSHORE LOCK

Millside Boatyard

weir !

lock

sluice

Pershore Town FC

market Co-op.

Town Centre

Abbey

Pershore

Pershore Lock

A4014

Pershore Bridge

P — A44 to Evesham

Tiddesley Wood

1. Take the centre arch at Pershore New Bridge and the largest arch at the old one.
2. Pershore Lock has a ground paddle which must be used first when filling the lock.
3. Care should be taken when mooring on the lock island or using the facilities on the opposite bank as these are located on the weir channel.

ENTRENCHED in the Vale of Evesham, the Avon makes its stately way past Tiddesley Wood, where the famous Pershore 'Egg' plum was discovered growing wild in 1833. Pollarded willows and swaying poplars betray the river's course as it meanders towards the sturdy tower of Pershore Abbey.

The original bridge at Pershore dates from the 14th century and contrives to look even older. Military men have always had a love/hate relationship with bridges, and the Cavaliers tried to demolish this one as they escaped from the Battle of Worcester in 1651. Thankfully it stood its ground. Seemingly nothing could mar the charm of its setting or its own inherent beauty. Nothing, that is, until the motor car came along, demanding construction of a straighter, flatter span. Built in 1928, it was the first concrete bridge in Worcestershire, but sadly not the last.

Pershore Mill was destroyed by fire early in the 1970s. It had been the last mill on the river in commercial use, and was also the source of the Avon's last commercial traffic. A little barge with the biblically appropriate name of *Pisgah* traded to and from the mill until the end.

However tight your schedule, it's virtually impossible to pass Pershore Recreation Ground without dropping anchor, so attractive are the free moorings provided there, so irresistible the urge to visit this fascinating Georgian town. WYRE LOCK is diamond shaped: many of the original Avon locks were of unusual configuration to reduce erosion of the chambers by the force of water from the sluices. LANT's offices and workshops are located in the old mill at Wyre.

Desirable residences create an enviable riverside environment for the villagers of Wyre Piddle. Well groomed gardens spill down to the riverbank where substantial cruisers are moored status symbols of an affluence which, once attained, has a perverse capacity for souring. How seldom boats like this seem to be used. They lie at their moorings waiting for their owners to make some symbolic gesture of escape, a way out of the morass of middle class conventions and routines that wealth has lumbered them with. But upstream the river soon loses itself amongst the fruit fields and orchards of this fertile valley. Herons and kingfishers abound. Time hangs motionlessly over the landscape like the cobwebby pendulum of an unwound grandfather clock. Fladbury flood bank dates from 1881. Four feet high, it has sluice valves built into its bank to protect the farmlands from the ravages of the river. The flood bank hasn't always been up to its task, as several high water marks in Fladbury village testify.

Pershore (Map 3)

Balconies blossoming from Georgian houses lend a holiday feel, an inherent *joie de vivre* to Pershore, best known nowadays, not for pears as the name implies, but for rich, ruby red plums. The Abbey, only marginally less imposing than Tewkesbury's, was only partially demolished following the Dissolution of the Monasteries. John Betjeman wrote of the abbey bells being rung for evensong in a poem called *Pershore Station*. Boaters are afforded easy access to the town centre over playing fields and past an impressive leisure centre beside a quaint and bustling indoor market.

 THE ANGEL INN - High Street. Old coaching inn. Lunches, teas, dinners and bar meals. Friendly service. Tel: 01386 552046.
BRANDY CASK - Bridge Street. Tel: 01386 552602. Brews its own beer, enjoys a big garden running down to the river, serves bar and restaurant food.
WHISTLERS - Broad Street. Tel: 01386 556900 Amiable first floor bistro overlooking the sweep of Broad Street. Balcony tables for warm days.
SUGAR 'N' SPICE - High Street. Unassuming tearooms housed behind a gift shop offering a surprisingly wide range of meals. Tel: 01386 553654.

Many boaters venture no further than the large Co-op Pioneer supermarket adjacent to the riverside recreation ground, but it would be a shame to miss out on the many antique and book shops dotted around the town. The indoor retail market (also close to the recreation ground) operates on Wednesday through Saturday and oozes with small town atmosphere.

BUSES - Services to/from Worcester and Evesham (not Sundays). Tel: 01905 763888.
TRAINS - Cotswold Line services by Thames Trains. Tel: 08457 484950.

Wyre Piddle (Map 3)

Straggling but affluent village on the road between Pershore and Evesham. Shopless, Wyre Piddle is perhaps best known for the popular ANCHOR INN - Tel: 01386 552799.

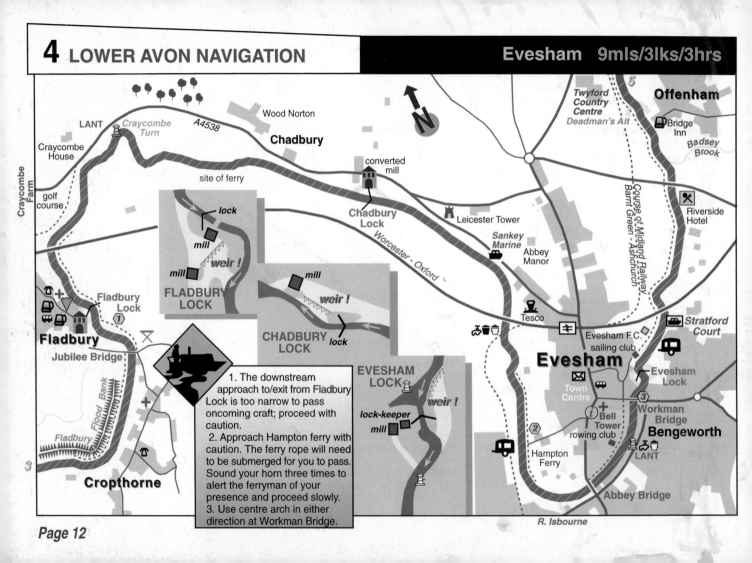

Offenham

Twyford Country Centre
Deadman's Ait

Bridge Inn

Badsey Brook

LANT

Craycombe Turn

A4538

Wood Norton

Chadbury

Craycombe House

site of ferry

converted mill

Chadbury Lock

Course of Midland Railway Barnt Green - Ashchurch

Craycombe Farm

golf course

Leicester Tower

Riverside Hotel

Worcester - Oxford

Sankey Marine

Abbey Manor

lock

mill

weir !

mill

FLADBURY LOCK

mill

weir !

Tesco

Stratford Court

Fladbury Lock

CHADBURY LOCK

lock

Evesham F.C. sailing club

Evesham

Evesham Lock

Fladbury

Jubilee Bridge

EVESHAM LOCK

weir !

Town Centre

Workman Bridge

Flood Bank

lock-keeper

mill

Bell Tower rowing club

Bengeworth

Fladbury

1. The downstream approach to/exit from Fladbury Lock is too narrow to pass oncoming craft; proceed with caution.
2. Approach Hampton ferry with caution. The ferry rope will need to be submerged for you to pass. Sound your horn three times to alert the ferryman of your presence and proceed slowly.
3. Use centre arch in either direction at Workman Bridge.

Hampton Ferry

LANT

Cropthorne

Abbey Bridge

R. Isbourne

EVESHAM marks the frontier between the Lower and Upper navigable sections of the River Avon. Between Cropthorne and Offenham the river practically boxes the compass on its gorgeous meanderings through the fruity vale.

In the 19th century the only way to cross the river at Cropthorne was to ford it. But in Queen Victoria's Jubilee year a bridge was built to span the river here, so that Fladbury lads could go courting Cropthorne lasses without necessarily getting their feet wet. One of the river's last working water-gates occupied the reach below Jubilee Bridge. These were devices for altering water levels without adversely affecting supplies to the mills. A conventional lock here would have lowered the water level to the detriment of the mill at Wyre. The water-gate provided a simple alternative. It consisted of a gate fitted with sluices set into a weir. In normal circumstances the gate would remain open until a boat passed through on its way upstream. Then the gate would be closed while the boat waited for a sufficient level of water to be built up to enable it to navigate up to Fladbury Lock. On the way back the sluices would be drawn on reaching the gate, and there a boat would wait until the levels had equalised and the gate could be opened.

The Avon at Fladbury is the stuff of dreams. Once there were two mills, that beside the lock being known as Cropthorne Mill in deference to its position. It is linked to the outside world by a private ferry. The other, quite naturally, was called Fladbury Mill and in later years a pair of Armfield 20hp turbines were installed to provide the village with electricity. Grandiosely known as the Fladbury Electric Light & Power Co., they charged ten shillings per light per annum to householders in the district.

The rhyming locks at Fladbury and Chadbury deserve a poem about them. Certainly there is plenty of inspiration in the landscape as the river winds past the orcharded flanks of Craycombe and Wood Norton. Craycombe House was built for George Perrott, an 18th century owner of the navigation. The novelist Francis Brett Young lived in it during the Thirties. Wood Norton House is used by the BBC as a training centre, but once belonged to the Duke of Orleans, a pretender to the French throne. Like most Avon mills, the one at Chadbury has been converted into a highly desirable private dwelling, but how one aches to see an Avon mill in business again, doing the job it was built to do, at no cost to the environment. Chadbury Lock was the first to be rebuilt by LANT in 1953. Much of the work was done by the Royal Engineers, a pioneering use of military resources on a civilian project.

Above the treetops bordering the next reach stands the Leicester Tower, built in 1840 as a memorial to Simon de Montfort, the Earl of Leicester, who came a cropper at the Battle of Evesham in 1265. The monks of Evesham Abbey planted vineyards on these south-facing slopes in the middle ages. Round the corner two railway bridges spanned the river. One remains, carrying the scenic Cotswolds & Malverns line. The other, a victim of Beeching, carried the Midland Railway route from Redditch to Ashchurch near Tewkesbury. If it had remained open north of Evesham at least, it might have been more than a little useful as a commuter link with Birmingham today, a mere 13 miles of railway permanently lost through dubiously reached and short-sighted, accountancy-led thinking.

Glass houses, glinting in the sunlight, emphasise Evesham's reputation as a fruit growing centre, as the river skirts its western suburbs and you pass the flourishing ferry at HAMPTON. This is one of only two public ferries still in existence on the Avon. It provides a popular short cut for the housewives of Hampton to reach Evesham's shops. There is an aesthetic pleasure in its to-ing and fro-ing which makes you sad that not more of the river's ferries have survived. Local authorities, one feels, might have done more to preserve such operations, if only to maintain the integrity of public rights of way.

A stately bridge, named after one of the town's Victorian mayors, spans the Avon in the centre of EVESHAM, and recreation grounds, bordered by an avenue of limes, create a gracious riverside environment. On hot days, with Evesham en fete, you might be reminded of Seurat's famous pointillistic masterpiece of the Ile de la Grand-Jatte. Evesham Lock is the highest upstream on the Lower Avon. A triangular-shaped lock-keeper's house spans the original, long since disused chamber.

HAMPTON FERRY · EVESHAM
FARES
Adults 50. EACH WAY.
Children 25. EACH WAY.

Between Evesham and OFFENHAM the river is left pretty much to its own devices. The railway and the by-pass cross the Avon but leave little impression on it. Beyond the watermeadows, and the likelihood of floods, the countryside is thick with regimented fruit trees. Deadman's Ait was the scene of heavy fighting during the Battle of Evesham. Many Welshmen were slaughtered in the vicinity, and large quantities of human remains were unearthed during the eighteenth century. The peace we associate with the English landscape had to be fought for.

Fladbury (Map 4)

Alas, a lack of suitable moorings renders the pretty village of Fladbury effectively beyond the reach of boaters - Temple Thurston would feel betrayed and Mrs Izod aghast that the ferry no longer operates for the benefit of the public and radish pickers. One becomes even more frustrated when one learns that THE CHEQUERS (Tel: 01386 860276) is an excellent inn offering good food, accommodation and locally-brewed beer, and that, though bereft of a general store, the village retains its butcher. Consolation can be found at CRAYCOMBE FARM, (accessible from the LANT moorings at Craycombe Turn - but *do* take care of the traffic) which does breakfasts, lunches and teas and offers locally grown produce, crafts and gifts - Tel: 01386 860473.

Evesham (Map 4)

One expects romantic things of Evesham, cynosure of its fruity vale, and at last the by-pass and pedestrianisation between them seem to have created a sense of calm that has been absent since the invention of the motor car. Highlights include: the Bell Tower, all that's left of an abbey demolished following the Dissolution. Compare its fate with Pershore, losing only its nave and Tewkesbury, surviving virtually intact. Time your visit to hear the tower's carillon. Nearby is The Almonry, housing the town's small museum, and one further building of note is the Round House

in the Market Place, a sprawling, half-timbered structure dating from 1450, not remotely circular and now home to a bank.

GREEN DRAGON - Oat Street. Home-brewed 'Asum' ales. Tel: 01386 446337.
TRUMPET INN - Merstow Green. Heavenly Hook Norton & food. Tel: 01386 446227.
RIVERSIDE HOTEL - Hotel restaurant located a mile or so above Evesham Lock with moorings for customers. Tel: 01386 446200.
ASK - Vine Street. Stylish Italian. Tel: 01386 424545.
THE LANTERN - Bridge Street. Highly retro cod & chips. Tel: 01386 47726

Bridge Street and High Street are the principal shopping thoroughfares, along with the River Side indoor shopping centre, the latter being the site for many of the well known chain stores. But don't ignore Bengeworth, east of the river, which has a good bakery, a bike shop, launderette, pharmacy, heaps of takeaways, an old-fashioned cinema called THE REGAL and an excellent secondhand bookshop called BOOKWORMS (Tel: 01386 45509) which doesn't open on Mondays or Sundays.

TOURIST INFORMATION - The Almonry, Abbey Gate. Tel: 01386 446944.
ALMONRY HERITAGE CENTRE - Abbey Gate. Tel: 01386 446944. Admission charge. The former home of the Abbey Almoner today houses a heritage centre detailing the history of the town.

BOAT HIRE - skiffs, motorboats and river trips - Tel: 01386 834070.
BUSES - Services to/from Pershore and Worcester (not Sundays). Tel: 01905 763888.
TRAINS - Cotswold Line services to/from Worcester, Pershore and Oxford by Thames Trains and First Great Western. Tel: 08457 484950.

Offenham (Map 4)

BRIDGE INN - riverside, Offenham. Tel: 01386 446565. Donnington beers from Stow-on-the-Wold, plus regular guests. Food daily and a nice setting beside the river but sadly the ferry has gone.

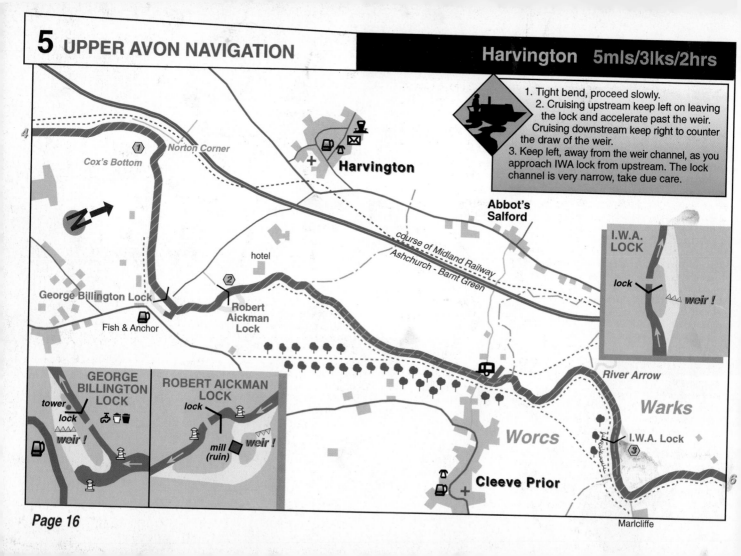

1. Tight bend, proceed slowly.
2. Cruising upstream keep left on leaving the lock and accelerate past the weir. Cruising downstream keep right to counter the draw of the weir.
3. Keep left, away from the weir channel, as you approach IWA lock from upstream. The lock channel is very narrow, take due care.

4

Norton Corner

Cox's Bottom

Harvington

Abbot's Salford

course of Midland Railway
Ashchurch - Barnt Green

hotel

George Billington Lock

Fish & Anchor

Robert Aickman Lock

I.W.A. LOCK

lock △△△ weir !

River Arrow

Warks

Worcs

I.W.A. Lock

GEORGE BILLINGTON LOCK

tower
lock
△△△ weir !

ROBERT AICKMAN LOCK

lock
mill (ruin) △△△ weir !

Cleeve Prior

Marlcliffe

DRIFTING through time and space, the Avon wends its secluded way between Evesham and Bidford. Substantially different in character to the lower river, the Upper Avon has a wilder feel to it, akin perhaps to the uppermost reaches of the River Thames between Oxford and Lechlade. It was appropriate, therefore, that second-hand paddle gear from Thames locks was used in the restoration of the Upper Avon. And what a mammoth undertaking it was, costing more than six times as much as the Lower Avon restoration project.

All the Upper Avon locks are named after individuals or groups associated with the restoration of the river. The work at GEORGE BILLINGTON LOCK was completed in just six weeks so as to enable its donor, who was terminally ill, was able to observe the effect of his benefaction before he died. ROBERT AICKMAN LOCK commemorates one of the most influential figures of the post war inland waterways renaissance. Aickman founded the Inland Waterways Association in 1946 and crusaded for the waterways cause for a further twenty years. Returning navigation to the Avon was dear to his heart, and he was on the council of both Trusts. A memorial plaque, set in an attractive sweep of brickwork, graces the lockside, paying homage to his achievements and single-minded determination. More practically, the boater is thankful for the provision of free overnight moorings on most Upper Avon lock cuts, many located in blissfully remote rural surroundings, welcome facilities that the Lower Avon and the Upper Thames are not so well endowed with.

Sir Arthur Quiller-Couch wrote of 'clouds of sweet-smelling flour' issuing from the doorway of Cleeve Mill, but virtually all trace of the lock, weir and mill at Cleeve has vanished. Up until the Second World War this was a popular venue for picnics. You could get cream teas at the mill and hire a skiff for a leisurely row up the river. The Avon broadened below the weir and was shallow enough to be crossed by hay carts at harvest time. A correspondent from Canada wrote to tell us that his great uncle once lived in the mill, commuting from Salford Priors station to Birmingham, where he was the conductor of the symphony orchestra and on personal terms with Tchaikovsky. What interesting people the Canal Companion readers are!

At the foot of its wooded escarpment, the setting at Cleeve remains seductive, though somewhat compromised by the presence now of a caravan park on the Warwickshire bank, and it is disappointing that boaters have no access to the pretty village of Cleeve itself.

Downstream of the IWA LOCK, the River Arrow has its confluence with the Avon. Consideration was given to making this navigable in the 17th century, but nothing materialised. The Arrow rises on the Lickey Hills and passes through the lower reservoir at Bittell beside the Worcester & Birmingham Canal, so you may well see it again. Likewise its tributary, the Alne, which follows the Stratford Canal for a while in the vicinity of Preston Bagot.

Marlcliffe is aptly named, for the Trust had considerable problems during the construction of the IWA Lock, due to the unyielding quality of the substrata. UANT's handbook describes many of the difficulties overcome during the restoration in a matter of fact way, a modesty which fails to disguise the vast amount of work they undertook - and continue to undertake - on our behalf.

Summary of Facilities

The benefits of civilization are left behind on this section of the river, unless you are prepared to make the lengthy trek to Harvington from either George Billington or Robert Aickman Lock. When you get there you'll find a post office stores and the GOLDEN CROSS (Tel: 01789 772420), an attractive pub with a good range of real ales, bar food and a vegetarian-friendly restaurant. Harvington is also the base for the Upper Avon Navigation Trust, their offices being housed in the former railway station.

Closer to the water, the FISH & ANCHOR (Tel: 01386 41094) beside George Billington Lock offers restaurant and bar meals as well as moorings for customers.

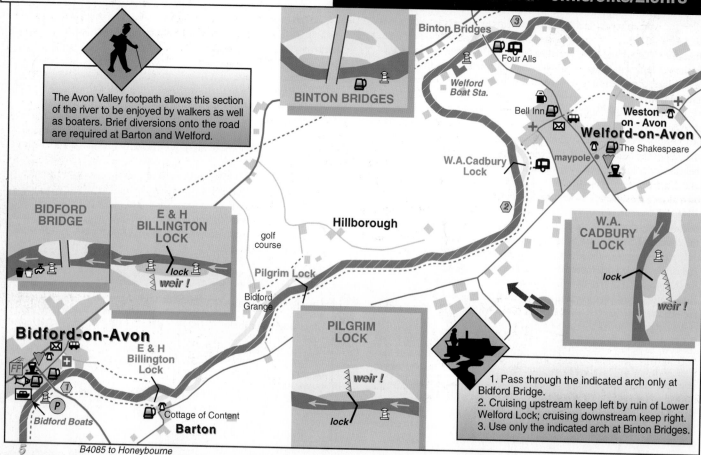

The Avon Valley footpath allows this section of the river to be enjoyed by walkers as well as boaters. Brief diversions onto the road are required at Barton and Welford.

BINTON BRIDGES

Binton Bridges

Four Alls

Welford Boat Sta.

Bell Inn

Weston - on - Avon

Welford-on-Avon

The Shakespeare

maypole

W.A.Cadbury Lock

BIDFORD BRIDGE

E & H BILLINGTON LOCK

lock

weir !

golf course

Hillborough

W.A. CADBURY LOCK

lock

weir !

Pilgrim Lock

Bidford Grange

PILGRIM LOCK

weir !

lock

Bidford-on-Avon

E & H Billington Lock

Bidford Boats

Cottage of Content

Barton

1. Pass through the indicated arch only at Bidford Bridge.
2. Cruising upstream keep left by ruin of Lower Welford Lock; cruising downstream keep right.
3. Use only the indicated arch at Binton Bridges.

B4085 to Honeybourne

THE Upper Avon is at its loveliest between Bidford and Weston. Locks come at satisfying intervals, but the rest of the time you have every justification for just sitting back and watching the peaceful landscape slip uneventfully astern. Neither is it absolutely necessary to be afloat to enjoy the seclusion of this part of the river, because an excellent public footpath stretches from Marlcliffe (Map 5) through Bidford to Stratford (Map 7), allowing those on foot to see more than just a tantalising glimpse of the river for once.

BIDFORD serves to further enhance the river's appeal. In high season it positively bristles with boaters, coming in to moor with varying degrees of proficiency, or threading their way gingerly through the single and narrow navigation arch of the 15th century bridge. There is only limited space available at the Recreation Ground but if you have a penchant for peace and seclusion, we can wholeheartedly recommend the UANT moorings at E. & H. Billington Lock, from where it is but a fifteen minute walk back into town along an exceedingly pleasant footpath.

UANT's locks are not always situated in exact accordance with those on the original navigation. For instance, E. & H. Billington and Pilgrim locks are located either side of the former lock at Bidford Grange. Similarly, there used to be separate locks at Welford which UANT replaced with the single W. A. Cadbury Lock. These changes were necessitated by the alteration of water levels in the intervening years between dereliction of the original navigation and the commencement of the new scheme in the early Seventies. The attitudes of landowners, local and water authorities also influenced the final shape of the UANT project. Sometimes such individuals were extraordinarily helpful, whilst others seemed determined to stop the scheme in its tracks. Inexplicably, as Robert Aickman put it, the restorers were not always seen to be on the side of the angels.

The river splits into several channels - only one of which is navigable - to pass beneath the ancient arches of BINTON BRIDGES. Nearby lies the trackbed of the old Stratford & Midland Junction Railway, one of those endearingly independent cross-country lines which seemed to lead from nowhere to nowhere. At plum-picking time as many as twenty wagons a day were loaded with fruit in the tiny siding at Binton. The line's most important trains were the banana specials operated by the Midland Railway between Avonmouth Docks and London in roundabout rivalry with the Great Western. The reach above Welford is overlooked by Thames-like boathouses and thatched cabins on stilts protect them from raised water levels.

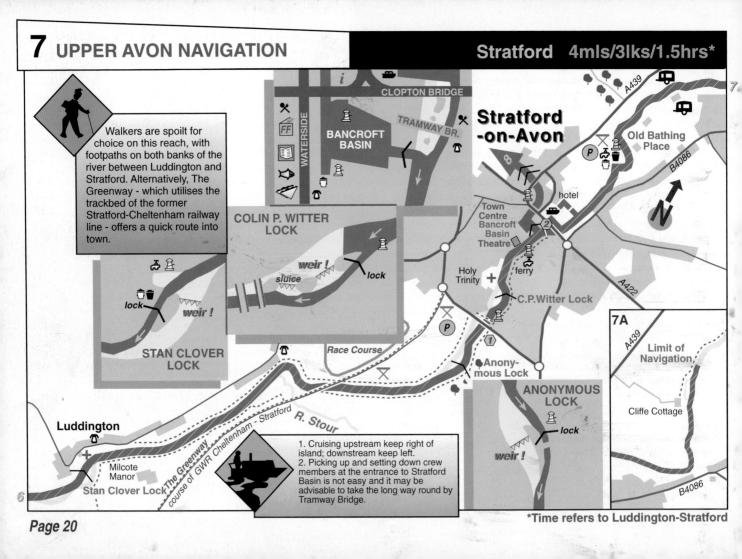

CLOPTON BRIDGE

TRAMWAY BR.

WATERSIDE

BANCROFT BASIN

Stratford -on-Avon

Old Bathing Place

A439

A4086

hotel

Town Centre Bancroft Basin Theatre

COLIN P. WITTER LOCK

weir !

sluice

lock

Holy Trinity

C.P.Witter Lock

ferry

lock

lock

weir !

STAN CLOVER LOCK

Race Course

Anony-mous Lock

A422

7A

Limit of Navigation

A439

Cliffe Cottage

Walkers are spoilt for choice on this reach, with footpaths on both banks of the river between Luddington and Stratford. Alternatively, The Greenway - which utilises the trackbed of the former Stratford-Cheltenham railway line - offers a quick route into town.

ANONYMOUS LOCK

lock

weir !

Luddington

Milcote Manor

R. Stour

The Greenway course of GWR Cheltenham - Stratford

Stan Clover Lock

1. Cruising upstream keep right of island; downstream keep left.
2. Picking up and setting down crew members at the entrance to Stratford Basin is not easy and it may be advisable to take the long way round by Tramway Bridge.

B4086

*Time refers to Luddington-Stratford

BOATERS have three river locks to contend with (plus a fourth if they are moving on to or off the canal at Stratford) as the Upper Avon winds from Luddington, past Stratford, to the present head of navigation at Alveston Weir.

Luddington Lock was renamed STAN CLOVER LOCK in 1997 in honour of one of UANT's loyal supporters. Just over a mile upstream the River Stour enters the Avon, having descended from the Cotswolds, its source being near the brewery town of Hook Norton. Above the confluence a large steel girder bridge carries the trackbed of the old Great Western Railway's Stratford-Cheltenham line. Now known as 'The Greenway', it stretches from Stratford to Long Marston, a useful escape route from the busy tourist town for walkers, cyclists and horse-riders.

ANONYMOUS LOCK commemorates all those who donated funds towards restoration of the Upper Avon, including the individual who made the staggering donation of £100,000. The late Queen Mother travelled from here to the next lock up by narrowboat during the opening ceremony of June 1st 1974, as celebrated in the poem *Inland Waterway* by John Betjeman.

The short reach separating Anonymous and Colin P. Witter locks is spanned by the Stratford & Midland Junction Railway bridge which was converted to carry road traffic. A footbridge also crosses the river at this point, making it easy for pedestrians to enjoy a circular walk beside the Avon. Blocks of highly desirable flats occupy the site of Lucy's Mill, which stood here for hundreds of years and was an important customer of the river barges until the advent of the railway.

Stratford New Lock was renamed COLIN P. WITTER LOCK in 1986. Massive steel frames protect the chamber from collapse threatened by high ground pressures. The bold steeple of Holy Trinity Church (Shakespeare's burial place) overlooks the lock, above which Stratford's passenger ferry boat operates by means of a submerged chain fed through a winch on the pontoon wound by the ferryman. Rowing boats may be hired from the ferryman.

Stratford's riverfront is familiar to people from all over the world. Indeed, you are seemingly more likely to overhear the accents of New York or Tokyo than Warwickshire. And everyone seems determined to get afloat. Barnacle-encrusted navigators of the Avon Ring can look imperiously down on rowers and punters and motor-boaters, but you have to keep a weather-eye peeled for sudden unexpected and unpremeditated lurches to port or starboard. A long river bank, backed by playing fields, extends between Colin P. Witter Lock and Tramway Bridge, providing an alternative, marginally less public berth to the canal basin, and on the opposite bank stands the Royal Shakespeare Theatre.

Upstream of the entrance lock to Stratford Basin the river is spanned by the TRAMWAY BRIDGE, a redbrick structure built in 1826 to carry the Stratford & Moreton Horse Tramway. It is now used by pedestrians. In contrast, the stone arches of CLOPTON BRIDGE date back to 1480. But the two bridges harmonise well with their shared environment, as though the gap of four centuries on their construction was just a twinkling ripple in the timespan of the river beneath them. Rowing skiffs and motor boats can be hired from the boathouse between the two bridges. Two backwaters lead to the boatyards of Stratford Marina and Bancroft Cruisers.

Beyond Stratford the Avon is currently navigable for another couple of miles or so as far as Alveston, but the Upper Avon Navigation Trust are promoting a bold scheme to extend navigation up the Avon and its tributary the Leam to a junction with the Grand Union Canal at Radford Semele to the south of Leamington Spa. Ten locks and sixteen miles seem modest by the standards of many inland waterway project proposals, and the boost to tourism and the benefits of improved flood control are manifest, but the concept has so far foundered on the reactionary response of riparian landowners.

But it would be churlish to leave the Avon on such a disappointing note. Boating enthusiasts have fifty miles of gorgeous river to play with thanks to the vision and graft of the two Trusts and their volunteers. Additional navigability is something to look forward to. Attitudes and personalities change. The river can bide its time.

Stratford-on-Avon (Maps 7 & 8)

That Stratford-on-Avon is second only to London in the esteem of foreign visitors, serves to emphasise the charisma surrounding Shakespeare. Without his omnipresence, one imagines Stratford's position in the league table of tourism would be academic. And yet, subtract the Shakespeare factor, and you are still left with an attractive town with a large helping of good architecture, its setting enhanced by the proximity of the Avon, and there is a hair-down demeanour about the people in the streets which becomes infectious. Contriving a dramatic analogy, Stratford delivers its lines and plays its part, but survives with its integrity and dignity intact, really being the rather nice place to visit as extolled by the tourist propaganda.

Sorting out the wheat from the chaff can be a foot-wearying experience, as indeed can be finding a free table on a warm summer evening, but we've attempted to do some of the spade work for you.

GEORGETOWN - Sheep Street. Tel: 01789 204445. Colonial Malaysian cooking.

THE OPPOSITION - Sheep Street. Tel: 01789 269980. Classy restaurant.

LAMBS - Sheep Street. Tel: 01789 292554. Ditto.

CAFE ROUGE - Sheep Street. Tel: 01789 263526. French chain.

THE BOATHOUSE - riverside between Tramway and Clopton bridges. Tel: 01789 297733. Thai restaurant.

SHAKESPEARE HOTEL - Chapel Street. Fine beams, fine beer, fine food. Tel: 01789 294771.

HATHAWAYS - High Street. Tel: 01789 292404. Old-fashioned tearooms.

THISTLE HOTEL - Waterside. Bar and restaurant meals as well as a choice of real ales. Lovely garden for eating *al fresco*. Tel: 01789 294949.

Market day is Friday and a good one it is too. Elsewhere the town bristles with quality shops engaged in the hectic business of emptying the bank accounts of visitors. But many of these shops have such character that you don't resent being plunged into the red. Even the chain stores, like Marks & Spencer on Bridge Street, appear to have more flair than branches elsewhere. The best policy, chaps, is to get here after the shops have shut and insist on an early start. A 24 hour branch of TESCO stands within easy reach of Bridge 65 on the canal.

TOURIST INFORMATION - Bridgefoot. Tel: 01789 293127.

GUIDE FRIDAY TOURS - Open top bus tours providing a good introduction to the town's attractions. Charge. Tel: 01789 294466.

ROYAL SHAKESPEARE THEATRE - Waterside. Whatever else you do in Stratford, try to catch a performance at the RST, or at one of the two other theatres in town, The Swan or The Other Place. Tel: 01789 295623.

THE WALK - A two hour guided walk around the Stratford streets that brings Shakespeare back to life. Starts and finishes at the Swan Theatre. Charge. Tel: 01789 412602.

THE SHAKESPEARE VISITOR CENTRE - Henley Street. Everything you always wanted to know about Shakespeare and were too afraid to ask your teacher at school. Good starting point for visiting the three 'Shakespeare houses' in town: Shakespeare's Birthplace (Henley Street), Nash's House and New Place (Chapel Street) and Hall's Croft (Old Town). Admission charge. Tel: 01789 204016.

COX'S YARD - Bridgefoot. Described as "a major celebration of the town's past, the colour, the characters, the lives, the legends." Features a working micro brewery and an 18th century industrial heritage site. Admission charge. Tel: 01789 404600.

STRATFORD BRASS RUBBING CENTRE - RST Summer House, Avonbank Gardens. Interactive experience for brass rubbing enthusiasts. Admission free. Tel: 01789 297671.

STRATFORD BUTTERFLY FARM - Tramway Walk, Swan's Nest Lane. Some light relief from all that Shakespeare stuff at Europe's largest butterfly farm. Attractions, if that's the right word, include deadly spiders. Admission charge. Tel: 01789 299288.

And if you can't find anything of interest there, then call at the TIC and they will no doubt have a hundred and one other suggestions to offer, including details of how to get afloat aboard punts, canoes, rowing boats or anything else that takes your fancy.

BUSES- Regular services to Birmingham, Oxford, Coventry etc. Tel: 01788 535555.

TRAINS - Fairly frequent services to Birmingham via Wootton Wawen and Henley-in-Arden. Also regular trains run to Leamington Spa for connections to all points south. Tel: 08457 484950.

stratford
CANAL

THE Stratford Canal holds a special place in the affections of a generation of canal enthusiasts, its southern section being the first great restoration success of the post-war canal movement. It was transformed from virtual dereliction and the threat of abandonment in 1958 to navigable status once again in 1964. The restoration project, managed by David Hutchings, was undertaken under the aegis of the National Trust, but in 1988 ownership of the canal passed to British Waterways.

Little evidence survives of former commercial activity at Stratford Canal (or Bancroft) Basin. Ice cream boats, baguette boats, and a floating art gallery lend it nowadays a Disneyland ambience, though it remains an entertaining spot to moor should you be able to find space. Quieter canal moorings are to be had through Bridge 69, an unobtrusive exit from the basin which begins (or, of course, ends) exploration of the Stratford Canal, and the canal's traverse of the town's eastern outskirts, through a quartet of locks, is surprisingly anonymous.

Above the locks, a hire base and boatyard create a sense of activity as the canal passes beneath two railway bridges (look out for Summer Sunday steam trains) and passes the town's little football stadium.

Well kept and easy to operate, WILMCOTE LOCKS, like Caesar's Gaul and strawberry cheesecake, are divided into three distinct parts: two outer threes and a middle five. For ease of maintenance and access to two canalside cottages, the status of the towpath here has been upgraded to that of a minor road.

BRIDGE 59 was the straw that almost broke the camel's back. Its deterioration caused the local authority to seek permission to abandon the canal back in 1958, so that they could divert the roadway across the bed of the waterway. Evidence as to the canal's use relied on the purchase of a solitary ticket for a canoe trip the previous year! The only real function that the canal performed at the time was as a source of water for engine cleaning at Stratford railway station. The canal narrows at the site of a former quarry and lime-burning wharf, and the abutments of a former tramway bridge recall this activity. Wilmcote boasts good moorings for visiting boaters.

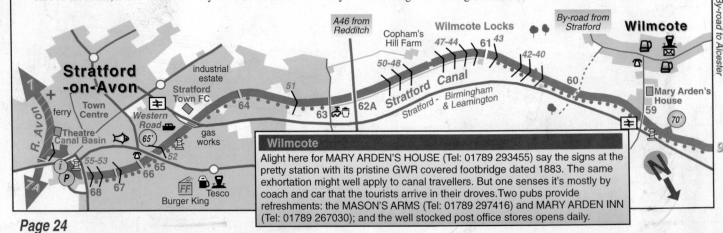

Wilmcote

Alight here for MARY ARDEN'S HOUSE (Tel: 01789 293455) say the signs at the pretty station with its pristine GWR covered footbridge dated 1883. The same exhortation might well apply to canal travellers. But one senses it's mostly by coach and car that the tourists arrive in their droves. Two pubs provide refreshments: the MASON'S ARMS (Tel: 01789 297416) and MARY ARDEN INN (Tel: 01789 267030); and the well stocked post office stores opens daily.

ODD Lock separates two lengthy and delightfully remote pounds between the locks at Wilmcote and Preston Bagot. EDSTONE AQUEDUCT - sometimes known as Bearley - is undoubtedly the Stratford Canal's most dramatic engineering feature. It consists of an iron trough resting on thirteen tapering brick piers. At 28 feet high and 475 feet long, it seems modest enough, but in the context of the gently rolling landscape, its sudden appearance has the majesty and startling effect of the renowned Pontcysyllte Aqueduct on the Llangollen Canal. The sunken towpath offers walkers a strange, fish-eye lens view of passing boaters. The aqueduct spans a by-road, a tributary of the River Alne and the twin tracks of the Birmingham & North Warwickshire Railway whose undistinguished diet of Sprinter units is supplemented on Summer Sundays by the steam-hauled 'Shakespeare Express'. Those with a trained railway eye will notice an overgrown trackbed curving away from beneath the aqueduct across the countryside in a north-westerly direction. This was the Great Western Railway's Alcester branch an ill-fated and relatively shortlived line which had its track lifted as an economy measure during the First World War, re-opened in 1923, then closed again at the beginning of the Second World War, apart from a semi-secret service operated for employees at a motor works evacuated from Coventry.

WOOTTON WAWEN AQUEDUCT is a more modest affair than Edstone, but it fights a running battle with juggernauts on the A34. On several occasions it has borne the brunt of high-sided vehicles whose drivers' grasp of measurements lacked finesse. Nevertheless, it has stood its ground since 1813 and should be good for a few years yet, especially as it has recently been refurbished with the help of Heritage Lottery funding.

Wootton Wawen

Wootton Hall is a 17th century mansion which once belonged to Mrs Fitzherbert, a mistress of George IV. The parish church is of Saxon origin and considered one of Warwickshire's finest. A handsome former paper mill straddles the Alne.

THE NAVIGATION - canalside by the aqueduct. Tel: 01564 792676. Bar and restaurant meals. Nice garden.

HERON'S NEST - Coffee shop at Yew Tree Farm. Tel: 01564 792701. Also does B & B.

General stores in the centre of the village and excellent farm shop selling fresh produce, home cooking (see above) and crafts.

TRAINS - hourly service to/from Birmingham and Stratford. Tel: 08457 484950.

A3400 from Stratford

Bearley Cross

Edstone Aqueduct

Odd Lock

Wootton Wawen

The Navigation
Anglo-Welsh

aqueduct

farm shop

mill

Hall

Bulls Head

DELICATE split cantilever bridges and barrel-roofed cottages are two ingredients which lend particular charm to the middle section of the Stratford Canal. Actually, they only serve to 'gild the lily', because this length of canal is especially lovely in any case. Between Wootton Wawen and Kingswood the waterway loses itself in the last vestiges of the old Forest of Arden.

From Preston Bagot to Lowsonford the canal winds its lonely way across Yarningale Common, crossing Yarningale Aqueduct, the baby of the Stratford Canal family. The barrel-roofed cottages by locks 34 and 37 have been incorporated into modern extensions, but those by locks 28 and 31 remain unspoilt. The unusual design of these cottages is said to have been brought about by the use of the same wooden frames used in the construction of the brick road bridges which span the canal.

The abutments of a former railway bridge frame the canal near Lowsonford. The bridge carried a branchline to Henley-in-Arden, closed when the route was made obsolete by the opening of the North Warwickshire Railway. Legend has it that the track was despatched to The Front during the Great War but ended up at the bottom of the English Channel. Frustratingly, it seems unlikely that the M40 will be as shortlived.

Woods border the canal, birdsong fills the air, the scent of wildflowers is intoxicating. Temple Thurston was equally taken with this part of the Stratford Canal. In 1910 he hired a narrowboat known as *The Flower of Gloster*, its captain Eynsham Harry, together with a horse called Fanny and set off on a journey of discovery which has remained a 'desert island' favourite of many canal enthusiasts ever since. Temple Thurston described the Stratford Canal as being 'right out of the track of the world'. He climbed the hillside to a farm at Yarningale for fresh milk, and Eynsham Harry bought beer from the wife of a lock-keeper. Reading *The Flower of Gloster* as you travel along the canal today leads inevitably to melancholy comparisons.

Lapworth 11
Bottom Lock

Leamington - Birmingham

26
39A
27
28
29
30
40

Fleur de Lys

Finwood

Lowsonford
41
31

32
42
43
33
44
34
46
35
45
aqueduct
47 38 37
36
48
60'
49
50
51

Preston Bagot

A4189 from Henley in Arden

Crab Mill

A4189 to Warwick

Yarningale Common

N

The towpath, though not always formally surfaced, is generally well kept and wide, though cycling is officially frowned upon.

David Alison

Edstone Aqueduct, Stratford-on-Avon Canal

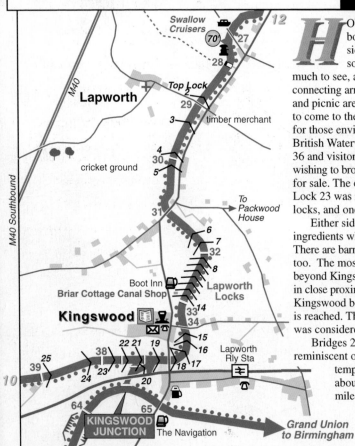

Swallow Cruisers 70' 27

28

Top Lock 2

29 *timber merchant*

3

4

30

5

To Packwood House

31

6

7

32

8

Boot Inn

Briar Cottage Canal Shop

Lapworth Locks

Kingswood

33 14

34

15

16 *Lapworth Rly Sta*

38 22 21 19

18 17

39 25

24 23 20

64

65

KINGSWOOD JUNCTION The Navigation

Grand Union to Birmingham

Grand Union to London To Baddesley Clinton Hall

M40 Southbound

Lapworth

cricket ground

12

10

OWEVER many times you've been there before, and whether you arrive by boat, by car or on foot, Kingswood Junction never fails to captivate. Either side of the junction the Stratford Canal continues with its unremitting locks, so boaters will be more than grateful to take a break here. Certainly there is much to see, and the configuration of the two briefly parallel canals, together with the connecting arm, allows plenty of opportunity for circular or figure-of-eight walks. A car park and picnic area, well masked by pine trees, encourage the non boat owning or hiring public to come to the junction, whilst the proximity of Lapworth railway station is advantageous for those environmentally aware folk who favour the use of public transport.

British Waterways use the old National Trust workshops and maintenance yard by Bridge 36 and visitors are made welcome whether seeking specific help or information or simply wishing to browse through an extensive display of local walks leaflets and books and souvenirs for sale. The original connection between the Stratford and the Grand Union Canal below Lock 23 was reinstated in 1996, offering GU boaters bound for Stratford a saving of two locks, and one of the former reservoirs has been adapted for long term moorings.

Either side of Kingswood there is much to look forward to encountering - all the tasty ingredients which create the Stratford Canal's unique flavour are encountered on this length. There are barrel-roofed cottages by Locks 21 and 25, and several of the charming split bridges too. The most dramatic section of the Lapworth flight lies between Bridges 32 and 33, beyond Kingswood Junction on the northern Stratford Canal. Here there are seven chambers in close proximity, presenting a spectacular view whether you are looking up or down. Leaving Kingswood bound for Kings Norton there are eighteen locks to negotiate before the summit is reached. The top lock is numbered '2' because the guillotine stop lock at Kings Norton was considered to be No 1.

Bridges 26 and 28 are lifting structures: the former of Llangollen pattern; the latter reminiscent of those found on the Oxford Canal. A winding hole by Bridge 27 marks the temporary terminus of the Stratford Canal between 1796 and 1800, a hiatus brought about by lack of capital. It actually took twenty-two years to build the twenty-five mile route between King's Norton and Stratford, which must be some sort of record.

The summit cost as much as the budget for the whole canal. The engineer was Josiah Clowes, who we will met again in this guide on the Thames & Severn Canal.

Lapworth Locks

Kingswood & Lapworth *(Map 11)*

Twin villages in North Warwickshire's commuter belt where the property prices routinely run into six figures.

THE NAVIGATION - canalside (Grand Union) Bridge 65. Unspoilt Bass pub with lovely garden for hot days and cool interior for *really* hot days. Tel: 01564 783337.

THE BOOT - canalside Bridge 33. Well appointed pub with sophisticated menu. Tel: 01564 782464.

Off licence by Bridge 65 (Grand Union), post office stores by Bridge 34 and basic groceries, as well as gifts etc, from the BRIAR COTTAGE canal shop by Bridge 33.

BADDESLEY CLINTON HALL AND PACKWOOD HOUSE - National Trust houses within walking distance of the canal. The former, a medieval manor house, lies one mile north-east of Bridge 65 (Grand Union), whilst the latter, a Tudor house, is one mile north of Bridge 31. Tel: 01564 783294 for details of both properties.

BRITISH WATERWAYS - Tel: 01564 784634. Helpful and friendly canal information on tap.

TRAINS - local services to/from Leamington Spa, Warwick and Birmingham. Tel: 08457 484950.

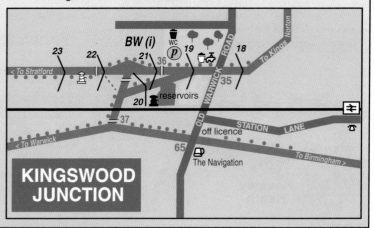

NORTH of Hockley Heath the canal assumes a mantle of trees which border the summit section. Oak, alder, hazel and willow predominate, creating a soothing, sylvan quality which, however beautiful, is apt to become soporific after a while. When you do catch glimpses of the surrounding countryside, it reminds you of the Home Counties, exuding an air of affluence epitomised by large detached houses, and horsey people, trotting down dappled lanes on dappled steeds.

The winding hole by Bridge 22 marks the site of a wharf once linked by tramway to the limestone quarries of Tanworth-in-Arden. Originally a branch canal had been planned to cater for this traffic. Near Bridge 19 an extensive miniature railway stands close to the canal, though hidden by a cutting. Privately owned, it does however, open to the public on selected dates.

At Earlswood an embankment carries the canal over Spring Brook and a feeder enters the canal from a trio of reservoirs which lie to the south-west. These Earlswood Reservoirs are a popular amenity, attracting ramblers, anglers and bird watchers.

Even if you have more enthusiasm for machinery than wildlife, the reservoirs are still worth visiting to see the old engine house on Lady Lane, to which narrowboats carried coal up the feeder until 1936. Earlswood Motor Yacht Club members use the feeder now for moorings.

Like a dart player's waistline, Birmingham's southern suburbs keep on expanding and a new housing estate now borders the canal at Dickens Heath. Significantly architects are now keen to incorporate canals into their vision, whereas a generation ago ugly boundary fences would have been erected and the houses would have turned their backs to the water. A new footbridge encourages residents to stride out and enjoy the splendours of the towpath.

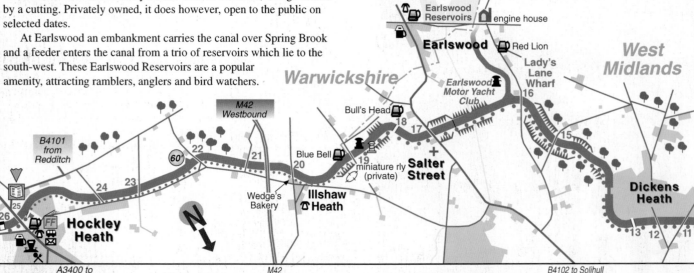

The Stratford Canal near Dickens Heath

From the road Hockley Heath looks like any other suburban settlement, the canal renders it more significant, if only for the facilities on offer.

NETTUNO - likeable Italian restaurant on A3400. Tel: 01564 784800.

NAG'S HEAD - Harvester Restaurant. Tel: 01564 784137. KAM SUNG - Chinese takeaway. Tel: 01564 782782.

WHARF TAVERN - canalside Bridge 25. Carvery meals and waterside garden overlooking stub of old wharf. Tel: 01564 782075.

General stores, post office and Shell garage with shop (and cash machine) on one side of Bridge 25, newsagent and butcher on the other.

BUSES - service X20 usefully links Hockley Heath hourly Mon-Sat with Birmingham, Henley-in-Arden and Stratford-on-Avon. Tel: 01788 535555.

Other Facilities on Map 12

At ILLSHAW HEATH, Wedge's Bakery continues to flourish in its unlikely rural setting in the shadow of the M42. Fresh bread, sandwiches made to order, pies in profusion and a vegetable stall make it difficult for passing canaller's to resist.

Several excellent pubs are within easy reach of the canal. By Bridge 19, the BLUE BELL is a rare cider house, though naturally, in this day and age, beer and food are also available - Tel: 01564 702328. Near Bridge 17, the BULL'S HEAD on Lime Kiln Lane is a charming county pub with a good choice of food (Tel: 01564 702335) and you can say the same for the RED LION a quarter of a mile south of Bridge 16 (Tel: 01564 702325).

ALTHOUGH the map emphasises how built-up these south-western suburbs of Birmingham are, the canal seems oblivious to the proximity of so many houses and people, retaining an aloof quality, like a recluse in a crowd. The boater's steady progress is interrupted by having to throttle down past moored boats at the bottom of gardens. Another obstacle to progress is Shirley Drawbridge, not so much a local-lass, more a wind-lass operated lift bridge on a busyish by-road, necessitating the use of barriers accessed with a British Waterways' Yale key. Nearby the canal crosses the River Cole which finds its way via the Tame, Trent and Humber to the North Sea.

Shakespeare looks inscrutably down from the western portal of Brandwood Tunnel. Brandwood was built without a towpath, so horses were led over the top while boats were worked through by the simple expedient of boatmen pulling on a handrail set into the tunnel lining. The horse path still provides walkers with a right of way and also offers access to some useful suburban shops.

Between the tunnel and King's Norton Junction stands a swing bridge with a history, a *cause celebre* in the embryonic days of the Inland Waterways Association. It was originally a lift bridge and, during the Second World War the Great Western Railway, who owned the canal at that time, clamped down the platform following damage by a lorry. Commercial traffic had ceased on the canal, but the IWA maintained that a right of navigation still applied. The GWR claimed that they would be only too happy to jack up the bridge to permit boats to pass as required, little realising that the IWA intended to organise as many boat passages as would be necessary to have the bridge fully repaired. Several campaign cruises ensued, but it was not until Nationalisation that the present swing bridge was installed. Often erroneously referred to as Lifford Lane Bridge, Bridge 2 is in fact on Tunnel Lane.

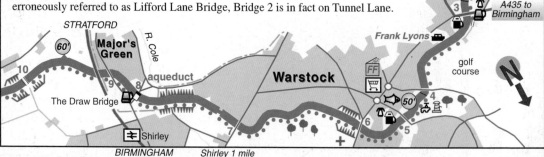

Summary of Facilities

WARSTOCK'S shops, including Kwik Save, post office, newsagent, butcher, pharmacy, McDonalds and a fish and chip shop, are just a short walk south from Bridge 5, where visitor moorings and a water point are provided. Above BRANDWOOD TUNNEL you'll find a general store, a fish & chip shop and an enterprising sandwich shop which will take advance orders on 0121 444 004. There's a pair of canalside pubs: The Drawbridge by Bridge 8 (Tel: 0121 474 5904); and The Horseshoe by Bridge 3 (Tel: 0121 443 3888).

worcester & BIRMINGHAM

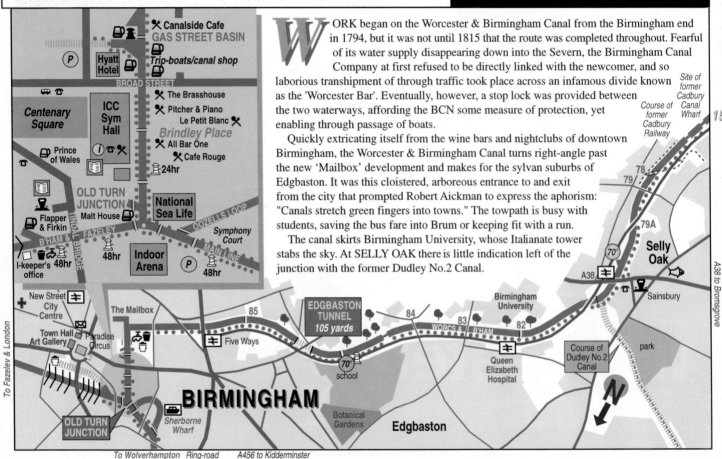

WORK began on the Worcester & Birmingham Canal from the Birmingham end in 1794, but it was not until 1815 that the route was completed throughout. Fearful of its water supply disappearing down into the Severn, the Birmingham Canal Company at first refused to be directly linked with the newcomer, and so laborious transhipment of through traffic took place across an infamous divide known as the 'Worcester Bar'. Eventually, however, a stop lock was provided between the two waterways, affording the BCN some measure of protection, yet enabling through passage of boats.

Quickly extricating itself from the wine bars and nightclubs of downtown Birmingham, the Worcester & Birmingham Canal turns right-angle past the new 'Mailbox' development and makes for the sylvan suburbs of Edgbaston. It was this cloistered, arboreous entrance to and exit from the city that prompted Robert Aickman to express the aphorism: "Canals stretch green fingers into towns." The towpath is busy with students, saving the bus fare into Brum or keeping fit with a run.

The canal skirts Birmingham University, whose Italianate tower stabs the sky. At SELLY OAK there is little indication left of the junction with the former Dudley No.2 Canal.

Map labels:

Canalside Cafe
GAS STREET BASIN
Trip-boats/canal shop
Hyatt Hotel
BROAD STREET
The Brasshouse
Pitcher & Piano
Le Petit Blanc
Centenary Square
ICC Sym Hall
Brindley Place
All Bar One
Cafe Rouge
24hr
Prince of Wales
OLD TURN JUNCTION
Malt House
National Sea Life
OOZELLS LOOP
Symphony Court
Flapper & Firkin
B'HAM & F. FAZELEY
LINDA BRIDGE
48hr
48hr
Indoor Arena
MAIN LINE
48hr
48hr
l-keeper's office
New Street City Centre
Town Hall Art Gallery
Paradise Circus
The Mailbox
Five Ways
85
EDGBASTON TUNNEL 105 yards
84
83
WORCS & B'HAM
82
Birmingham University
70'
school
Queen Elizabeth Hospital
Course of Dudley No.2 Canal
Selly Oak
79A
70'
A38
Sainsbury
park
A38 to Bromsgrove
Site of former Cadbury Canal Wharf
Course of former Cadbury Railway
15
78
79
To Fazeley & London
BIRMINGHAM
Sherborne Wharf
OLD TURN JUNCTION
Botanical Gardens
Edgbaston
To Wolverhampton Ring-road   A456 to Kidderminster

A VON RING travellers pass from the Stratford to the Worcester & Birmingham at King's Norton. The old guillotine stop lock which once jealously guarded waters of the two canals is still intact, and though long disused, a fine and photogenic survival. A sizeable paper mill formerly overlooked the canal junction and large quantities of coal were brought here by narrowboat from Black Country mines for many years. Nail-making was another facet of the local economy which brought trade to the canal.

Canal trade was even more brisk to and from Cadbury's famous chocolate factory at Bournville. Commercial activity on the canal is sadly no longer considered a viable proposition, but leisure boating does bring its fair share of visitors to Cadbury World for which there are moorings alongside Bournville railway station.

Bournville's garden village owes its existence to the altruism of Quakers Richard and George Cadbury, who built a chocolate factory on a greenfield site in the vicinity in 1879. It was George in particular who had vision's of a worker's paradise, commissioning the architect Alexander Harvey to design artisans dwellings on a 120 acre site. Each house was to have a garden with fruit trees and a vegetable patch to provide an element of self-sufficiency - one cannot live on chocolate alone.

At 2,726 yards, WAST HILL TUNNEL is the Worcester & Birmingham's longest. It takes around half an hour to pass through and, whilst appearances can be deceptive, rest assured that there is room to pass oncoming craft inside its gloomy depths. Like all Worcester & Birmingham tunnels (except Edgbaston), it has no towpath and walkers must negotiate the depressing environs of a large Hawkesley housing estate before rejoining the canal.

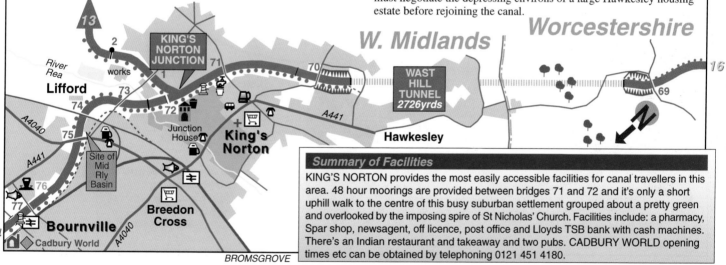

Summary of Facilities

KING'S NORTON provides the most easily accessible facilities for canal travellers in this area. 48 hour moorings are provided between bridges 71 and 72 and it's only a short uphill walk to the centre of this busy suburban settlement grouped about a pretty green and overlooked by the imposing spire of St Nicholas' Church. Facilities include: a pharmacy, Spar shop, newsagent, off licence, post office and Lloyds TSB bank with cash machines. There's an Indian restaurant and takeaway and two pubs. CADBURY WORLD opening times etc can be obtained by telephoning 0121 451 4180.

POST-WAR Alvechurch overspills up its hillside to impinge upon the canal, but barely deflects from its dreamy, lockless progress above the valley of the River Arrow. There are panoramic views eastwards towards Weatheroak Hill crossed by the Roman's Ryknild Street. A feeder comes in from Upper Bittell Reservoir beside an isolated canal employee's cottage near Bridge 66. The Lower Reservoir, rich in wildfowl, lies alongside the canal and is given a gorgeous wooded backdrop by the Lickey Hills. Only the Upper Reservoir feeds the canal, the Lower was provided to compensate millers whose water supplies from the Arrow had been detrimentally affected by construction of the canal. A short section of the canal was re-routed in 1985 to accommodate construction of the M42 motorway. Bridge 62 carries the electrified commuter line from Redditch

through Birmingham to Lichfield. A deep cutting - thick with the scent of wild garlic - leads to the 613 yard Shortwood Tunnel. The horse-path across the top, unlike that at Wast Hill, is well defined and offers a most enjoyable diversion from the confines of the towpath.

Summary of Facilities

There are canalside pubs by bridges 67 and 61: the HOPWOOD HOUSE INN (Tel: 0121 445 1716) is a large, refurbished roadhouse; THE CROWN (Tel: 0121 445 2300) is unspoilt and old fashioned. Alvechurch lies twenty minutes' walk down from the canal but boasts a useful range of shops: general store, pharmacy, butcher, off licence, and bakery, but no bank. There are Chinese (Tel: 0121 447 8085) and Indian (Tel: 0121 445 5660) takeaways. THE WEIGHBRIDGE, a boaters club/cafe open to non members at Alvechurch Boat Centres' yard by Bridge 60, where a canal shop also sells a modest range of provisions. There are trains to Redditch and Birmingham (Tel: 08457 484950).

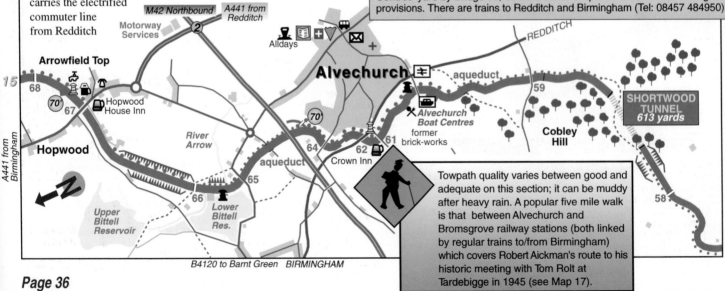

Towpath quality varies between good and adequate on this section; it can be muddy after heavy rain. A popular five mile walk is that between Alvechurch and Bromsgrove railway stations (both linked by regular trains to/from Birmingham) which covers Robert Aickman's route to his historic meeting with Tom Rolt at Tardebigge in 1945 (see Map 17).

TARDEBIGGE represents a boater's Rite of Passage. Once you have tackled this flight which, coupled with the neighbouring six at Stoke, amount to thirty-six locks in four miles, other groups of locks, however fiendish, however formidable, pale into insignificance. The thirty chambers of the Tardebigge flight raise the canal over two hundred feet, the top lock - somewhat removed from the rest - being, at 14 feet, one of the deepest narrowbeam locks on the system; it replaced a lift prone to malfunction and water wastage. Well maintained and surrounded by fine countryside, with wonderful views to the Malvern Hills, Tardebigge Locks are there to be enjoyed, not dreaded. And in the summer months you'll have plenty of fellow travellers with whom to share the experience, not to mention the work! Tardebigge's 18th century church, with its slender 135ft spire, is an inspirational landmark.

Tardebigge holds a special place in the story of the inland waterways movement. It was to here that Robert Aickman and his wife made their way from Bromsgrove railway station to meet Tom and Angela Rolt aboard their narrowboat home *Cressy* which had been moored above the top lock throughout the Second World War. As a direct result of their meeting the Inland Waterways Association was formed. A plinth adjacent to the lock tells the story though it is generally accepted that the meeting took place in 1945 and not a year later as originally recorded.

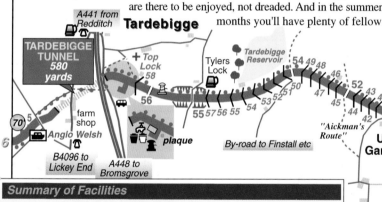

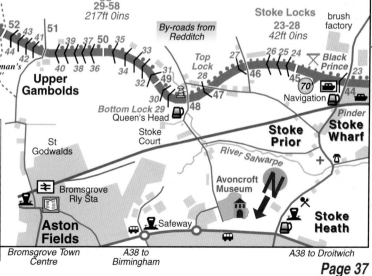

NOWADAYS, Britain's salt industry is largely confined to Cheshire but, as the name Droitwich suggests, this part of Worcestershire was once a centre of salt making too. The salt obsessed Romans built a special road between Droitwich and Alcester to carry this valuable commodity. Similarly, the Worcester & Birmingham built the short Droitwich Junction Canal from Hanbury Wharf to carry the same cargo. Barely two miles long, it included seven locks and passed briefly into the River Salwarpe before meeting the previously established Droitwich Canal at Vines Park near the town centre. Both the Droitwich canals had lapsed into dereliction before the end of the Thirties. In recent years they have undergone varying degrees of restoration: at Hanbury Wharf the first three locks have been restored and the top pound of the Junction Canal has been re-watered and is in use as private moorings. The summit of the widebeam Droitwich Canal is also in water and a day boat is available for hire from the Droitwich Canal Company - see page 95. Full restoration is earmarked for 2007.

At the end of the 18th century, John Corbett, son of a local boatman, discovered large deposits of brine at Stoke Prior and developed one of the largest saltworks in the world on the site. It made his fortune. He met an Irish woman in Paris, married her and built a replica French chateau for her on the outskirts of Droitwich, a town he transformed from one of industrial squalor into a fashionable spa. In its heyday the canalside works at Stoke was producing 200,000 tons of salt a year. The company had a fleet of narrowboats and hundreds of railway wagons. Corbett died in 1901 and is buried at the pretty little church of St Michael's, Stoke Prior (Map 17). His vast works, later part of ICI, was demolished in the 1970s.

Attractive countryside returns at ASTWOOD LOCKS, as canal and railway drift lazily through lush farmland overlooked by the wooded slopes of Summer Hill to the east. Westward views encompass Abberley and Woodbury hills beyond the River Severn. Closer at hand are the twin 700ft high masts of Wychbold radio transmitting station. Opened in 1934, its call sign "Droitwich Calling" became known throughout Britain and in many parts of Europe. During the Second World War Droitwich's long range transmitter broadcast the 'voice of freedom' throughout occupied Europe.

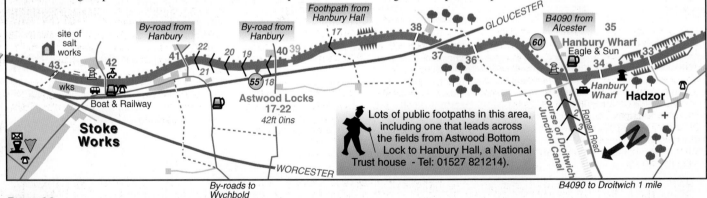

site of salt works

By-road from Hanbury

By-road from Hanbury

Foothpath from Hanbury Hall

GLOUCESTER

B4090 from Alcester 35

Hanbury Wharf
Eagle & Sun

43 42

wks

Boat & Railway

41 22 21 20 19 40 39 17 38 37 36 60

55 18

Astwood Locks 17-22
42ft 0ins

Stoke Works

Lots of public footpaths in this area, including one that leads across the fields from Astwood Bottom Lock to Hanbury Hall, a National Trust house - Tel: 01527 821214).

33 34

Hanbury Wharf

Hadzor

Course of Droitwich Junction Canal

Roman Road

WORCESTER

By-roads to Wychbold

B4090 to Droitwich 1 mile

Droitwich (Map 18)

Droitwich is a twenty-five minute walk from Hanbury Wharf along the Salt Road (how nice it will be to cruise into town along the Droitwich Junction Canal), but it really is well worth making the effort. Despite nestling almost under the armpit of the M5 motorway, this is a genteel place, as befits a former spa town. The High Street is particularly appealing, with a number of interesting and highly individual shops. The TOURIST INFORMATION CENTRE (Victoria Square) doubles as a Heritage Centre detailing the history of the town's salt trade as well as the story of the nearby Wychbold radio transmitting station. Tel: 01905 774312.

Stoke Works (Map 18)

The BOAT & RAILWAY (Tel: 01527 831065) is a Banks's pub with a nice canalside terrace, good choice of beers and a wide range of bar meals (not Sundays) and a skittle alley. The Worcester & Birmingham Canal Society regularly meet here. Also in Stoke Works, the BOWLING GREEN (Tel: 01527 861291), accessed from Bridge 41, has a nice garden with a children's play area. There's a butcher and a post office stores on a housing estate half a mile north of bridge 42.

Hanbury Wharf (Map 18)

At Hanbury Wharf the EAGLE & SUN (Tel: 01905 770130) is perennially popular with boaters, perhaps on account of the generously-sized bar meals that are served.

Shops are conspicuous by their absence hereabouts, although a range of basic provisions is available from the boatyard along with guides, maps and postcards.

THE canal skirts the mellow settlements of Shernal Green, Dunhampstead, Oddingley and Tibberton and, in site of being sandwiched by the railway and motorway, seems remote and untouched. High clumps of sedge border the canal, swaying with the passage of each boat and somehow emphasising the loneliness of the landscape. At Shernal Green the Wychavon Way - a 42-mile long distance footpath running from Holt Fleet on the River Severn to Winchcombe in Gloucesterhire - makes its way over the canal. 'Severn & Avon Ring' boaters will encounter the path again at Cropthorne where it crosses the River Avon by way of Jubilee Bridge.

DUNHAMPSTEAD TUNNEL is tiny compared to the 'big three' to the north, but like them it has no towpath, forcing walkers to take to the old horse-path through deciduous woodlands above. A hire base adds traffic to the canal at this point, whilst a craft shop and convivial country pub provide an excuse to break your journey.

ODDINGLEY consists of little more than an ancient manor house, a tiny church and a level-crossing keeper's cabin of typical Midland Railway style. Murder was done here in 1806!

A4538 from Evesham
M5 Southbound

Tibberton
Speed the Plough
Bridge Inn
70'
25
24A
24
26
27 **Oddingley**
28
29
70'
The Firs
Forge Studio
30 **Dunhampstead**
Brook Line

DUNHAMPSTEAD TUNNEL 236 yards

Shernal Green
B'HAM
31
32

M5 Northbound
16
15 14 13 12
23 11
22A
20
A449 to Worcester
rugby ground
6
M5 Southbound
A4538 to Droitwich

Offerton Locks 11-16
42ft 0ins

TIBBERTON is a long, straggling village of largely modern housing. Good moorings are provided to enable boaters to avail themselves of the amenities on offer. By the time you have negotiated OFFERTON LOCKS in a southbound direction, Worcester's industrial fringe begins to make its presence felt; rugby players stomp across the footbridge at the tail of Lock 11, and Hindlip Hall (4934 to fans of the old GWR), headquarters of the County Constabulary and refuge, in its original Elizabethan guise, of two members of the Gunpowder Plot, dominates the nearby ridge.

Summary of Facilities

The quiet hamlet of Dunhampstead is able to offer both a canalside craft shop and a comfortable pub, THE FIR TREE INN (Tel: 01905 774094), serves a good range of food including pre-booked breakfasts. Inside you can learn about the dastardly Oddingley Murders. Tibberton's amenities include a post office stores which also sells newspapers (lunchtime closing and early closing Wed,Sat & Sun) and two Bank's pubs, the BRIDGE INN (Tel: 01905 345684) is the more canal orientated, having a large waterside garden and offering a good choice of food; however the SPEED THE PLOUGH (Tel: 01905 345602) can also be recommended. Buses connect the village with Worcester - Tel:

WATERSIDE Worcester has always enjoyed a flagrant love affair with the Severn, but in recent times the canal has come into its own. From Tolladine down, the towpath is designated a 'pedway' and popular with pedestrians and cyclists alike. Burgeoning industrial estates accompany the canal but do little to spoil it. Cadbury's once had a busy wharf at Blackpole linked by water transport to their premises at Bournville (Map 15) and Frampton-on-Severn (Map 28). A leisure centre and municipal golf course border the canal above Bilford Upper Lock. Worcester City, a non league football club, have a substantial ground, signposted by tall floodlights, beside Bridge 12. North of Bridge 11 school playing fields are overlooked by an imposing pavilion.

A shapely railway bridge spans the canal by

Lowesmoor Wharf. It has a hole cut out of it, presumably to lessen the weight of the structure. Lowesmoor Wharf is a good spot to moor securely close to the city centre - just slip beneath the roving bridge and ask permission at the boatyard office.

An Italianate clock tower peeps over the canal by Bridge 8, the former Engine Works of 1864. In contrast new retail units have been

Map labels:

19 · A449 from M5

22

Tolladine Lock 7ft 0ins

industrial estate

Black Pole Lock 7ft 0ins

21 · By-road from Hindlip

20

DROITWICH · By-road from Heath

9

19

rems of Cadbury wharf · 18

17

16

A449 to Kidderminster

golf course

Leisure Centre · 15 · 8 · 14

Gregory's Mill Locks 14ft 0ins

Bilford Locks 14ft 0ins

7 · 6 · 13 · 5

Worcester City F.C.

WORCESTER

LOWESMOOR · 70 · 9 · 8 · 10

Viking

Shrub Hill

Blockhouse Lock 11ft 0ins

Sidbury Lock 11ft 0ins

5A · 6 · 4 · 4 · 3

Cathedral

9 · 8

10

City Centre

Foregate St.

11 · 12

Steamer Quay

Race Course

rowing boats for hire

Diglis Canal Locks 18ft 0ins

Diglis River Locks

WEIR

2 · 3

ferry

cricket ground

Worcester Bridge

21

Fort Royal Park

cafe · Commandery

Fownes Hotel · cinemas

3 · Royal Worcs

City Centre · P

Diglis Basins

basin · basin

drydock · lock-keeper

W&B

RIVER SEVERN

pontoon

N

provided with a new linking footbridge numbered 5A. Fownes Hotel was once a glove factory. Almost opposite stands The Commandery. Charles II used this building as his headquarters during the Civil War Battle of Worcester in 1651, though it was originally a hospital and dates from as early as the 15th century. There is space here for some half a dozen boats to moor overnight within mellifluous earshot of the cathedral clock. Sidbury Lock lies near the site of a gate in the city wall where a thousand Royalist troops are said to have been killed. Cromwell's men had captured the nearby fort and turned its canons on the escaping Cavaliers. The elevated fort is a pleasant park now, easily reached from the Commandery moorings. A panoramic plaque identifies major incidents of the Battle of Worcester and the gardens offer a marvellous view over the city.

Industry reasserts itself as the canal passes the famous Royal Worcester porcelain works and Townsend's Mill. The latter was once an intensive user of water transport, via both canal and river, but nowadays the only traffic hereabouts is of the pleasure variety, all regular trade on this waterway having ceased by the Sixties. New apartments are being built overlooking the canal here, eroding much of the old latent atmosphere of working boat times.

DIGLIS BASINS opened in the 19th century to facilitate transhipment of cargoes between river and canal. In the absence of commercial traffic they have an atmospheric backwater of residential boats. It would be invigorating to see the basins packed with sailing trows and narrowboats once again, but instead they are the subject of a controversial redevelopment scheme by British Waterways and Bryant Homes, which is being doggedly resisted by locals and canal groups worried that Diglis's heritage will be swamped by out of scale housing. Modern history suggests they have every right to be concerned. If, like us, you have savoured the latent ambience of lost trade at Diglis in the past, the moral is to go and taste it again soon before it is too late.

Two broad locks separate the basins from the river. They are closed overnight, re-opening about eight in the morning when the lock-keeper comes on duty. Mostly he doesn't get involved in operating them, but it's good to know he's about should you require his help or advice. Entering or leaving the river can pose problems, especially if the current is flowing quickly, and getting your crew on or off for the locks needs careful consideration. One of the easiest access points is the sanitary station pontoon immediately downstream of the lock entrance. Downstream there is a third Diglis Lock, in fact an automated pair, that on the east bank being the smaller of the two.

Worcester (Map 20)

Descending from Birmingham to Worcester, the West Midlands are left intuitively behind, and you find yourself in streets where the patois has a distinct West Country burr. 'Royal' Worcester suffered more than most at the hands of the developers during the Sixties (Ian Nairn, the late architectural writer and broadcaster, was incensed, and James Lees-Milne got into hot water for permitting his *Shell Guide to Worcestershire* to be too critical) but much making of amends has been done in recent years to enhance the city's fabric. The Cathedral, gazing devoutly over the Severn, belongs - along with Gloucester and Hereford - to a golden triangle of ecclesiastical paragons which share Europe's oldest music festival, 'The Three Choirs'. From the deep well of Worcester's history you can draw inspiration from almost any era that captures your imagination. This was the 'faithful city' of the Civil War from which Charles II escaped following the final defeat of the Cavaliers. It was the home, for much of his life, of Sir Edward Elgar. Home too of the manufacturers of Royal Worcester porcelain and that ensign of the empire, Lea & Perrins sauce. And here you'll find one of the country's loveliest cricketing venues, Worcestershire's New Road ground - Tel: 01905 748474. So in any boating itinerary, Worcester deserves to be allotted at least half a day in your schedule.

BROWNS RESTAURANT - Quay Street. Tel: 01905 26263. Worth blowing the budget here (lunch Tue-Fri & Sun approx £20, dinner Tue-Sat approx £35) for the ambience (former riverside mill) let alone quality of the cooking.

Diglis Locks

HODSON - High Street. Tel: 01905 21036. Long established cafe restaurant near the Cathedral and Elgar's statue.

SAFFRONS BISTRO - New Street. Tel: 01905 610505. Highly recommended restaurant open daily for lunch & dinner.

DIGLIS HOUSE HOTEL - riverside. Tel: 01905 353518. Best to moor in basins and walk back for good bar and restaurant meals; nice views over the Severn.

CROMWELLS PANTRY - The Commandery. Coffees, teas, light snacks in adjunct to museum. Canalside or courtyard al fresco on warm days.

SALMON'S LEAP - Severn Street. Quiet real ale pub within easy reach of Diglis.

THE ANCHOR - Diglis Basin. Down to earth Banks's boozer for prodigious Swallowers and Amazons only.

Worcester is an excellent city in which to shop. Two refurbished shopping areas are The Hopmarket and Crown Passage. The Shambles, Friar Street and New Street feature numerous fascinating little shops and small businesses. Crown Gate is the main shopping precinct with adjoining street markets on Tue, Wed, Fri & Sat. If you are making the *faux pas* of boating through non-stop, then a butcher and pharmacy can be reached from Sidbury Lock.

TOURIST INFORMATION CENTRE - The Guildhall, High Street. Tel: 01905 726311. Worcester appears to have more visitor centres than any other provincial city of its size. A thorough list defies our space limitations, but obvious highlights are: THE COMMANDERY (canalside by Sidbury Lock - Tel: 01905 361821) which was Charles II's headquarters during the Civil War; ROYAL WORCESTER (Severn Street, near Sidbury Lock again - Tel: 01905 746000), the porcelain and bone china makers; and THE CATHEDRAL (Tel: 01905 611002, dating from the 11th century and the burial place of King John. WARNER CINEMAS (close to Sidbury Lock) can be contacted on 01905 617737.

BUSES - Midland Red West services throughout the area and local Citibus services. Tel: 01905 763888.

TRAINS - stations at Foregate Street and Shrub Hill. Services to/from the Malverns (nice idea for an excursion), Droitwich, Kidderminster, Birmingham etc. Tel: 08457 484950.

RIVER TRIPS - 45 minute cruises hourly March to October aboard the ex Irish tugboat *Marianne* from South Quay near the Cathedral. Tel: 01905 831639. Longer journeys to Stourport or Upton are provided by the vessels of the New Worcester Steamer Company from North Quay - Tel: 01905 354991.

river
SEVERN

A MODERN, and inevitably concrete, road bridge takes Worcester's southern by-pass over the river half a mile south of its confluence with the Teme. Like a deferential waitress coming to clear the dishes, the Teme makes little impact on the haughty Severn. But on its way down from the Welsh Marches, past Ludlow and through lush Herefordshire pastures, this lovely river hits heights of beauty that the Severn never attains.

William Sandys, who was originally responsible for making the River Avon navigable, acquired the rights to make the Teme navigable up to Ludlow in the 17th century, but he never got around to doing anything about it. Perhaps the Civil War impeded his plans. Just a canon ball's trajectory from here the first skirmish of that conflict took place at Powick Bridge on September 23rd 1642. The Parliamentarians lost that battle but came from behind to win the war by defeating the Royalist forces on virtually the same battlefield nine years later.

South of Worcester the Severn pursues an undemonstrative course. There are brief glimpses of the Malvern Hills beyond the river's high, and largely uninspiring, banks. But if the scenery momentarily falters, the novelty of deep, wide water has yet to wear off.

KEMPSEY comes bravely down to the riverbank but the passing boater sees little more than a long line of pontoon moorings belonging to the Seaborn Yacht Company boatyard. The A38 trunk road bisects the village and much modern housing has engulfed the core of the original settlement.

An old ferry house marks the site of a former river crossing at PIXHAM. In his informative account of fords and ferries on the Severn in Worcestershire (published locally in 1982), H. W. Gwilliam relates that the ferry here was capable of carrying motor vehicles until it ceased operating around the time of the Second World War. It seems that there was no formal road approach to the ferry stage on the Kempsey side, so cars had to be driven across the field as best they could. The local hunt used the ferry too and it must have been some sight to see the hounds packed aboard the vessel - except for the unfortunate fox, of course.

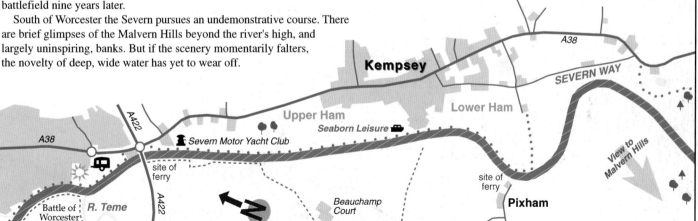

UNDER the watchful eye of the Malverns, the River Severn winds past occasional outcrops of sandstone rock - welcome interludes of drama amid the monotony of the willow-lined banks. This is probably the prettiest part of the river between Worcester and Tewkesbury, and though there are few formal moorings, owners of shallow-draughted cruisers seem prepared to tie up to overhanging tree trunks and enjoy a peaceful picnic.

CLEVELODE is a pleasant little community of orchards and cottages but just downstream lies one of those caravan parks that the Severn seems fated to attract. There were ferries both here and at RHYDD. The sandstone outcrop extended across the bed of the river and caused problems with navigation before the locks were built.

If the rocky bluffs have a Rhineland quality about them, then, in the context of the Severn Plain, the Malverns are positively Alpine. They represent the highest point along Latitude 52 between the Black Mountains of Wales and the Harz Mountains in Germany. It is impossible not to be moved by their brooding presence. They were the inspiration behind much of Sir Edward Elgar's music, though the Severn also played a part in exciting his muse. 'I am still at heart the dreamy child who used to be found in the reeds by Severn side with a sheet of paper, trying to fix the sounds and longing for something great'.

An ostentatious, castellated mansion towers above the woods at SEVERN BANK and an old boathouse stands on the river below SEVERN END, but barely any trace survives of the former quay at HANLEY CASTLE. In bygone days isolated villages like these would have relied on the river for transport, coal being brought in by barge and local agricultural produce taken away.

A38

Severn Stoke

Severn Bank

Clifton

Sheepcote Farm

SEVERN WAY

21

Cliffey Wood

site of ferry

site of ferry

Severn End

Clevelode

B4424

Rhydd

Hanley Castle

23

B4211 to Malvern

PTON-ON-SEVERN'S fleshpots come as welcome relief to the Severn's somewhat repetitive scenery. Two road bridges span this section of the Severn. The present bridge at UPTON dates from the Second World War. It replaced a swing bridge, the abutments of which can still be seen. Each plod along the road of Progress apparently rids us of something worthwhile: fords give way to ferries, ferries to swing bridges, swing bridges to fixed structures devoid of any character. And now we can travel so quickly that the average journey makes no impression on us whatsoever, all of which succinctly explains the appeal of inland waterway travel. The railway bridge which carried the Malvern and Tewkesbury line over the Severn would have been well worth seeing too, as it originally was equipped with a sliding central section which could be moved aside to permit tall-masted vessels to pass.

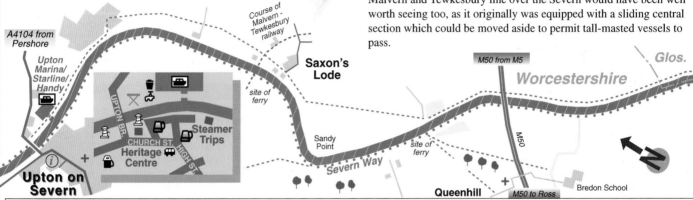

Upton-on-Severn

The spirit of the Severn pervades this charming little town, lending it the atmosphere of a small coastal port, an illusion enhanced by the resemblance of the cupola-topped old church to a lighthouse. Limited visitor moorings are provided either side of the bridge.

THE CORNER HOUSE - High Street. Stylish modern restaurant in ancient half-timbered setting. Tel: 01684 591222.
PUNDITS - Old Street. Cosy Bangladeshi restaurant and takeaway. Tel: 01684 591022.

WHITE LION HOTEL - High Street. Comfortable hotel with popular Brasserie. Tel: 01684 592551.
Numerous pubs and takeaways to choose from as well.

Shopping as it should be in a number of highly individual shops, good delicatessens, bakers, butchers and greengrocers; Lloyds TSB and HSBC banks. Interesting specialist map shop, old-fashioned sweet shop, chocolate-maker and secondhand bookshop. Small SPAR and CO-OP supermarkets.

TOURIST INFORMATION - High Street. Tel: 01684 594200.
UPTON HERITAGE CENTRE - Church Street. Small museum tracing Upton's history. Tel: 01684 592679.
THE TUDOR HOUSE - Church Street. 'Upton Past and Present'. Admission charge. Tel: 01684 592447.
BOAT TRIPS - Severn Leisure Cruises. Market Day waterbus to Tewkesbury every summer Wednesday. Tel: 01684 593112.
BUSES - Services to/from Worcester Tel: 01905 763888.

Tewkesbury

Deerhurst

Odda's Chapel

Town Centre

abbey

for Tewkesbury detail see Map 1

Lower Lode rowing club

SEVERN WAY

Chaceley Stock

Yew Tree

25

Tewkesbury Marina

mill

ferry

flour mill

Severn Ham

Avon Lock

water works

Lower Lode

By-road to Chaceley

1

The Mythe

WEIR !

By-road to Forthampton

Mythe Bridge

Upper Lode Lock

A438 to Hereford

A38 from Worcester

course of Midland Railway Ashchurch - Malvern line

SEVERN WAY

Glos.

Worcs.

N

Summary of Facilities

Two excellent riverside pubs provide the refreshment opportunities along this length of the Severn. The LOWER LODE HOTEL (Tel: 01684 293224), with BW moorings close by, has a fine restaurant, a good range of beers and an attractive garden. The YEW TREE INN at Chaceley Stock (Tel: 01452 780333) is a former cider making house offering bar and restaurant meals in a pleasant setting.

IN contrast to the aesthetic shortcomings of the two bridges upstream, MYTHE BRIDGE is handsome in the extreme, a single iron span dating from 1825. You only have to see it to guess that it is the work of that Botticelli of bridge builders, Thomas Telford. This is one of half a dozen bridges that Telford built across the Severn; its setting, below the wooded heights of Mythe Cliff, is sublime.

The confluence with the navigable channel of the Avon soon follows, but if you're bound for Gloucester or Sharpness you proceed to UPPER LODE LOCK, which was built in 1858 to alleviate the problem of shallows experienced upstream, particularly in the vicinity of Upton. A second channel of the Avon enters the Severn at LOWER LODE, from where the view of Tewkesbury Abbey, with Bredon Hill as a backdrop, is quite breathtaking. A passenger ferry operates here in the summer months and is popular with walkers, cyclists and patrons of the Lower Lode Hotel.

How sad it is that access to Deerhurst and its Saxon church are denied to the boater, no mooring facilities being provided here. In bygone days the river formed an islet at this point. It was a constant irritant to bargemen who were often marooned in the shallows and forced to seek solace in the local inn.

Thomas Telford's Mythe Bridge over the River Severn

Keith Goss

Apperley (Map 25)

Once a village known for apple growing and salmon fishing, Apperley now exists chiefly as a commuter base for folk who work in Gloucester and Cheltenham and there is no longer enough daytime activity to support a shop.

THE COAL HOUSE - riverside with pontoon moorings. Tel: 01452 780211.

Haw Bridge (Map 25)

A British Waterways mooring pontoon and two good inns make this a popular staging post for boaters.

THE NEW INN - riverside to north of bridge. Tel: 01452 780275. Charmingly old fashioned and well regarded for its steaks and grills; nice garden to rear.

HAW BRIDGE INN - riverside to south of bridge. Tel: 01452 780275. A convivial Wadworth pub.

RED LION - riverside but *no* easy mooring. What Severn Way walkers lose over Ashleworth, they gain with this well-appointed inn at the foot of Wainlode Hill. Tel: 01452 730251.

Ashleworth (Map 25)

There no longer being a ferry, walkers on the Severn Way are denied access to Ashleworth and its National Trust owned, but still agriculturally functioning tithe barn.

THE BOAT - riverside, mooring pontoon. Justly celebrated unspoilt pub which has been run by the same family for generations. Catering is restricted to lunchtime rolls and the varying choice of beer represents the output of many small local breweries whose ales come into their own at the pub's annual beer festival each autumn. Tel: 01452 700272.

The Severn at Haw Bridge with Wainlode Hill in the distance.

PASSING villages so reluctant to dip their toes into the flood plain of the Severn that they hang half a mile back from its banks, the river suddenly finds itself baulked by the high flank of Wainlode Hill. Erosion has carved a bluff grey rockface here, rising sheer from the water's edge like a seaside cliff. The deep water channel hugs the northern bank and old barges have been beached on the south side to prevent further incursions into the river's bank.

The River Chelt sidles in from the east. Nearby is the ruined entrance lock of the Coombe Hill Canal, built to carry Forest of Dean coal to the spa town of Cheltenham, though it never actually got that far and was abandoned as early as 1876. Old riverside inns punctuate this length of the river. Once they existed to quench the prodigious thirsts of the bargemen,

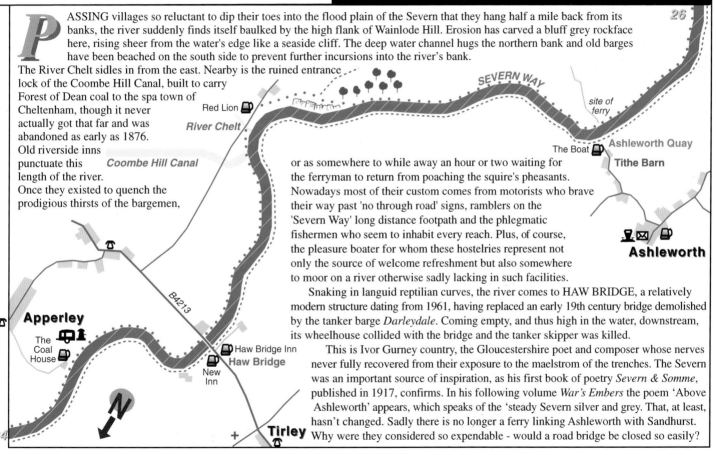

or as somewhere to while away an hour or two waiting for the ferryman to return from poaching the squire's pheasants. Nowadays most of their custom comes from motorists who brave their way past 'no through road' signs, ramblers on the 'Severn Way' long distance footpath and the phlegmatic fishermen who seem to inhabit every reach. Plus, of course, the pleasure boater for whom these hostelries represent not only the source of welcome refreshment but also somewhere to moor on a river otherwise sadly lacking in such facilities.

Snaking in languid reptilian curves, the river comes to HAW BRIDGE, a relatively modern structure dating from 1961, having replaced an early 19th century bridge demolished by the tanker barge *Darleydale*. Coming empty, and thus high in the water, downstream, its wheelhouse collided with the bridge and the tanker skipper was killed.

This is Ivor Gurney country, the Gloucestershire poet and composer whose nerves never fully recovered from their exposure to the maelstrom of the trenches. The Severn was an important source of inspiration, as his first book of poetry *Severn & Somme*, published in 1917, confirms. In his following volume *War's Embers* the poem 'Above Ashleworth' appears, which speaks of the 'steady Severn silver and grey. That, at least, hasn't changed. Sadly there is no longer a ferry linking Ashleworth with Sandhurst. Why were they considered so expendable - would a road bridge be closed so easily?

L ONG Reach leads to Upper Parting. These old river names have an evocative resonance. And there were deeper subtleties: the navigable channel downstream of the Parting was known to working boatmen as 'Skipper's Length', whilst that above was known as 'Mates'. The tradition was that barge skippers would be at the wheel for the tortuous, narrow exit channel from Gloucester, being relieved once Upper Parting had been reached by the mate.

The now unnavigable western channel of the Severn, which loops past the village of Maisemore, was used to gain access to the Herefordshire & Gloucestershire Canal, a 34 mile rural waterway which took fifty years to build. Within forty years of completion in 1845 it had largely been converted into a railway. Twenty years ago

Approaching Gloucester Lock off the Severn, beware the current drawing you towards the unnavigable weired channel to Lower Parting. The quay wall to your left has chains through which a line should be looped until the green light signals that you can enter the lock.

KEY

1. Custom House	8. Philpotts Warehouse
2. Flour mill	9. Brittannia Warehouse
3. North Warehouse	10. Albert Warehouse
4. Lock Warehouse	11. Vinings Warehouse
5. Victoria Warehouse	12. Reynolds Warehouse
6. Herbert Warehouse	13. Shipton Warehouse
7. Kimberley W'house	14. Alexandra Warehouse

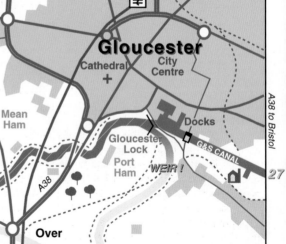

no one would have considered that the Hereford & Gloucestershire could ever be made navigable again, but other 'impossible' restoration projects have been achieved, and 'never' is no longer a word in any self-respecting canal activist's dictionary. In recent years the junction basin at Over on the western outskirts of Gloucester has been cosmetically restored, though being on a tidal reach of the Severn it cannot be accessed by inland waterway craft.

The navigable, eastern channel of the Severn must have demanded all the barge skipper's fund of experience. If you have been used to the motorway breadth of the river down from Tewkesbury, this B road backwater comes as something of a shock. It forms a surreptitious approach to the city, for the overhanging willows hide any view which might otherwise be had of the cathedral. A series of bridges span the river as roads and railways converge on the city centre, before you reach the long wall of the old River Quay, where vessels which had navigated the tidal Severn used to berth prior to the development of the docks and the ship canal from Sharpness. Downstream of the Quay the river branches again, the right hand unnavigable channel leading round to Lower Parting. Head instead for Gloucester Lock, which dates from 1812 and was originally in the form of a staircase pair. Now it is one deep chamber, mechanised and spanned by a swingbridge carrying a busy road around the docks. As the lock fills, GLOUCESTER DOCKS are gradually revealed in all their grandeur and it is with a sense of exhilaration that you proceed into the Main Basin to seek out a mooring amidst these splendid surroundings.

Gloucester was given the formal status of a port way back in Elizabeth I's reign. Navigational problems on the Severn, however, restricted the port's development and it was only with the opening of the Gloucester & Berkeley (later Sharpness) Canal in 1827 that its fortunes began to rise. Gloucester's basins have become a centre of pleasure boating, whilst the warehouses have enjoyed refurbishment. With a direct link to the inland waterway system, it is therefore highly appropriate that this should be the site of the National Waterways Museum.

Gloucester (Map 26)

Charles Dickens was amazed to find merchant seamen wandering conspicuously along the streets of what he imagined would be a quiet cathedral city. He followed one and discovered 'endless intricacies of dock and huge three-masted ships'. Naturally, there are no sailors to be followed today, and, in any case, one has one's reputation to consider. Also, most users of this guidebook will be wondering what Gloucester *itself* is like, having already become acquainted with the docks. In truth it's a bit of a curate's egg, a bit of a Mahler symphony, consisting of serene passages and alleyways interspersed with strident concrete shopping precincts. Here and there remains evidence of the Roman 'Glevum', stressing Gloucester's longevity. The city has, however, in its cathedral, a masterpiece of medieval architecture, an act of faith which transcends the shortcomings of modern life. Here is the largest stained glass window in England, the tomb of King Edward II and, in one shadowy corner, a moving memorial to a battalion of the Gloucestershire Regiment who made an heroic stand in the Korean War. Ignore the car parks, the concrete and the chain stores, this is the city's true testament.

NEW INN - Northgate. Tel: 01452 522177. Rare example of a medieval galleried inn. Bar and restaurant food and accommodation. Local brews in the Ale Bar.

BLACK SWAN INN - Southgate. Tel: 01452 523642. Victorian hotel transformed into modern bistro. Food, accommodation and real ale.

Tourists flock to the MERCHANTS QUAY shopping zone in the docks, you may wish to escape the water for a while and immerse yourself in the city centre shopping districts. Collectors of antiques will enjoy the ANTIQUES CENTRE housed in a former warehouse beside the entrance lock.

TOURIST INFORMATION - Southgate Street. Tel: 01452 396572.

NATIONAL WATERWAYS MUSEUM - Gloucester Docks. Tel: 01452 318200. Admission charge. The nation's premier waterways museum.

HOUSE OF THE TAILOR OF GLOUCESTER - College Court. Tel: 01452 422856. Shop and museum devoted to the world of Beatrix Potter.

CITY MUSEUM & ART GALLERY - Brunswick Road. Tel: 01452 396131. Roman and medieval displays, plus paintings, furniture, clocks etc.

BUSES - services throughout the area. Tel: 01452 527516.

TRAINS - services to/from Birmingham, London and Bristol and through the Golden Valley. Tel: 08457 484950.

gloucester & SHARPNESS

THE Gloucester & Sharpness Canal certainly seeks out the shabby side of town as it makes its departure from the Docks. By any standard this is an unsightly stretch of canal; unless, of course, you happen to be an enthusiast of industrial archaeology and maritime heritage, in which case you will be enthralled by what remains of the canal's commercial past - the docks and quays, the mills, warehouses and associated industries once sited specifically to take advantage of the transport facilities provided by the waterway.

Imagine the banks of the canal as the working boatmen saw them, cornucopias of railway-threaded wharves where it was necessary to fight, sometimes literally, for a space to berth. Look out (on the east bank) for the elegant 19th century Pillar Warehouses, one of which has been converted into 'The Waterfront' pub/restaurant. Then a little further on are the former maltings and provender mill. Behind here the old Midland Railway dockyard sidings and vast Gloucester Railway Carriage & Wagon Works have disappeared, replaced by a retail park and cinema complex. The wagon works once had a small 'timber pond' where timber used in the construction of rolling stock could be stored in the wet to prevent it from drying out and cracking prior to use. This was one of several such ponds that flanked the canal between Llanthony and Hempsted bridges. Meanwhile, on the west bank of the canal - still riddled with rusty railway lines - a tall flour mill remains in use alongside Monk Meadow Dock.

Leaving the docks astern, the remains of an old swing bridge, which carried a Midland Railway dockyard branch firmly into Great Western territory on the far bank of the canal, may be observed as the waterway bends slightly towards Hempsted Bridge. Hempsted is the first of many swing bridges, all automated and operated by British Waterways keepers, which span the canal at regular intervals between here and Sharpness. Stonebench is a good spot for viewing the Severn Bore.

Two miles out from Gloucester the hitherto relatively straight waterway essays an S bend, closely followed by a pair of swing bridges, the second of which is graced by an ornately classical keeper's house, notable for its Doric-columned portico. These charming structures are to become increasingly familiar as the canal journeys south to Sharpness. North of Sellars Bridge the canal widens at the site of an oil terminal which received supplies by coastal vessels trading from South Wales until the early 1980s.

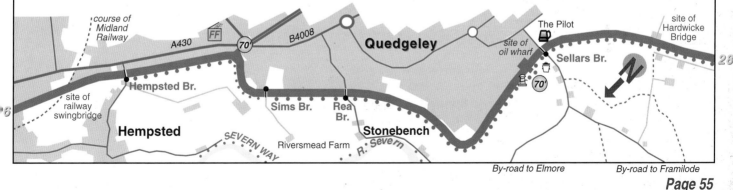

ACCOMPANIED by pylons and power lines, the Gloucester & Sharpness Canal traverses an apparently remote, low-slung landscape lost in a topographical void between the Cotswolds and the Forest of Dean. The fields focus on farms which, in their loneliness - and yours - assume a heightened significance. Between Parkend Bridge and Saul Junction the waterway is slightly elevated above the surrounding countryside with echoes of East Anglia in its reedy margins and reflections of high, wide skies.

SAUL JUNCTION will once again be able to live up to its name when the ambitious Cotswold Canals restoration project is realised. The Stroudwater Canal predated the G&S by almost fifty years and was formally abandoned in 1954, though trade had ceased a dozen years earlier. We follow its fascinating course from Map 31 onwards.

Saul Junction remains, pending restoration of the Stroudwater Navigation, an engaging location dominated by the high crane of a busy boatyard. Conglomerations of moored craft resonate with its strategical past and there is much for the canal history devotee to imbibe. Only refreshments are lacking: for them you'll have to walk to Frampton or Framilode.

British Waterways have a maintenance yard beside Sandfield Bridge. Then at Frethern Bridge you encounter a sizeable canalside works which once belonged to Cadburys. Waterbourne trade between here and the company's other premises at Blackpole (Map 20) and Bournville (Map 15) was intensive and it is disheartening to observe such a deep and wide waterway bereft now of all commercial traffic.

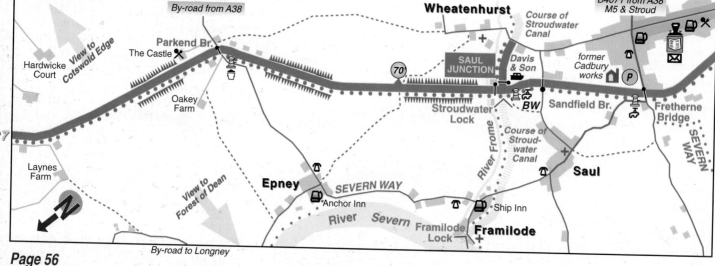

Frampton-on-Severn *(Map 28)*

Exiles and Anglophiles fantasise about villages like Frampton where Fair Rosamund (see Map 45) is reputed to have been born. Rosamund's Green incorporates a cricket pitch, duckponds and an array of horse chestnuts overlooked by a heterogeneous collection of houses from the large to the small, from the ridiculous to the sublime. Peacocks call from the 18th century purlieus of Frampton Court and many of the trees on the green have circular seats just made for watching the world go by.

THE BELL INN - The Green. Tel: 01452 740346. Good food and accommodation.

THREE HORSESHOES - The Green. Tel: 01452 740463. Convivial village local.

GILBERT BROWN - The Green. Tel: 01452 740077. Pretty little restaurant open Wed-Sun for breakfasts, coffees, lunches and teas.

Handsomely contained within a Georgian frontage, Frampton's excellent post office stores is obviously a focus of Frampton life. Wide range of provisions plus hot snacks for hungry walkers.

BUSES - services to/from Gloucester. Tel: 01452 527516.

Epney *(Map 28)*

Severnside hamlet with a good pub called THE ANCHOR - Tel: 01452 740433. Also worth noting by Parkend Bridge is THE CASTLE (Tel: 01452 720328) a restaurant alongside the canal noted for its home-cooking.

Framilode *(Map 28)*

Back of beyond village with an interesting Victorian church overlooking the wide Severn. THE SHIP INN (Tel: 01452 740260) offers food and comes personally recommended by our publisher.

Saul *(Map 28)*

Shopless, publess, but not devoid of interest, particularly in that a number of its houses feature unusual friezes above their front doors.

Swing-bridge and classical keeper's house at Fretherne.

HAVING acquired the mantle of the 'Severn Way', the canal continues its delightfully bucolic progress making its way past willow-fringed dykes draining fields extending down to the flood bank of the Severn, a seething, boiling mass of cafeteria tea-coloured water at high tide. Frampton's isolated parish church overlooks Splatt Bridge, whilst a ramshackle bungalow borders the entrance point to the once partially navigable River Cam, now used simply as a feeder to the canal. Such bungalows were a common feature of the Gloucester & Sharpness from the 1930s onwards. Built intially as holiday homes, many were gradually upgraded for domestic use throughout the year. Often self-built by their owners on land owned by the Sharpness Dock Company, some were actually constructed from materials brought along the canal by barge. Once there were almost a hundred of them, now less than half a dozen remain inhabited.

Slimbridge is derived from 'slyme bridge', a reference to the once marshy nature of the surrounding landscape. The New Grounds are exactly that, land reclaimed from the river's tidal grasp during the 16th and 17th centuries. They provide rich pastures for cattle and once featured a number of decoys for the catching of duck. Nowadays, of course, it is with the preservation of duck and wildfowl that the area is concerned, since Peter Scott's establishment here of the Slimbridge Wildfowl and Wetland Trust in 1946. Son of the famous Antacrtic explorer, Sir Peter Scott was the original Vice-President of the Inland Waterways Association, a close friend of Robert Aickman and one time husband of the novelist Elizabeth Jane Howard. In the early days of the Wildfowl Trust he brought a converted narrowboat called *Beatrice* to Shepherd's Patch to provide accommodation for visiting ornithologists. In 1950 *Beatrice* undertook a lengthy voyage of the northern canals as vividly described by Robert Aickman in *The River Runs Uphill*.

By-road from Cambridge & A38

By-road from Slimbridge & A38

Shepherd's Patch

Cam Bridge

Slimbridge Boat Station

Tudor Arms

Ryall's Farm

Patch Bridge

Church End

Splatt Bridge

SEVERN WAY

New Grounds

River Severn

Slimbridge Wildfowl & Wetlands Trust Centre

SEVERN WAY

The Warth

28

30

*T*HE canal moves languorously through a landscape which feels as if it's about to fall off the edge of the globe. In the old days map-makers would have written "here be monsters" beyond the floodbank of the Severn. For all its proximity, the Forest of Dean might as well be on another planet.

Presently the canal curves round to Purton past a treatment plant which extracts its water on behalf of the population of Bristol. A pair of swing bridges span the waterway as it winds around to the very edge of the Severn, whose banks are reinforced with the hulls of old barges berthed with a permanent cargo of silt and reeds. Then you reach the remains of a much grander swing bridge, which once carried a railway, not only over the canal but over to the far side of the Severn as well. It consisted of twenty-one fixed arches spanning the estuary and a moveable arch, propelled by steam, over the ship canal. The base of the moveable arch and a couple of masonry arches remain, but the rest of the structure was demolished by a pair of oil tankers, heading for Gloucester in the mists of October 1960, which had

missed the entrance to Sharpness Docks. It would have been nice to know Sharpness then, to have luxuriated in the aural backdrop of steam whistles and the accompanying cacophony of clanking couplings and banging buffers. The vessels which locked mysteriously up from the Severn into the dock precincts would have been of more classical maritime design too, but at least this is not, by any definition, a dead port. No, Sharpness thrives! Annual tonnage here is in the region of half a million - coal, grain, fertilizer, steel in, scrap metal out. And although, due to fast turnarounds, the quays often appear empty, the last time we were here no less than four ships were berthed at the quaysides.

The original course of the canal veers to the right, making its approach to the former entrance lock along an arm now used for moorings. The docks lie ahead, beyond two swing bridges. Stay a bit and soak up the atmosphere. Go and check if the tide is running and vessels making to use the entrance lock, from which there are views downstream towards the Severn bridges. Enjoy !

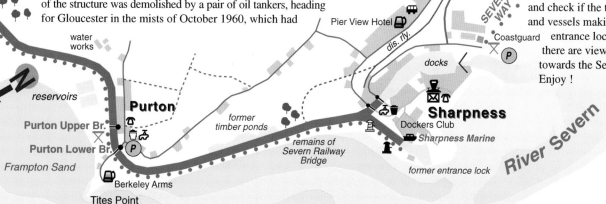

Slimbridge *(Map 29)*

The village straggles down from the A38 to Shepherd's Patch, beyond which the road crosses the canal swing-bridge and makes a bee-line for the Wildfowl & Wetlands Trust centre.

TUDOR ARMS - adjacent Patch Bridge. Tel: 01453 890306. Popular country inn with a good restaurant known far and wide for its 'Rorty Crankle' steaks. Refreshments are also available at the WWT Centre and from a small cafe at the Boat Station.

SLIMBRIDGE BOAT STATION - canalside Patch Bridge. Tel: 01453 899190. Enterprising establishment offering bike hire and day-boat hire facilities plus chandlery, a small range of groceries, a cafe, gifts and souvenirs. WWT SLIMBRIDGE - half a mile north-west of Patch Bridge. Tel: 01453 891900. Open daily year round, Slimbridge has the world's largest collection of rare and endangered ducks, geese and swans and offers brilliant views across the Severn from its observation tower. Not to be missed!

Purton *(Map 30)*

BERKELEY ARMS - unspoilt pub tucked inconspicuously away between the canal and the river. Limited opening times. Tel: 01453 810291.

Sharpness *(Map 30)*

Like a maritime version of 'Brigadoon', it strikes one as implausible to enter or leave this small dockland village by any means other than water. The dockscape is characterised by high concrete silos and a military camp like network of roads. Two timber piers jut into the tidal river and rows of coastguard and pilot cottages increase the seafaring atmosphere.

PIER VIEW HOTEL - in village to east of docks. Tel: 01453 811255. Food and accommodation. SHARPNESS DOCKERS CLUB - dock precincts. Tel: 01453 811477.

POST OFFICE STORES in dock precincts and Co-op store in village.

BUSES -infrequent services to reality but not necessarily back again. Tel: 01452 527516.

The Docks, Sharpness

cotswold
CANALS

OPENED in 1779, and measuring eight miles in length with thirteen locks, the Stroudwater Navigation enjoyed considerable prosperity before the Railway Age. And even thereafter, up until the Second World War, a moderate amount of local trade, predominantly in the guise of Forest of Dean mined coal, continued to use the route. Now it is due to be restored, along with the Thames & Severn Canal, at a cost approaching a hundred million pounds, to enjoy a new era of leisure-based boating. The first mile from Framilode to Saul Junction, however, is not to be made navigable again, because the Severn downstream from Gloucester is far too treacherous a river for inexperienced boat crews to be let loose upon. Thus this first section will remain the province of the walker who will be in a unique position to compare the characteristics of the waterway before

and after regeneration, and in doing so draw their own conclusions, however ambivalent they might be, concerning the Cotswold Canals' new lease of life.

Don't start off too quickly walking eastwards: contemplate the Severn; gaze across its broad expanse to the hilly outline of the Forest of Dean; pay a visit perhaps to St Peter's; then set your face towards the Cotswold escarpment - Sapperton Tunnel is almost twenty miles away and three hundred feet higher above sea level.

Framilode Lock was tidal and lies buried in a garden now. A reedy length of canal, more or less 'in water', runs past the Ship Inn, is culverted beneath the by-road to Saul, then promptly peters out as the path to Saul Junction follows the southern bank of the River Frome, channelled beside pollarded willows, to reach the Gloucester & Sharpness Canal at Saul Junction.

The first few hundred yards of the Stroudwater east of Saul remained

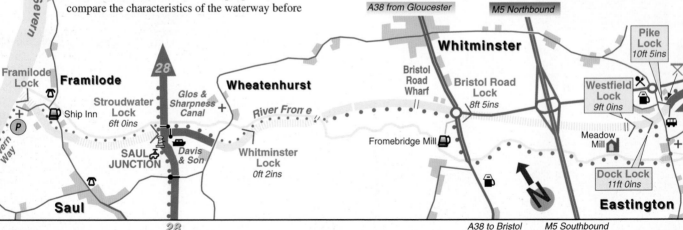

Already navigable section of the Stroudwater Navigation

in use as linear moorings after the navigation was officially abandoned in 1954. These end abruptly at the site of a swing-bridge. The by-road it carried from Wheatenhurst will need to be raised to provide navigable headroom when restoration takes place.

East of here the navigation is likely to be merged with the River Frome to facilitate passage beneath the A38 and M5, construction of which obliterated sections of the original route. In the meantime, walkers can follow at least some of the towpath as far as the site of Bristol Road Wharf before being forced into their own detour via the river bank. A fine hump-backed occupation bridge remains intact and two old pillboxes permit you to indulge in fantasies of invasion and resistance, whilst a peculiarly rust coloured form of duckweed renders the water in the canal bed reminiscent of an asphalt tennis court.

Fromebridge Mill has been converted into a popular pub and restaurant. Walking beside the Frome would be an idyllic exercise but for the racket emanating from the M5, an immense and unceasing barrier of noise of El Alamein artillery barrage intensity. At least, in passing through the dark confines of the tunnel beneath the motorway, you can pretend to be a rock star emerging from your dressing room to a stadium filled with roaring fans.

Passing Meadow Mill you reach the northern outskirts of the village of Eastington and rediscover the original course of the navigation at Westfield Lock, currently buried, yet still discernible if you know what to look for. Dock Lock derived its utilitarian name from the presence of the Stroudwater company's boatyard and maintenance depot at this point. Pike Lock is overlooked by a cottage which latterly provided accommodation for a lock-keeper, but which originally - and hence its name - was a toll house on the local turnpike road.

BEYOND Pike Lock restoration has already taken place and the Cotswold Canals Trust use the section as far as the Birmingham-Bristol railway as a showpiece with regular trip-boat operations. Blunder Lock is just that, having gained its amusing name from a miscalculation of water levels when the canal was being built. Newtown Lock was re-opened (in heavy rain) by the Prince of Wales in 1992. The towpath changes sides at Roving Bridge and proceeds to Bond's Mill Bridge, the world's first plastic lift bridge - sturdier than it sounds. Nice hill views are revealed to the south-east, down as far as Hetty Pegler's Tump!

On its high embankment, the main line railway presents an expensive challenge to the restorationists. A culvert of navigable dimensions will have to be inserted, and whilst this is not too difficult an engineering exercise, the fines imposed in disrupting rail traffic are likely to be costly.

'The Ocean' is a wide pool which probably predated the navigation, being overlooked by Stonehouse Court, an extensive Elizabethan building renovated by Lutyens and now an hotel. Next door is the charming little church of St Cyr's which apparently relinquished part of its churchyard to the canal builders.

Comparatively little work needs to be done to restore navigability as far as Ryeford Double Locks. Two attractive houses abut Nutshell Bridge and are curiously linked by a passage beneath it. The route of the old Midland Railway line to Nailsworth crosses the canal on a cast iron bridge and there was once a transhipment wharf here. A private swingbridge spans the canal at Ryeford as the Cotswold Way swoops down on its hundred mile way from Chipping Campden to Bath.

Ryeford Locks are one of only two staircase pairs on the Cotswold Canals. Behind their isolated lock cottage you can see the unusual French Gothic church tower of Bodley's hillside church at Selsley. Ebley Mill provides a handsome landmark as the navigation nears Stroud. As we went to press, new lengths of canal were being excavated.

BIRMINGHAM

Newtown Lock 7ft 5ins

31

Blunder Lock 7ft 5ins

Roving Bridge

A419

Bond's Mill

N

hotel

'The Ocean' Nutshell Bridge

Upper Mills

BRISTOL

Wycliffe College

Stonehouse

Cotswold Way

A419

Stanley Mills

Ryeford Double Locks 16ft 10ins

Course of M.R. Nailsworth branch

Ebley

Ebley Mills

SWINDON

A419

Foundry Lock 8ft 7ins

Dudbridge Lock 8ft 7ins

A46 to Bath

Selsley

B4066 to Dursley

THE Stroudwater Navigation and Thames & Severn Canal meet at Wallbridge Basin on the outskirts of Stroud. The latter was completed across its astonishing summit in 1789, thereby linking two of Britain's greatest rivers and providing new transport opportunities for the manufacturers of the Forest of Dean and of South Wales, not to mention the cloth-makers of the Stroud Valley. Much celebrating took place on that November day towards the end of the 18th century, and will undoubtedly do so again when the Severn and the Thames are reconnected in the not too distant future.

Much altered in recent years by road building and redevelopment, Stroud's canalscape can only be improved by restoration. Sadly, though, no one has suggested bringing back the Stroud Brewery whose derelict coal chutes remain discernible between the locks.

Another remnant of lost endeavour is the Midland Railway's blue brick viaduct which curves tantalisingly through the valley of the Frome, its last train having puffed into the sunset as long ago as 1949. In a contrast of fortunes, the former Great Western Railway viaduct remains in use, its tracks forming a close companionship with the canal all the way up to Sapperton.

Wallbridge Upper Lock is gated and makes a symbolic declaration of intent in the vanguard of full restoration. The railway spans a presently infilled section of canal and walkers are faced with a short detour past a Waitrose supermarket before regaining the canal as it regains its shape - though not as yet its depth - in a rewarding section stretching as far as Hope Mill Lock. The Frome passes beneath the canal and establishes itself on the towpath side, broadening into a

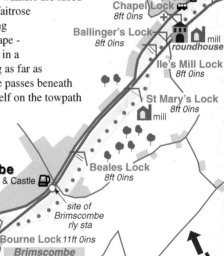

Chalford

Bell Lock
10ft 0ins

Chapel Lock
8ft 0ins

Ballinger's Lock
8ft 0ins
roundhouse mill

Ile's Mill Lock
8ft 0ins

St Mary's Lock
8ft 0ins
mill

Beales Lock
8ft 0ins

Stroud
Town Centre
mus
Waitrose

site of Midland rly sta

Wallbridge Upper Lock
11ft 0ins

Wallbridge Lower Lock
9ft 0ins

Bowbridge Lock
10ft 0ins

Stanton's Br.

Griffin Mills

Jubilee Br.

Griffin's Mill Lock
10ft 0ins

Ham Mills

Ham Mill Lock
9ft 0ins

Bagpath Br.

Hope Mill Lock
8ft 0ins

Gough's Orchard Lock
8ft 0ins

Brimscombe
King & Castle

Ship Inn

Bourne Lock 11ft 0ins

site of Brimscombe rly sta

Brimscombe Port

34

lagoon at the site of Arundel Mill. New housing overlooking Bowbridge Lock has had the wit to use local stone in deference to its location. Remedial work carried out in the early days of the Cotswold Canal Trust in the 1970s has created the illusion of a working canal by Stanton's and Jubilee bridges. The latter is an attractive structure of cast iron latticework built to enable workers to reach the mills from their houses up on the hillside beyond the railway. The present day industrial premises along the valley floor perhaps lack the visual appeal of the earlier mills and one suspects that the majority of their workforces arrive and depart by road.

Beyond Bagpath Bridge the canal bed grows thicker with reeds and then becomes infilled at the site of Hope Mill Lock. Briefly, by Gough's Orchard Lock, the canal line returns, but this proves just a brief illusion as Brimscombe Port is reached where a good deal of imagination is required to envisage the former layout of the canal and its associated wharves.

No avid canal enthusiast would have been immune to the fascination of Brimscombe in its heyday. The need for an inland port was brought about by the necessity of transferring goods between vessels of a different gauge: Severn 'trows' and Thames barges of the 'western' kind as well as a requirement to store items pending final delivery or further transport. Locks on the Stroudwater and Thames & Severn, though widebeam, were of differing dimensions, the former being 68/9ft long by 16ft 1/2ins wide, the latter originally 90-93 feet in length by 12ft 9ins or 13ft wide. To save water the Thames & Severn locks were reduced in length around 1841 and in the final years of trade carriers found the ubiquitous narrowboat a more suitable craft for working on the Thames & Severn than the wide-beam barges of old.

Brimscombe basin offered a hundred and seventy five thousand square feet of capacity and was said to have been able to accommodate up to a hundred vessels simultaneously. Notable features included the company's head offices, a transit shed, warehousing and a boat weighing machine used for establishing tolls. A central island was incorporated for the secure storage of goods which might, unprotected, have caught the attention of the thieving classes. The main warehouse found unusual use as a school following the demise of the canal and was unfortunately demolished in 1964. Thereafter, as so often is the case, the old port became an industrial estate. The most handsome survival is Port Mill, premises now of Tempus Publishing, whose list appropriately contains many titles devoted to the history of canals. In 2002 British Waterways seized the opportunity to purchase the site of Brimscombe Port, thereby paving the way for restoration. Meanwhile walkers face a short detour (past a tempting fish & chip bar) before regaining the line of the canal by Bourne Lock, beyond which the canal is punctured again by the railway, following which it re-establishes itself as far as Chalford, a beguiling section upon which the Golden Valley begins to cast its spell.

A pub called the King & Castle recalls the existence of Brimscombe railway station alongside the canal. Here a small engine shed provided bankers for the climb to Sapperton summit. On to St Mary's, canal and railway - accompanied by the Frome chuckling transparently over it's gravel bed -create a mutually exclusive environment away from the traffic on the A419. An access lane to St Mary's Mill swoops down to cross the railway by way of a traditionally gated level crossing guarded by a tiny signal box. Piped beneath the railway yet again, the canal briefly loses confidence before reappearing at Ile's Lock overlooked by a mellow and now domesticised Clayfield Mill, at least one occupant of which is proficient at the piano.

It grows increasingly difficult not to be overawed by the beauty of the canal's surroundings, as indeed was Temple Thurston on his famous (though perhaps over-imagined) voyage along the canal with the *Flower of Gloster* in 1910. He likened the surrounding scenery to Switzerland, something hacks are over-inclined to do when faced with precipitously hilly districts of England. Nevertheless his heart was in the right place and you too will be entranced by these 'blue slate roofs' viewed against a 'golden distance'. At Chalford you come upon the first of the Thames & Severn's keynote roundhouses and a gable end advertising 'James Smart - Coal, Stone & Sand Merchant, Dealer in Staffordshire Bricks'. Smart's barges traded here until abandonment finally took place in the 'Thirties; a priceless survival!

Stonehouse (Map 32)

Stonehouse will come into its own when boaters begin to use the Stroudwater Navigation once again. In the meantime, walkers will probably want to press on to Stroud where the facilities are closer to hand. Wycliffe College was founded in 1882. The remains of its original boathouse still stand beside the canal, though nowadays the boat crews are put through their paces on the Gloucester & Sharpness Canal at Saul Junction. In the 18th and 19th centuries, Stonehouse flourished, as other settlements along the Frome Valley, as a centre for the wool trade. Shops, banks, takeaways and other trappings of modern life are to be found in the vicinity of the railway station north of the canal.

Stroud (Map 33)

A codicil to the Cotswolds, with a spirited tradition of independent outlook, the textile town of Stroud tumbles down the valley side with the profile of a dry ski slope. With one end of the town six hundred feet lower than its counterpart, one can well imagine that yesteryear's urchins must have lost many of their marbles in the canal; restoration will reveal rich treasure trove. Gradients apart, Stroud is a likeable place to wander around, several fine buildings vying for attention, none finer than the splendidly classical Subscription Rooms of 1833. In its heyday as a wool town Stroud was famous for its military tunics, now those mills left in production - out of the hundred and fifty which once functioned in the Frome Valley - are renowned for the production of snooker table baize and Wimbledon tennis ball felt.

MILLS - The Shambles. Tel: 01453 752222. Pleasant wholefood cafe with pavement tables under a canopy within yards of where John Wesley preached from a butcher's block.

THE RETREAT - Church Street. Lively cafe/bar. Tel: 01453 750208.
CLOTHIERS ARMS - Bath Road. Tel: 01453 763801. Pub offering accommodation within easy reach of canal.
THE BELL HOTEL - canalside Wallbridge Upper Lock. Tel: 01453 763556. Food and accommodation.

Stroud's precipitous High Street is refreshingly bereft of chain stores (they lurk down in the ubiquitous Merrywalks Shopping Centre and can, as such, be left to their own anodyne devices) and congenially populated by individual retailers of more enterprising outlook, notably INPRINT (Tel: 01453 759731), a stylish secondhand bookshop with a choice collection of local subject matter. MADE IN STROUD (Tel: 01453 758060) on Kendrick Street reflects the area's status as a haven for craftsmen and artists, and has links with the FARMER'S MARKET held in The Cornhill on the first and third Saturdays of each month.

TOURIST INFORMATION - Subscription Rooms, George Street. Tel: 01453 760960.
THE MUSEUM IN THE PARK - Stratford Park. Tel: 01453 763394. Local heritage in a lovely setting.

TRAINS - Wessex and First Great Western services along the Golden Valley to/from Gloucester and Swindon with many through trains to/from London Paddington. Tel: 08457 484950.
BUSES - Stagecoach services throughout the area, offering the opportunity of excursions to the likes of Dursley (a pretty market town); Wootton-under-Edge; or Slad (Laurie Lee country). Service No.54 threads its way through the Golden Valley via Brimscombe, Chalford and Sapperton to Cirencester Mon-Sat and is consequently of good use to towpath walkers. Tel: 01453 763421.

Brimscombe (Map 33)

Re-establishment of Brimscombe Port can only add lustre to this roadside settlement east of Stroud. Useful facilities for passing walkers include the SHIP INN (Tel: 01453 884388), KING & CASTLE (Tel: 01453 884388), a fish & chip shop, post office and newsagents.

Chalford (Map 33)

Cuddled in the lap of the Golden Valley, Chalford deserves to be savoured in its own right rather than just an adjunct to the canal. Indeed, there is something to be said for the walker detouring along the gorgeous by-road between Bell Lock and Golden Valley Lock to get a more intimate view of the higgledy-piggledy houses which define its character. The church of 1724 overlooks the canal roundhouse and features Pre-Raphaelite glass and 'Arts & Crafts' furnishings. Railway enthusiasts will remember Chalford as the eastern terminus of a push & pull service from Gloucester until 1964.

NEW RED LION - canalside above Bell Lock. Tel: 01453 882384. Friendly little pub with a cool interior. Beers include Wiltshire-brewed Moles from Melksham. Bar meals.
POST OFFICE TEA ROOMS - Tel: 01453 882288.

Post Office stores on by-road east of Bell Lock. Groceries and newspapers. Bike shop by Chapel Lock should your tyres or your ego need inflating.

BUSES - Stagecoach service 54 runs Mon-Sat between Stroud and Cirencester calling also at Sapperton. Tel: 01453 763421.

PENNINE overtones assail the Thames & Severn as it climbs through the Golden Valley. The Cotswold landscape is softer of course, yet you are still reminded of the constricted valleys of the Calder or the Colne, the Tame or the Roch. Here it was the course of the Frome which aided and abetted the canal builders, and the little river comes flowing transparently down its valley with the self-confidence of a child empowered by an important errand.

Thicker and thicker grow the locks, and the walker feels the climb, though not as much as the boaters will once navigation is restored. Clowse Bridge gained its name from the canal's resident engineer, Josiah, the man responsible for realising Robert Whitworth's blueprints in bricks and mortar. Narrowing, the constricted valley suffers lack of space, its hillside houses, so mellow, so apparently organic in origin, scattered haphazardly on shelves and terraces like the contents of a tiny corner shop.

With the railway, it seems, intent on climbing harder, faster and attached to the neighbouring ridge on a remarkable sequence of arches, the canal reaches Valley Lock, whereafter the houses and mills are largely left behind and woodland creates a very real sense of remoteness. In these woods, while Eynsham Harry prepared a mid-day meal of wild hops, Temple Thurston counted seventeen varieties of wild flower. Short-changed by poetic impulse, Pearson was much more attracted to the redbrick and rounded windows of Chalford's erstwhile waterworks, enigmatic in decay. Dating from 1890, quite late in the canal's commercial career, coal for the furnaces was brought in by boat. On the towpath a milepost informs you that you have journeyed five miles from Wallbridge , and that a further twenty-three and

three-quarters remain to be covered before reaching the Thames at Inglesham.

By Baker's Mill Upper Lock the Frome widens into a reservoir created by the canal company for water supplies. In doing so they were forced to acquire Puck's Mill in 1791 and close it down in order to guarantee a sufficient head of water. An inn once overlooked Puck Mill Upper Lock, an important thirst-slayer on the long haul to the summit. Look out for a delightful (and occupied) dovecot attached to the end wall of a canalside house above the lock: footpaths splay off into the woods, begging to be explored.

The Golden Valley lives up to the implications of its name as the canal winds through woodland never out of earshot of the Frome. Walkers on the Thames & Severn towpath are joined at Whitehall Bridge by fellow travellers on the Wysis Way, a 55 mile path linking Offa's Dyke with the Thames Path. 'WD 1784' engraved on the arch of Whitehall Bridge refers to the mason William Dennis responsible for constructing this section of the canal. You are now entering the Sapperton Valley Reserve of the Gloucestershire Wildlife Trust and it is to be hoped that the return of boats does nothing to upset the fragile balance of flora and fauna in the vicinity.

Even in the canal's heyday, working up or down the final flight of seven locks to and from the summit at Daneway was often problematical given the paucity of water supply. Consumption was reduced by about 20% following shortening of the lock chambers. A series of sideponds had already been added in 1823, but every drop of water continued to count. Encountering just one other boat (captained by an elderly lady humming quietly to herself at the tiller) Temple Thurston remarked that in places they barely floated at all, much to the chagrin of Fanny the boat horse. A quarter of a century later the author Geoffrey Boumphrey and a companion were unable to progress this far even by canoe as described in his book *Down River*, an account of a tour on the Severn and the Thames and, where possible, the Cotswold Canals, published in 1936. In the event Boumphrey and his pal 'George' had to portage their canoes by car between Chalford and Cricklade. They must have been reading William Bliss's, *Art and Practise of Canoeing on English Rivers, Navigations and Canals* , which records that he was charged 25 shillings to have his own canoe conveyed by road between Chalford and Cricklade!

The canal widened into a wharf and basin between the two Daneway locks, the upper of which was overlooked by an inn, once the Bricklayer's Arms now The Daneway. The higher lock has been infilled to provide the pub with a car park; future patrons of the beer garden will have the preferable ring-side view of an excavated lock chamber.

The summit lies 362 feet above sea level, but it rapidly becomes apparent as you twist in an easterly, becoming south-easterly direction away from Daneway, that the canal can go no further save by subterranean methods. And indeed, within less than half a mile, the neighbouring ridge rears suddenly up in defiance and the western portal of Sapperton is revealed, battlemented as if it means business, an entrance into Hades.

3,808 yards long- impressive enough, but roundly beaten by the Huddersfield Narrow Canal's Standedge tunnel which is 5,698 yards long - and up to 200 feet below the surface of the Cotswold landscape it burrows through, Sapperton Tunnel was five years in the making. George III came to inspect it on Saturday 19th July 1788 as an antidote to taking the waters in nearby Cheltenham. Contemporary accounts suggest that His Majesty expressed astonishment. So, more practically, did Temple Thurston, who lay on his back with Eynsham Harry for four and a half sepulchral hours to propel the *Flower of Gloster* through the tunnel in time honoured fashion. In its working days a four-hourly cycle of entry times was the order of the day. A realisitic account of a boat being legged through the tunnel enlivens the opening pages of C. S. Forester's adventure *Hornblower and the Atropos*. Pending restoration, we have to walk across the top in the footsteps of the old boat horses and mules. For a heady moment one imagines that the dung on the road through Sapperton village is still steaming from those animals, until it becomes apparent that horse-riding is a popular activity amongst the rides of Oakley Wood.

WALKING over the top of Sapperton Tunnel gives you plenty of time to marvel at its existence - and perhaps yours as well. From time to time you catch sight of spoil heaps planted with beech trees which bring to mind all the activity of the human moles who dug the tunnel over two centuries ago. Spare a thought too, for the almost parallel railway tunnel completed in 1845 which is a mere 1 mile and 95 yards long. This is said to have been bored outwards from vertical shafts because the railway company wasn't yet in possession of the land at the ends of the tunnel!

If you were enamoured of the Gothic portal at the western end of the canal tunnel, you will probably be surprised to discover not a mirror image at the eastern end, but a design of quite different Classical style: a sort of double-A-side in pop single terms. It was restored by a local stonemason in 1977 and the Cotswold Canal Trust operate trips into the tunnel for a short distance on selected dates. Above, and to the left of the portal, stands the Tunnel House Inn, erected during construction of the canal to provide accommodation and refreshment. It still fulfils the latter purpose admirably though the original third storey was destroyed by a fire in 1952.

Recalling George III's visit, the cutting between the tunnel mouth and Tarlton Bridge is called 'King's Reach'. It is succeeded by the second Thames & Severn roundhouse encountered by westbound travellers. Coates Roundhouse differs from Chalford in two ways: it is (currently at any rate) uninhabited, but more significantly, its roof, though conical, is inverted, as a means of gathering rainwater for domestic use. Before the railway arrived it must have been a lonely

Map labels:

36

Park Leaze Bridge

site of Smerrill Aqueduct

Halfway Bridge

site of former rly Bridge

By-roads to Ewen

A433 from Cirencester

Course of G.W.R. Cirencester Branch

R. Thames

Thames Path

A419 from Stroud

34

sawmill

Coatesfield Bridge

Summit Section 362 ft.

By-road from Coates

Source of R. Thames

site of pumping engine

Thames Head Inn

Sapperton Tunnel 2mls 288yrds

N

Tunnel House Inn

Tarlton Bridge

Coates Roundhouse (ruin)

The Tavern

Kemble

Course of G.W.R. Tetbury Brnach

By-roads to Tarlton

A433 to Tetbury

A429 to Malmesbury

location for the resident company employee and his family. Forcibly closed by the local authority on health grounds in the 1950s, it now resembles an abandoned lighthouse, especially as glimpsed from passing trains.

The summit section of the Thames & Severn is 8 miles 13 chains in length. Sadly the canal east of Sapperton is not so well defined as in the Golden Valley. At Coatesfield Bridge it ceases to be a right of way and walkers are forced to join a field path which soon passes the official Source of the Thames. Meanwhile the canal passes beneath the Roman Road which links Lincoln with Exeter, the famous Fosse Way, and comes upon the site of a pumping house which, in its various guises ranging from a windmill, through a Boulton & Watt beam engine to a second-hand steam pump from a Cornish mine, supplied three million gallons of water a day to the summit until 1912. The last engine was scrapped as part of the war effort in 1941, though the rebuilt pumphouse remains, off limits and in domestic use.

Walkers, unfortunately, miss all this, their route lying to the south along the Thames Path as far as the enchanting village of Ewen, beyond which they rejoin the canal at Halfway Bridge, alongside a three-arched, stone-built bridge which formerly carried the Kemble-Cirencester branchline over a by-road and the canal. Halfway Bridge marks the halfway point of the Thames & Severn Canal and it was rebuilt in 1997, a small, yet important gesture which kept up the impetus of the canal's eventual restoration. However charming the Thames, especially in its strippling state, it feels good to be re-united with the canal, which for half a mile or so, is convincingly defined, if predominantly as dry as the stone walling which delineates its towpath side from neighbouring farmland. How the rabbits who make its dry banks their home, or the rooks who nest in the high tops of trees which overhang the canal will react to an invasion of dumper-drivers and membrane-layers is anyone's guess, but nature has a ready knack of making restitution. Presently, it becomes necessary to detour on to the adjacent by-road as the towpath becomes impassable and the canal bed peters out. Cirencester Council used the canal as a linear refuse tip in less enlightened times: one trusts that any surviving councillors have the grace to express regret in what must now be their dotage.

Frampton Mansell (Map 34)

Vertiginous village overlooking the Golden Valley. Nice walk up to the CROWN INN (Tel: 01285 760601) from Puck Mill.

Sapperton (Map 34)

Idyllic settlement perched above its famous tunnel offering easy access to view the western portal. Historic links with proponents of the Arts & Crafts movement. Unfortunately no shops, but a very good pub called THE BELL (Tel: 01285 760298). Buses to Cirencester and Stroud - Tel: 01453 763421.

Daneway (Map 34)

Hamlet at the head of the Golden Valley best known in canal circles for its eponymous canal boatmen's pub the DANEWAY INN (Tel: 01285 760297) a charming Wadworth house.

Kemble (Map 35)

Over the years, housing schemes have enlarged Kemble, whose prime role had hitherto been as host to the railway junction of the branchlines to Cirencester and Tetbury, the latter famous for its isolated station called Trouble House Halt which featured in Flanders & Swann's elegiac song *Slow Train*. The branchlines and their railbuses have gone now, but the splendid Tudoresque station remains a popular railhead for this well-heeled district as evinced by copies of *Country Life* in the well-appointed waiting room - 'Paddington - 81 minutes' !

TUNNEL HOUSE INN - adjacent eastern portal of Sapperton Tunnel. Tel: 01285 770280.

THAMES HEAD INN - Fosse Way. Tel: 01285 770259.

THE TAVERN - adjacent Kemble railway station. Tel: 01285 770216.

The Post Office stores in village centre is the only shop anywhere remotely close to the canal between Chalford and Siddington.

TRAINS - excellent service linking Swindon with Gloucester and Cheltenham. Stroud is a comfortable 15 mile walk away. Tel: 08457 484950.

BUSES - connections with Cirencester and Tetbury. Tel: 01285 653985 or 01452 425543.

TAXIS - Tel: 01285 642767.

AT Bluehouse you can detour to see a former lengthsman's cottage, but otherwise your way lies via public footpaths and by-roads to Siddington, site of the former junction of an arm which led into Cirencester itself and the beginning of the mainline's descent to the Thames at Inglesham. The majority of the arm lies beneath an industrial estate now. Another Whitchurch, another Leek; enlightenment deepening the regret that the lines of their canals have been lost beneath hasty redevelopment.

The quartet of locks at Siddington lower the canal by almost forty feet, the lowest being buried beneath a new house which provocatively carries a narrowboat on its name plaque. One imagines it will have to be moved or demolished to effect restoration unless they fancy a cellar with a working lock chamber as a conversation piece. Between the third and the fourth chambers, another transport casualty, less likely to be revived, is the Midland & South Western Railway, one of those wonderful cross country lines of no apparent use to anyone but railway enthusiasts, though this line, which linked Cheltenham with Southampton, did bizarrely flourish briefly as a route for northerners bent on emigrating to Australia.

Cowground Bridge is intact and of traditional hump-back appearance. It is followed by the remains of a swing-bridge, and then the Thames & Severn crossed the River Churn: the original masonry aqueduct has been replaced in recent years by a wooden footbridge. The Churn rises high up on Cotswold to the south of Cheltenham and has its confluence with the Thames at Cricklade. It was one of a baker's dozen of tributaries lyrically described by the poet and topographical writer Brian Waters in his *Thirteen Rivers to the Thames* published by Dent in 1964. In it he noted that water-mills are as frequently encountered on the Thames and its tributaries as public houses along an English road: forty years

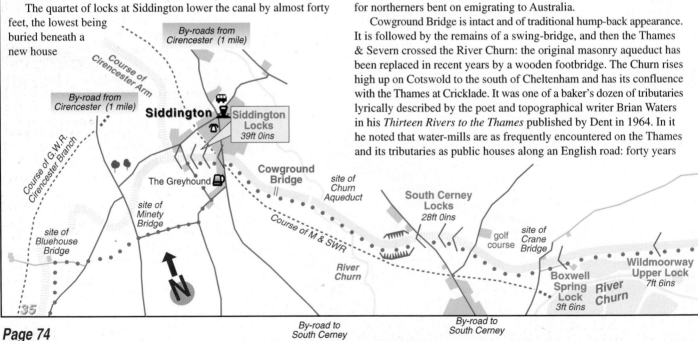

of contestable progress have not dealt kindly with this observation. There is still, however, if you look closely enough, evidence of a fascinating irrigation system which once permitted the meadowlands beside the Churn to be deliberately flooded in winter so as to protect the grass beneath from freezing and also to allow rich nutrients in the river water to enhance the grazing properties of the meadows the following spring. A seat commemorating Councillor David Fox, a keen advocate of restoration, offers the chance to dally in such delightful surroundings. Close your eyes and imagine the approaching clip clop of a boat horse, a dripping towline, and a western Thames barge laden with Cotswold stone whilst, to your rear, the South Express (through carriages Liverpool Lime Street to Southampton) shuffles past in a vapoury dream of soot and oil.

Claymeadow Cutting precedes South Cerney Wharf where locally baked bricks once provided regular cargoes. The wharf house remains in domestic use. Will its owners welcome a canal on their doorstep? All three locks in the South Cerney flight are buried but should provide no undue difficulties in re-establishing them. Crossing the road, one walks at 45 degrees across a field overlooked by one of Gloucestershire's many wartime aerodromes, regaining the line of the canal at Northmoor Lane where a new golf course provides ramblers and canal enthusiasts with interesting contrasts in the use of leisure time. A pleasant length of canal follows, though the increasing decibels of 'noises off' earmark the impending intrusion of a busy dual-carriageway. The well preserved chamber of Boxwell Spring Lock is a mere 3ft 6ins deep. It wasn't originally intended that there should be a lock here at all, but a miscalculation in water levels rendered its construction a necessity. The towpath progresses through an avenue of ivy-clad tree boles to Wildmoorway Upper Lock where rotting tail gates lie submerged within inky black pools of brackish water.

QUITE apart from the canal's present state of dereliction, the 18th or 19th century boatman would be hard pressed to recognise his surroundings, the present landscape of flooded gravel workings bounded by the busy A419 trunk road, not being one which he would either be familiar with nor necessarily comfortable in. The character of the 21st century manifests itself most strongly below Wildmoorway Lower Lock where a new spine road, car park and picnic site encourage road-based visitors to enjoy the charms of the Cotswold Water Park: leisure for the masses needs to be ring-fenced and manufactured now.

Tall reeds swaying in the shallow waters of the canal mask the visual, if not the aural, impact of the main road as the towpath forms the boundary between Gloucestershire and Wiltshire. Cerney Wick Lock is overlooked by the third of the Thames & Severn's five roundhouses; as at Chalford the roof points conically upward. The lock chamber has top gates but the adjoining road bridge is levelled and the canal culverted beneath. Across the Churn The Crown offers an opportunity for refreshment and meditation.

Latton Basin marked the junction of the Thames & Severn and North Wilts canals for a number of years. The North Wilts opened in 1819 and created a nine-mile link with the Wilts & Berks Canal at Swindon, its chief benefit lying in its ability to provide a more reliable route to Abingdon than via the rather less than reliable upper Thames, though its gauge was constrained by a dozen narrow locks. Formally abandoned in 1914, though

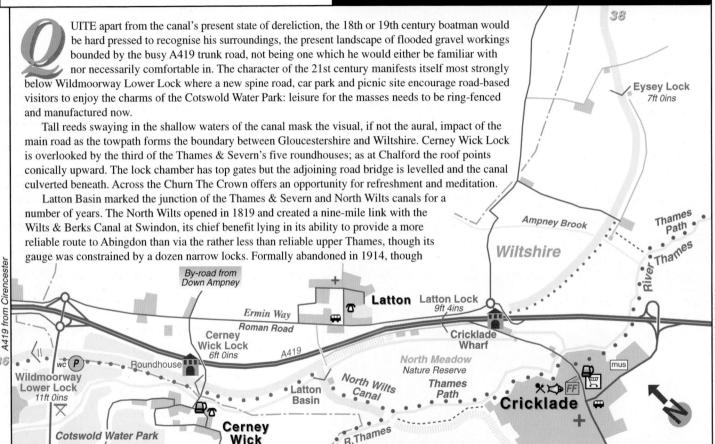

denuded of trade long before that, the North Wilts ironically provides present day walkers with the best option for progress pending restoration, because the Thames & Severn between Latton and Inglesham is for the most part infilled and no longer a right of way. A solid path follows the dry bed of the North Wilts to the banks of the Thames where the Thames Path can be joined for an enjoyable onward walk via Cricklade to Inglesham, a distance of approximately ten miles. Diehards may progress along the line of the Thames & Severn to Cricklade Wharf, but the A419 compromises much of the original canal bed and it is a matter of walking along a desultory access road too close to the noisy dual-carriageway to be considered enjoyable.

Cricklade Wharf retains its original, and imposing, Thames & Severn wharf building, but it turns its rear to the road and is off limits to the general public. Frustratingly the best view is from the A419, and that, by definition, a fleeting glimpse. The basin at Cricklade Wharf was infilled long ago but a major victory was achieved by the canal lobby when the A419 dual carriageway was constructed with a navigable culvert in 1997.

Beyond Cricklade we would advocate use of the Thames Path or an alternative route promulgated by Gerry Stewart in his equally practical and lyrical book *The Cotswolds Canal Walk (ISBN* 0 952787 03 2) which recommends a network of public footpaths via Down Ampney (birthplace of the composer Ralph Vaughan Williams), Marston Meysey and Kempsford.

Siddington *(Map 36)*

Over-run by Cirencester's expanding suburbs, Siddington nevertheless offers canal walkers a post office stores and THE GREYHOUND (Tel: 01285 653573) an amenable Wadworth pub with food and a skittle alley.

Cricklade *(Map 37)*

The ancient Wiltshire town of Cricklade is dominated by the turreted 16th century tower of the parish church of St Samson of Dol. Otherwise, one main street defines the town, sloping from the Jubilee Clock of 1897 steadily, widely, and agreeably down to the Town Bridge over the Thames past St Mary's, Britain's 'oldest Catholic church'. A small museum celebrating the town's rich history opens on Wednesday and Saturday afternoons.

RED LION - foot of High Street. The first pub on the way into town from the Thames Path and difficult to better. Moles ales and guests, Tel: 01793 750776. No food as such, though the mouthwatering possibility of pasties from Michael Hart's - see below.

WHITE HART - High Street. Tel: 01793 750206. Old coaching inn offering Swindon-brewed Arkells, food and accommodation.

CRICKLADE CAFE - High Street. Tel: 01793 750754. Filling food for famished walkers.

ANCIENT RAJ - High Street. Indian restaurant and take-away. Tel: 01793 750303.

TIGER LEE - High Street. Chinese take-away. Tel: 01793 751177.

CROWN INN - Cerney Wick. Tel: 01793 750369. Popular pub offering food and accommodation on the edge of the Cotswold Water Park and within easy reach of the towpath.

Facilities include a pharmacy, 'One Stop' convenience store, and a Lloyds TSB bank with cash machine, but best of all is MICHAEL HART'S butchers shop (Tel: 01793 750213) which purveys championship-winning sausages, pies and pasties, not to mention oven-ready pheasants.

BUSES - Stagecoach services to/from Swindon and Cheltenham via Cirencester. Tel: 01793 522243.

SHYNESS, as already hinted, overcomes the Thames & Severn between Cricklade and Inglesham, and until restoration takes place it is not feasible for members of the general public to follow the line of the canal in a satisfactory, let alone enjoyable manner. There are, however, one or two highlights that the diligent explorer will find of interest. A public footpath affords access to the site of Marston Meysey Wharf, private property now but retaining an overbridge and a roundhouse which has been tastefully incorporated into a modern dwelling. Enjoy a view of it, by all means, but respect its new owner's privacy as with all such mementoes of the canal in its prime. Old maps are required to make sense of the canal's eastward progress, the next convincing proof that it passed hereabouts being Oatlands Bridge, a high and dry remnant in a field close to the road on the outskirts of Kempsford. According to David Viner's invaluable *The Thames & Severn Canal - History & Guide* (ISBN 0 7524 1761 4), at least one of its bricks is embossed with the name of the Stonehouse Brick & Tile Co, evidence surely of materials being conveyed by boat along the line of the canal, if not for construction, then at least for maintenance in later years.

Kempsford lies on the Thames, and the two watercourses lay closely parallel for some distance, though nowadays, owing to access constraints, the Thames Path runs away from the riverbank in this locality. When the Thames & Severn was first being surveyed, consideration was given to making its junction with the Thames here rather than at Inglesham. Long ago the river formed the boundary between Mercia and Wessex at this point - now it contents itself with dividing Glos. from Wilts.

Wharf Lane reminds villagers that they once had a canal on their doorstep, and one imagines that most of them will be glad to have it back, not least the landlords of the village's two pubs. East of Kempsford the canal continues infilled and all but invisibly on the last lap to its junction with the Thames at Inglesham.

Marston Meysey

Old Speckled Cow

roundhouse

Oatlands Bridge

RAF Fairford

By-road from Fairford

Axe & Compass
The George

Kempsford

Ham Barn

River Thames

Red Lion

Castle Eaton

Wiltshire

Gloucestershire

Thames Path

By-road from Cricklade

37

By-road to Highworth

By-road to Highworth

upper
THAMES

OVERLOOKED by the last of its five characteristic roundhouses, the Thames & Severn Canal and River Thames meet at Inglesham a mile upstream of Lechlade.

As a declaration of intent, Inglesham Roundhouse was purchased by British Waterways in 2003 to pave the way for restoration. It is intended that in due course it will be available for holiday hire, and it is difficult to think of a more appealing dwelling for those of an inland waterway bent seeking a peaceful retreat for a week or two. Presumably, in due course, bearing in mind the target of 2010 for completion of the canal's restoration, the canal itself will once again before long become accessible, both on foot and afloat, and therefore the interesting double lock at Dudgrove, where the lower,

shallow chamber was considered to be of a temporary nature, will be once again revealed for public scrutiny. A mouth-watering prospect indeed!

Inglesham is generally recognised as the head of navigation on the River Thames as far as motor vessels are concerned, yet, legally, small unpowered craft such as canoes can get as far upstream as Cricklade. But as far as this guide is concerned, we concentrate now on the Upper Thames, and in particular the thirty lonely, twisting, shallow but very lovely miles between Lechlade and Oxford, one of the most rewarding inland waterway experiences in Britain.

As befits the largest - indeed the *only* - town on the upper reaches, Lechlade has been shaped, commercially and culturally by the presence of the Thames on its doorstep. Today a marina provides boating activity where once stone and cheese and wool were the prevalent cargoes. Lechlade or Halfpenny Bridge dates from 1793, its colloquial name derived from the toll paid by pedestrians (unless bound for church) until 1839. Downstream the Thames essays

By-road from Fairford

River Coln

Cotswold Hire/ Lechlade Marina

Lechlade

Inglesham Lock
6ft 2ins
Inglesham Roundhouse

Thames Path

70'

Lechlade Bridge

P

Dudgrove Farm

Thames & Severn Canal

Wiltshire

River Cole

Oxon.

Glos.

Dudgrove Double Lock
11ft 6ins

River Thames

Thames Path

St John's Bridge

The Trout

St John's Lock
2ft 10ins
Tel: 01367 252309

River Leach

Gloucestershire

Oxon.

40

38

a charming course overlooked by the spacious customer moorings of the New Inn, and the soaring Perpendicular spire of St Lawrence, together with a number of gracious private gardens, some sporting elegant gazebos. Informal public moorings are available on the south, Wiltshire bank of the river against a wide expanse of watermeadows. Idyllic indeed!

St John's Lock is the highest on the Thames, but if you travel all the way to Teddington you will arguably be unable to find one better tended. It is graced by a reclining statue of Father Thames, postcards of which are obtainable from the lock-keeper. It is the work of R. Monti and was sculpted for the Crystal Palace in 1854. Between 1958 and 1974 it graced the source of the Thames at Thames Head, but was prone to the attention of philistines and vandals, and this lockside was considered a safer spot for the old man's contemplation of his river.

Downstream of the lock cut two Thames tributaries join the channel: the River Cole, from the south flows off the Marlborough Downs below of Swindon and forms the boundary between Wiltshire and Oxfordshire; the River Leach rises high up on the Cotswolds, lends its name to the Fosse Way village of Northleach, and travels fifteen miles to meet the Thames - once it was said to yield 'the finest watercress in England' which was loaded on to a train each evening at Lechlade station for transit to Covent Garden.

Lechlade *(Map 39)*

Cause or effect ? - it would be difficult to manufacture a more amenable town to accompany the head of navigation on the River Thames. Formerly at the meeting place of four counties, Lechlade graces the south-eastern corner of Gloucestershire with thoroughfares of mellow 'Cotswold' stone. Cricklade and Cirencester have their towers, perfectly Perpendicular St John's at Lechlade has its spire, a landmark amongst the watermeadows for miles. Shelley came here in 1815 and wrote a poem about it - its gargoyles are remarkable! As befits a visitor-orientated town, rowing boats and motor boats are available for hire, as are bicycles Tel: 01367 253599.

NEW INN - Market Square. Tel: 01367 252296. Old coaching inn offering bar and restaurant meals and accommodation. Customer moorings at the foot of its lengthy garden.

COLLEYS SUPPER ROOMS - High Street. Tel: 01367 252218. Elaborate six-course dinners and Sunday lunches for discerning gourmets.
J A FLONG - Market Square. Tandoori restaurant and takeaway. Tel: 01367 252956.
RED LION - High Street. Tel: 01367 252373. Arkells, steaks and accommodation.
BLACK CAT TEAROOMS - High Street. Cafe/restaurant. Tel: 01367 252273.
THE CAFE - Market Square. Tel: 01367 253990. Upstairs cafe over a wine merchant plus pavement tables for warm days.
THE RIVERSIDE - Thames Street. Tel: 01367 252229. Popular riverside pub.
THE TROUT - riverside St John's Bridge. Tel: 01367 252313. One of three 'Trouts' on the Upper Thames. Bar and restaurant meals, nice big garden, customer moorings.
There's a fish & chip shop in Lechlade open daily except for Sundays.

A LONDIS minimarket (offering 'cashback' on purchases) is located in the Market Square and provides most day to day necessities, though there is also a butcher and delicatessen and wine merchants with an exceptionally good choice of bottled beer. There's also a pharmacy, post office, and branches of Lloyds TSB and Barclays banks, though neither of the latter featured cash-points at the time of writing (but see Londis above). Several antique, craft and gift shops provide counterpoint to day to day requirements, notably a shop selling Christmas goods all year round!

BUSES - since the closure of its railway station back in the Sixties, there is regrettably (and irrationally) no longer a public transport link with Oxford. There are, however, reasonable bus services to/from Swindon and Cirencester - Tel: 01793 522243.

OCCASIONALLY, in its inexperience, this youthfully navigable Thames coils itself up like an intestine, producing fiendishly difficult bends for the steerers of anything longer than a cabin cruiser to deal with. From the relative safety of the Thames Path, ramblers can watch the less-adept's attempts to extract themselves from sandbanks with feigned concern and hidden glee: it was always thus. But whether walking or boating, or simply picnicking on its banks, there is no escaping the inherent beauty of the river, nor its capacity for filtering out the less admirable excesses of 21st century living.

Parcels of land at Buscot are within the care of the National Trust. The riverside parsonage can be visited, though only by prior appointment. Its car park occupies the site of a wharf where, amongst other items, local cheese was despatched by barge to Oxford and London. Frustratingly, however, all trace of the vast Berkshire Distillery which stood upstream of the lock, has vanished. Brainchild of Robert Campbell,

the mid 19th century Australian denizen of Buscot Hall, and part of his 'great agricultural experiment', whereby the estate was intensively farmed for the production of sugar beet, distilled into alcohol and exported to France for brandy making. Another endeavour was a brick and tile works which had its own wharf at the end of a short canal off the main river channel.

Eaton Footbridge marks the site of the last flash lock on the river, extant until as relatively recently as 1937. It was operated by an arcane arrangement of 'rymers' and 'paddles' far too complicated to unravel here. A pub called The Anchor overlooked the river here until it burnt down with loss of life in 1979.

But it is perhaps Kelmscott Manor which is the cynosure on the reach between the locks at Buscot and Grafton. Sixteenth century in origin, with its mellow stonework masked from the river by a raucous high-rise community of rooks, it is inevitably for its associations with William Morris and the Pre-Raphaelites that the house is valued now. Morris arrived here in 1871, initially sharing the manor with Dante Gabriel Rossetti who paid rather

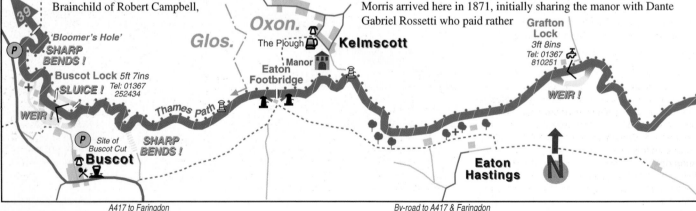

too much attention to Jane Morris (who sat for many of his best known paintings) for the household's equilibrium. A man of tremendous energy - political activist, forward thinker, designer of wallpapers, stained glass windows and furniture, early supporter of the Arts & Crafts movement, founder of the Society for the Protection of Ancient Buildings, and writer of poetry and prose - Morris employed Kelmscott as a summer retreat for quarter of a century and relished in particular its proximity to the Thames, alongside which his busy workaday life was spent at Hammersmith. His Utopian work of fiction, *News From Nowhere*, describes a dream-voyage upstream from London to Kelmscott (in 2003 of all years), encountering above Oxford 'whispering beds of reeds and willows dipping into the stream'. He must, presumably lie most contentedly in Kelmscott churchyard alongside his wife Jane and daughter May.

The Pre-Raphaelites busied themselves hereabouts: the tiny church at Eaton Hastings features glass by Burne-Jones. Grafton lock is typical in its remoteness. Opened in 1896 it had to wait until 1960 to receive the benefit of electricity.

Buscot *(Map 40)*

A model settlement dating from 1879, thankfully unimpinged upon by the A417, though you will have to brave its verges should you wish to visit the National Trust's Buscot House. The Old Parsonage is also a NT property, though only accessible by written request. The village shop may offer meagre provisions, but in its role as a tea room, with tables in the garden, it would be difficult to beat. BUSCOT HOUSE - Tel: 01367 240786. 18th century neo-classical house set in fine parkland 1 mile south-east of the river. Generally open April to September Wed-Sun.

Kelmscott *(Map 40)*

Morris's opinion that Kelmscott represents 'heaven on earth' is not much wide of the mark. His beloved Manor House is managed by the Society of Antiquaries and flings its doors open to an appreciative public on Wednesdays and Saturdays from April to September - Tel: 01367 252486. Refreshments are available at such times and a shop deals in Morris memorabilia. The PLOUGH INN (Tel: 01367 253543) has flagstone floors - always a reassuring sign - and offers food and accommodation.

A plethora of drainage dykes and channels serves to emphasise how marshy this district once was. Predominantly flat and just over two hundred feet above sea level, it is a profoundly strange parcel of emptiness despite its proximity to Oxford and Swindon. Second World War fortifications provide a surreal accompaniment to the river which, like the Kennet & Avon Canal twenty miles to the south, was perceived as a strategic line of defence in the event of a German invasion. They look foolish now and inadequate, but conflict is always just around the corner, as the American war planes flying out of Brize Norton to the north all too frighteningly confirm. One feels safer with antiquities such as Radcot Bridge, 13th century in origin and generally regarded as the oldest on the Thames, though possibly predated

by a Saxon structure. All of which is academic to boaters, who pass beneath an upstart new bridge engineered by William Jessop in 1790 as part of improvements to the Upper Thames carried out in conjunction with the opening of the Thames & Severn Canal. With its humped-back and simple single arch it has all the hallmarks of a canal bridge, but its location on a double bend, requires care and concentration from steerers. The old navigation channel has been adopted for private moorings.

Radcot Lock is exceptionally pretty; the keeper being the proud guardian of a delightful clinker-built skiff where most make do with functional punts. There are views south to folly-topped Cromwell's Battery at Faringdon. From Old Man's Bridge you can walk along blissful lanes to the mellow little town of Bampton. In 1954 an American B47 bomber crashed beside the river at Old Man's Bridge in mysterious

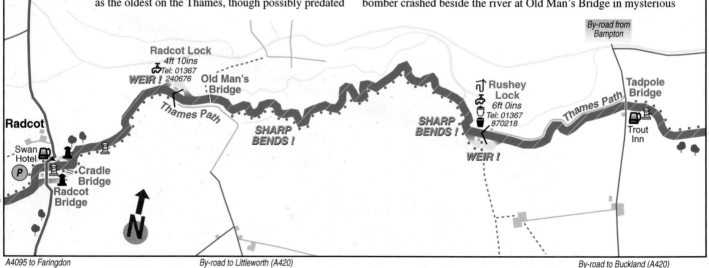

circumstances at the time of the Cold War.

    Sequences of sharp bends characterise the river's progress between Radcot and Rushey locks: narrowboat captains have their work cut out to follow the channel; walkers are tempted to cut corners! More embarrassingly, one can run out of superlatives describing these Upper Thames locks, somehow more charming than their mechanised brethren from Godstow downstream. In a way they are reminiscent of country stations, resonating with suspended activity between the appearance of boats as branchline

stations did between trains, leaving the lock-keeper, like the stationmaster of yore, to tend his geraniums and cogitate upon eternity.

    The steeple of Bampton church plays hide and seek with you on the reach between Rushey and Tadpole Bridge. The towpath changes sides, becoming a metalled access road to Rushey Lock. Tadpole Bridge was built in 1802 and consists of a single arch. A coal wharf once presented a busy scene where moorings are now provided beside the Trout Inn.

Radcot *(Map 41)*

The older bridge has been fought over down the centuries, but now the only hullabaloo is the traffic on the Witney to Faringdon road, slowed by the presence of traffic lights on each narrow bridge. THE SWAN HOTEL (Tel: 01367 810220) boasts a congenial landlord, a gorgeous waterside garden, has Old Speckled Hen on tap, and provides food and accommodation.

Bampton

Once widely known as Bampton-in-the-Bush, on account of its inaccessibility by road, this delightfully mellow old town lies two miles to the north of Tadpole Bridge, or a pleasant walk of similar distance via field paths from Rushey Lock. It is a celebrated centre of Morris Dancing as evinced by the MORRIS CLOWN (Tel: 01993 850217) a Free House where Aunt Sally is played. THE TROUT (Tel: 01367 870382) at Tadpole Bridge offers Archers, accommodation and a sophisticated menu.

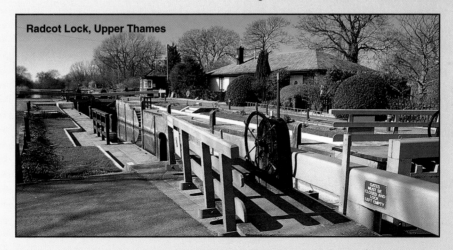

Radcot Lock, Upper Thames

THIS, you'll discover in due course, is an altogether different Thames from the floating-gin-palace-infested waters of the middle river. Thank Oxford's low-slung Osney Bridge for that, as well as the restricted depth and convoluted nature of the upper reaches, and the fact that the majority of boaters feel more at home in the lowest common denominator comfort zone of Henley and Windsor. Up here, in highest common factor country, perseverance and initiative are rewarded by an absence of crowds, the only likely observers of your progress being geese and swans and sheep. It also becomes apparent why the upper Thames bargemen of the 19th century favoured the North Wilts and Wilts & Berks canal route between Cricklade and Abingdon over this narrow and winding watercourse. Pollarded willows frame the river's course pleasingly - electricity pylons less so. Cattle stoop to drink where the banks have become eroded into sandy bays: it's all very bucolic and satisfyingly remote.

The Thames hereabouts used to form the boundary between Oxfordshire to the north and Berkshire to the south. Regrettably, it is Oxon. on both banks now: topic for discussion - is change invariably a dynamic for good, or a chronic human mechanism designed to compensate for inactivity? We oscillate from reorganization to reorganization, yet remain as far as ever from the rainbow's end of perfection.

Shifford derives its name from 'sheep ford' and was once a much busier spot than the farm and Victorian chapel encountered today. Alfred the Great held a parliament here in 885. Shifford Lock is the youngest on the river, having been opened in 1898 as part of a new cut by-passing the lengthy loop through Duxford, though small craft may still explore this side arm up as far as the old ford itself. The Thames Path adopts this route as well, temporarily deserting the river east of Tenfoot Bridge.

By-road from Cote

Shifford

By-road from Aston

Chimney

Shifford Lock
7ft 4ins
Tel: 01367 870247

41

Thames Path

SHARP BENDS !

Tenfoot Bridge

Duxford

ford

Thameside Farm

Thames Path

Harrowdown Hill
325ft

N

Thames Path

By-road to Hinton Waldrist ☎

Footpath to Longworth ☎ 🍴

IT can be disorientating to discover the Thames flowing *north* as is the case in the vicinity of Bablock Hythe. Without the natural obstacle of Cumnor Hills, it might have missed Oxford entirely (and where would the dark blue boat crew then be ?) and headed directly for the sea via Abingdon, only half a dozen miles from Bablock Hythe by road, but nearly twenty by water. Ideally you need copies of Matthew Arnold's *The Scholar Gypsy* and *Thyrsis* with you, lengthy mid-19th century poems which echo the mellow, elegiac beauty of the Upper Thames: 'Or in my boat I lie, Moor'd to the cool bank in the summer heats, 'Mid wide grass meadows which the sunshine fills,' are lines which boaters can readily relate to. The Scholar Gypsy crossed the stripling Thames at Bablock Hythe, and so too can present-day walkers as long as the ferry, owned by the landlord of The Ferryman Inn (Tel: 01865 880028) is operating. Quite what Matthew Arnold, let alone Thyrsis, would make of the caravan park which

lines the riverbank at Bablock Hythe, is probably best not dwelt on. Less intrusive, are the dwellings with boathouses which line what was formerly the Berkshire bank of the river south of Northmoor Lock. Marked by four tall poplar trees, Northmoor Lock dates from late 19th century improvements to the Upper Thames. Footpaths lead from this isolated spot to the villages of Appleton and Northmoor. Similarly, each village can be reached from Hart's Footbridge, the site of an old flash weir. A mid 18th century weir-keeper's daughter here was wooed and won by an aristocratic Oxford undergraduate. They married in Northmoor Church in 1766.

Newbridge illustrates the folly of ever calling anything 'new'. New Bridge is the second oldest on the river, dating from the middle of the 13th century, and being

A415 from Witney

R. Windrush

Newbridge
The Rose Revived

Thames Path

By-road from Stanton Harcourt

By-road from Northmoor

Bablock Hythe

The Ferryman ferry (seasonal)

44

Public right of way from Northmoor

Northmoor Lock
4ft 1in
Tel: 01865 862923

Thames Path

WEIR !

Public footpath to Appleton

By-road to Cumnor

'new' only in relation to Radcot. The River Windrush has its source near Bourton-on-the-Water up in the Cotswolds, and flows down through Burford and the blanket-making town of Witney. Wilson MacArthur wrote a book about it, published by Cassell as part of a series of river-following books, after the Second World War, when, grateful for having held on to what we might well have lost - as a nation and as individuals - there was still a market for such homespun topographical titles. Now we prefer our vicarious travels to be conducted ideally in more exotic climes. It would be pleasant to lean over the lichened parapet of one of its upstream facing arches, watch the waters of the Windrush adding their weight to the Thames, and consider the scene here in 1644 when Cromwell's troops captured the bridge from the Royalists following the briefest skirmish, were the Abingdon to Witney road not so busy nowadays. The Thames Path detours away from the river north of Bablock Hythe, returning by Farmoor Reservoir. If the ferry is operating, walkers have the option of using it to cross the river and continue along the former towpath on the east side of the river, rejoining the Thames Path at Pinkhill Lock.

Newbridge *(Map 43)*

THE MAYBUSH - riverside (south bank), customer moorings. Tel: 01865 300624. Convivial riverside pub vying for trade with its better known rival on the opposite bank. Good bar meals.
THE ROSE REVIVED - riverside (north bank), customer moorings. Tel: 01865 300221. Hugely popular, this spacious and historic inn attracts a wide variety of patrons from far and wide. Bar and restaurant food; gondola hire in the summer months!

Bablock Hythe & Northmoor *(Map 43)*

THE FERRYMAN INN - riverside. Tel: 01865 880028. Another famous Upper Thames hostelry continuing to trade on its historic reputation. Bar and restaurant food, and accommodation. Tea dances and music hall shows! Operators of the ferry in summer months.
For a quieter pint, try the Red Lion *in Northmoor - Tel: 01865 300301*
BUSES - Stagecoach service No.18 offers Mon-Sat links with Oxford and Bampton, making this a useful staging post for Thames Path walkers - Tel: 01865 772250.

Appleton *(Map 43)*

Sleepy village on the old Berkshire side of the Thames accessible on foot from Northmoor Lock. Post office stores and a pub called the PLOUGH INN (Tel: 01865 862441).

Eynsham *(Map 44)*

Picturesque and soporific, Eynsham is a worthwhile walk along a pavemented road from the Thames at Swinford Bridge. Shops, pubs and takeaways (though no bank as far as we could see) give you an excuse for the exercise involved. Closer to the river, you'll find the TALBOT INN - Tel: 01865 881348. Frequent buses to Oxford railway station - Tel: 01865 772250.

LOW-BANKED, and at its most northerly, the Thames arcs around the poet Matthew Arnold's 'green-muffled' Cumnor Hills. Deciduously wooded, and roamed by deer, Wytham Hill rises to 539 feet, the highest point of the Cumnor 'range'. One of the Thames's most gorgeous tributaries, the River Evenlode, makes its entry a little over a mile downstream of Eynsham Lock. The Evenlode's source lies near Stow-on-the-Wold and flows down through the remnants of the ancient Forest of Wychwood. It was too shallow and meandering a river ever to be practically navigable, but at the beginning of the 19th century, the Duke of

Marlborough funded the construction of Cassington Cut, a canal not quite a mile long, mainly to serve the mill at Cassington but also as an outlet for Eynsham malt. It was last used around 1870, but remains a useful drainage channel. Cassington was a 'halt' on the Oxford to Fairford railway. Predominantly hauled by 'Pannier' tank locomotives, the last passenger train trundled off stage forever in 1962, though the line had enjoyed an Indian Summer of busyness during the Second World War, bringing men and materials to the army camps and military aerodromes in the area. Paul Jennings wrote wistfully about its demise in *Just A Few Lines*, long

out of print but reasonably easily obtained secondhand.

SWINFORD TOLL BRIDGE was built in 1777 and many consider it one of the most handsome on the Thames. Three of its nine honey-coloured stone arches span the water. A classically-styled toll house abuts its northern approach, but the keeper spends most of his time in a plastic shelter nowadays, bamboozled by levels of road traffic that the 18th century Earl of Abingdon can never have envisaged when he bought out the ferry and commissioned William Taylor to design the bridge. Much of Oxfordshire derives its water supplies from Farmoor Reservoir which in turn draws its water from the Thames.

Map labels

- Eynsham
- The Talbot
- Swinford Toll Bridge
- Pinkhill Lock — 3ft 6ins — Tel: 01865 881452 — WEIR !
- Eynsham Lock — 2ft 9ins — WEIR ! — Tel: 01865 881324
- Thames Path
- B4044
- Oxford Cruisers
- waterworks
- pumping station
- Farmoor Reservoir
- Farmoor
- Wytham Great Wood
- Cassington Cut
- R. Evenlode
- Course of Fairford
- Oxford Rly
- A40 from Cheltenham
- A40 to Oxford
- Thames Path
- B4017 to Abingdon
- B4044 to Oxford

KING'S LOCK, depending on your direction of travel, is the first or last on the Upper Thames to be hand-operated - Godstow, in contrast, is mechanised. Just upstream of King's, a backwater leads to the Duke's Cut offering access (for boaters, *not* walkers) to the Oxford Canal. Working narrowboats passed through the Duke's Cut until the 1950s with Warwickshire coal for the paper mills at Wolvercote.

Godstow Lock is overlooked by the ruins of a 12th century nunnery indelibly associated with Rosamund Clifford, the 'Fair' mistress of Henry II. When the lock cut was being dug workmen disturbed the bones of long departed nuns.

The Thames' entry into Oxford (or exit from) is magnificently made along the banks of Port Meadow against a backdrop mostly consisting of 'dreaming spires' with one or two less salubrious 21st century additions. Between Godstow and Binsey the reach is often busy with schoolboy rowing fours and eights accompanied by the sharp but cultured megaphone assisted bark of sports masters.

A second opportunity to make for the Oxford Canal comes via the Sheepwash Channel upstream of Osney's low headroom bridge (7ft 6ins max): full details of the canal are to be found in *Pearson's Canal Companion to the Oxford & Grand Union Canals,* whilst the Thames downstream of Osney as far as Reading is covered in the *Kennet & Avon + Middle Thames Canal & River Companion.* Whichever route you decide to take, great adventures await you, but you will find nothing more lovely than the Upper Thames.

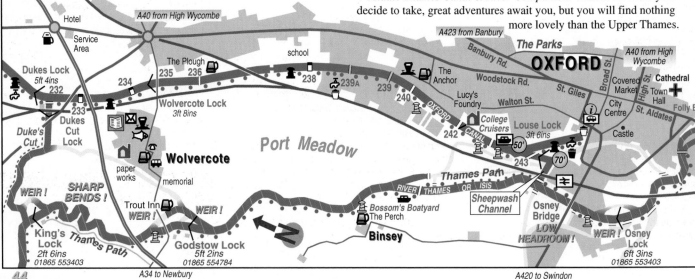

*Figures relate to River Thames between King's Lock and Osney Lock

Oxford (Map 45)

Oxford's pressures seem not so much 'Town & Gown' nowadays, as 'Town & Tourism'. Yet it can still remind you of an exclusive club, where the best the casual visitor can do is press their nose up against the lattice windowpane and peer enviously at the academically privileged world revealed within. Like Thomas Hardy's hero, we are all 'Obscure Judes', in awe of this world-renowned seat of learning. In Oxford - perhaps more than in any other English city - time stands quite literally still. Whole quadrangles and cloisters seem frozen into a medieval eternity where only the undergraduates ubiquitous bicycles break the chronological spell. From the perspective of the river boat, or the open-topped tourist bus, the sightseer can derive a vicarious wisdom. After all, you can now truthfully recall: "When I was at Oxford."

WATERMANS ARMS - riverside above Osney Lock. Tel: 01865 248832. Cosy local, bar food.

LAMB & FLAG - St Giles. Ancient inn associated with C.S. Lewis and Tolkien and, in recent years, one Endeavour Morse. Lunchtime food. Tel: 01865 515787.

THE NOSEBAG - St Michael's Street. Tel: 01865 721033. Long established wholefood cafe/restaurant.

FISHERS - St Clements. Close to Magdalen Bridge. Fish and seafood restaurant. Tel: 01865 243003.

THE PERCH - Thames-side, Binsey. Thatched riverside inn set back behind a mask of trees. Large garden, wide menu. Tel: 01865 240386.

LIVEBAIT - The Turl. Tel: 01865 324930. Contemporary seafood restaurant.

BROWNS - Woodstock Road. Tel: 01865 319655. Well established brasserie converted from former Morris garage.

LE PETIT BLANC - Walton Street. Tel: 01865 510999. Raymond Blanc owned restaurant hidden away in the backstreets of Jericho.

RESTAURANT ELIZABETH - St Aldates. An Oxford institution, predominantly French cooking. Tel: 01865 242230.

Drawing on a wide range of custom and taste, Oxford's shops are inspired to an admirable eclecticism. The COVERED MARKET (off High Street) hosts the most wonderful cross-section of retailers and those who have travelled the length and breadth of this guide from Bristol will find a resemblance to the market there. As befits a seat of learning, there are some good bookshops, though not, sadly, as many secondhand and antiquarian outlets as we seem to remember.

TOURIST INFORMATION - The Old School, Gloucester Green. Tel: 01865 726871. Assemble here for guided walking tours relating to many aspects of Oxford.

GUIDE FRIDAY - open top bus rides with running commentary. Regular departures from the railway station and city centre stops. Tel: 01865 790522.

THE OXFORD STORY - Broad Street. Ride through Oxford's rich history. Tel: 01865 728822.

MUSEUM OF OXFORD - St Aldates. Tel: 01865 815559.

ASHMOLEAN MUSEUM - Beaumont Street. Tel: 01865 278000. Britain's oldest public museum (not Mons) displaying European, Egyptian and Near Eastern antiquities.

CARFAX TOWER - Carfax. 99 steps to heaven for a bird's eye view of the city of dreaming spires.

PUNT HIRE - Oxford's most traditional means of seduction can be hired from boat houses at Folly Bridge on the Thames and Magdelan Bridge on the Cherwell.

COLLEGES - over thirty colleges make up Oxford University. Many of them are world famous such as Balliol and Merton which are both of 13th century origin; Magdalen (pronounced 'Maudlin') which dates from 1458; and Christ Church founded in 1525 by Cardinal Wolsey. The general public may look around most of them in the afternoons.

OPEN SPACES - much of Oxford's charm rests in the proliferation of green spaces, the city's lungs. These include: The Parks, Christ Church Meadow and Port Meadow. A stroll - or a picnic - on any of them comes as a refreshing experience after the hurly burly of the main thoroughfares and helps put Oxford in the context of its riverside setting.

TRAINS - services along the Thames Valley to/from Reading and London and connections to/from the midlands and the north. Tel: 08457 484950.

BUSES - contact the Oxford Bus Company on 01865 785400.

Godstow (Map 45)

THE TROUT - adjacent weir channel. Arguably the most famous of the three Upper Thames' 'Trouts'. Foaming weir and foaming pints. Wide range of food. Tel: 01865 554485.

How to use the Maps

There are forty-five numbered maps whose layout is shown by the Route Planner inside the front cover. Maps 1 to 7 cover the River Avon; Maps 8 to 13 cover the Stratford Canal; Maps 14 to 20 cover the Worcester & Birmingham Canal; Maps 21 to 26 cover the River Severn; Maps 27 to 30 cover the Gloucester & Sharpness Canal; Maps 31 to 39 cover the yet to be restored Cotswold Canals; and Maps 39 to 45 cover the upper reaches of the River Thames. The maps are easily read in either direction. The simplest way of progressing from map to map is to proceed to the next map numbered from the edge of the map you are on. Figures quoted at the top of each map refer to distance per map, locks per map and average cruising time. An alternative indication of timings from centre to centre can be found on the Route Planner. Obviously, cruising times vary with the nature of your boat and the number of crew, so quoted times should be taken only as an estimate. Neither do times quoted take into account any delays which might occur at lock flights in high season or against strong current conditions on the river sections.

Using the Text

Each map is accompanied by a route commentary, and details of most settlements passed through are given close by. Regular readers will already be familiar with our somewhat irreverent approach. But we 'tell it as we find it', in the belief that the users of this guide will find this attitude more valuable than a strict towing of the tourist publicity line.

Towpath Walking

The simplest way to go canal exploring is on foot. It costs largely nothing and you are free to concentrate on the passing scene; something that boaters are not always at liberty to do. Unfortunately the same cannot always be said of rivers where, down the centuries, landowners have cordoned off many ancient rights of way. The Avon is a typical case in point, long sections of its banks being inaccessible to pedestrians. Thankfully, the Severn and the Thames are now accompanied by long distance paths, though

again there are sections out of bounds to the general public, making detours necessary. In the course of preparing this guide we have walked every yard of the relevant towpaths and a good proportion of the river paths and can thoroughly recommend them as a means of getting to know these inland waterways without a boat. As usual the maps show the quality of the towpath, and whilst it does vary from area to area, none of it should prove problematical for walkers.

Towpath Cycling

Cycling canal towpaths is an increasingly popular activity. At present it is theoretically necessary for cyclists wishing to use towpaths to acquire a free of charge permit from a British Waterways office - see opposite page for appropriate addresses. Unfortunately significant sections of the Worcester & Birmingham and Stratford-on-Avon canals are currently out of bounds to cyclists, but British Waterways will be able to advise when you apply for a permit. Cycling on the river path is not formally encouraged and the surface, in any case, rarely conducive to a pleasurable journey.

Boating

Boating on inland waterways is an established, though relatively small facet of the UK holiday industry. There are over 20,000 privately owned boats registered on the canals, but in addition to these numerous firms offer boats for hire. These range from small operators with half a dozen boats to sizeable fleets run by companies with several bases. Most hire craft have all the creature comforts you are likely to expect. In the excitement of planning a boating holiday you may give scant thought to the contents of your hire boat, but at the end of a hard day's boating such matters take on more significance and a well equipped, comfortable boat, large enough to accommodate your crew with something to spare, can make the difference between a good holiday and an indifferent one.

Traditionally, hire boats are booked out by the week or fortnight though many firms now offer more flexible short breaks or extended weeks. All reputable hire firms give newcomers tuition in boat handling and lock working, and first-timers soon find themselves adapting to the pace of things 'on the cut'. Turn to page 94 for contact details of boat hire operations.

Navigational Advice

LOCKS are part of the charm of inland waterway cruising, but they can be potentially dangerous environments for children, pets and careless adults. Use of them should be methodical and unhurried, whilst special care should be exercised in rain, frost and snow when slippery hazards abound. We lack space for detailed instructions on lock operation: trusting that if you own your own boat you will, by definition, already be experienced in canal cruising; whilst first-time hire boaters should be given tuition in the operation of locks before they set out. Briefly, however, those new to these cruising waters should note that the locks on the Stratford and Worcester & Birmingham canals are of the narrow variety and pose no undue difficulties, whereas the locks on the rivers Avon, Severn and Thames are of widebeam dimensions and thus capable of taking narrowboats side by side. Landing stages are provided up and downstream of each chamber to enable crews to get on and off their craft. Travelling upstream boats should be secured with lines fore and aft once they are in the lock chamber to prevent them being buffeted by turbulence as the lock fills. The locks on the River Severn are automated. A guide to boating on the River Severn and the Gloucester & Sharpness Canal is obtainable from BW in Gloucester. On the Upper Thames all the locks are usually manned. Their telephone numbers appear on our maps. We recommend boaters on the Thames acquire a copy of the Environment Agency's *A User's Guide to the River Thames*.

MOORING on the canals featured in this guide is per usual practice - ie on the towpath side, away from sharp bends, bridge-holes and narrows. An open bollard symbol represents visitor mooring sites, either as designated specifically by British Waterways or, in some cases, as recommended by our personal experience or that of our regular correspondents. Of course, one of the great joys of canal boating has always been the opportunity of mooring wherever (sensibly) you like. In recent years, however, it has become obvious that there are an increasing number of undesirable locations, particularly in urban areas, where mooring is not recommended for fear of vandalism, theft or abuse.

CLOSURES (or 'stoppages' in canal parlance) traditionally occur on the inland waterways between November and April, during which time most of the heavy maintenance work is undertaken. Occasionally, however, an emergency stoppage, or perhaps water restriction, may be imposed at short notice, closing part of the route you intend to use. Up-to-date details are normally available from hire bases. Alternatively, British Waterways provide a recorded message for private boaters, the number to ring being: 01923 201402. Information is also available on BW's internet site at www.british-waterways.org

Useful Contacts

BRITISH WATERWAYS
Stratford and Worcester & Birmingham canals - British Waterways Lapworth, Brome Hall Lane, Lapworth, Solihull, West Midlands B94 5RB. Tel: 01564 784634 722859.
River Severn, Gloucester & Sharpness Canal, Cotswold Canals - British Waterways, Harbour House, West Quay, Gloucester Docks, Gloucester GL1 2LG. Tel: 01452 318000.
British Waterways operate a central emergency telephone service - Tel: 0800 4799947.

RIVER AVON
UPPER AVON NAVIGATION TRUST - Bridge 63, Harvington, Evesham, Worcs WR11 5NR. Tel: 01386 870526.
LOWER AVON NAVIGATION TRUST - Mill Wharf, Mill Lane, Wyre Piddle, Pershore, Worcs WR10 2JF. Tel: 01386 552517.

RIVER THAMES
Environment Agency, Kings Meadow House, Kings Meadow Road, Reading RG1 8DQ Tel: 0118 953 5000.

The Inland Waterways Association was founded in 1946 to campaign for retention of the canal system. Many routes now open to pleasure boaters may not have been so but for this organisation. Membership details may be obtained from: Inland Waterways Association, PO Box 114, Rickmansworth WD3 1ZY. Tel: 01923 711114. Fax 01923 897000.

The Cotswold Canal Trust is an affiliation of bodies determined to see the Stroudwater Navigation and Thames & Severn Canal restored to navigable status to effect a broad beam link between the Severn and the Thames. Tel: 01285 643440.

The Stratford-on-Avon Canal Society was formed in 1962, for further information telephone 01789 205571.

Hire Bases with boating facilities

ALVECHURCH BOAT CENTRES - Alvechurch, Worcs & Birmingham Canal, Map 16. Tel: 0121-445 2909. One of four bases.

ANGLO WELSH - Tardebigge, Worcs & Birmingham Canal, Map 17. Tel: 0117 924 1200. One of eleven bases.

ANGLO WELSH - Wootton Wawen, Stratford-on-Avon Canal, Map 9. Tel: 0117 924 1200. One of eleven bases.

BIDFORD BOATS - Bidford, River Avon, Map 6. Tel: 01789 773205.

BLACK PRINCE HOLIDAYS, Stoke Wharf, Worcs & Birmingham Canal, Map 17. Tel: 01527 575115. One of six bases.

BROOK LINE - Dunhampstead Wharf, Worcs & Birmingham Canal, Map 19. Tel: 01905 773889.

COLLEGE CRUISERS - Oxford, Oxford Canal, Map 45. Tel: 01865 554343.

COTSWOLD BOAT HIRE - Lechlade, River Thames, Map 39. Tel: 01793 700241.

EVESHAM MARINA - Evesham Marina, River Avon, Map 4. Tel: 01386 48906.

HANDY BOATS - Upton Marina, River Severn, Map 23. Tel: 01684 593594.

OXFORDSHIRE NARROW BOATS - Eynsham, River Thames, Map 42. Tel: 01865 881698.

SHERBORNE WHARF - Birmingham, BCN, Map 14. Tel: 0121 455 6163.

STARLINE NARROWBOATS - Upton-on-Severn, River Severn, Map 23. Tel: 01684 593443.

VIKING AFLOAT - Worcester, Worcs & Birmingham Canal, Map 20. Tel: 01905 612707. One of four bases.

Boatyards with a range of facilities

BOSSOM'S BOATYARD - Oxford, R. Thames, Map 45. Tel: 01865 247780.

R. W. DAVIS & SON - Saul, Gloucester & Sharpness Canal, Map 28. Tel: 01452 740233.

HANBURY WHARF - Worcs & Birmingham Canal, Map 18. Tel: 01905 771018.

LECHLADE MARINA - Lechlade, River Thames, Map 39. Tel: 01367 252181.

FRANK LYONS - Warstock, Stratford-on-Avon Canal, Map 13. Tel: 0121 474 4977.

MILLSIDE BOATYARD - Pershore, River Avon, Map 3. Tel: 01386 552849.

JOHN PINDER & SONS - Worcester & Birmingham Canal, Stoke Prior, Map 17. Tel: 01527 876438.

OXFORDSHIRE NARROWBOATS - Eynsham, River Thames, Map 42. Tel: 01865 881698.

SANKEY MARINE - Evesham, River Avon, Map 4. Tel: 01386 442338.

SEABORN LEISURE - Kempsey, River Severn, Map 21. Tel: 01905 820295.

SHARPNESS MARINE - Sharpness, Gloucester & Sharpness Canal, Map 30. Tel: 01453 811476.

SWALLOW CRUISERS - Hockley Heath, Stratford-on-Avon Canal, Map 11. Tel: 01564 783442.

TEWKESBURY MARINA - Tewkesbury, River Avon, Map 1. Tel: 01684 293737.

UPTON MARINA - Upton-on-Severn, River Severn, Map 23. Tel: 01684 593111.

WELFORD BOAT STATION - Welford, River Avon, Map 6. Tel: 01789 750878.

WESTERN ROAD MARINA - Stratford-on-Avon, Stratford Canal, Map 8. Tel: 01789 263772.

Day Boat Hire

ANGLO WELSH - Wootton Wawen, Stratford Canal, Map 9. Tel: 01564 793427.

Tardebigge, Worcester & Birmingham Canal, Map 17. Tel: 01527 873898.

BANCROFT CRUISERS - Stratford-on-Avon, River Avon, Map 7. Tel: 01789 269669.

COTSWOLD BOAT HIRE - Lechlade, River Thames, Map 39. Tel: 01793 700241.

DROITWICH CANAL CO - Ladywood, Droitwich Barge Canal. Tel: 01905 458352.

HANDY BOATS - Upton Marina, River Severn, Map 23. Tel: 01684 593594.

HANDSAM - Evesham, River Avon, Map 4. Motor and rowing boats. Tel: 01386 834070.

OXFORDSHIRE NARROW BOATS - Eynsham, River Thames, Map 42. Tel: 01865 882235.

RIVERSIDE - Lechlade, River Thames, Map 39. Motor and rowing boats. Tel: 01367 252229.

SLIMBRIDGE BOAT STATION - Gloucester & Sharpness Canal, Map 29. Tel: 01453 899190.

TELSTAR CRUISES - Tewkesbury, River Avon, Map 1. Tel: 01684 294088. Day boat hire. Book direct.

Trip Boats

BANCROFT CRUISERS - Trips on the Avon at Stratford, Map 7. Tel: 01789269669.

BICKERLINE - Trips on the Severn at Worcester, Map 20. Tel: 01905 831639.

GLOUCESTER LEISURE CRUISES - trips from Gloucester Docks, Map 25. Tel: 01452 318200.

HANDSAM BOAT CO - river trips from Evesham, Map 4. Tel: 01386 834070.

NEW WORCESTER STEAMER CO. - river trips from Worcester, Map 20. Tel: 01905 617070.

SALTERS - scheduled services from Oxford southwards on the Thames, Map 45. Tel: 01865 243421.

SEVERN LEISURE CRUISES - trips from Upton-on-Severn, Map 23. Tel: 01684 593112.

TELESTAR - river trips on the Avon from Tewkesbury. Tel: 01684 294088.

Disabled Boats

DART - Gloucestershire Disabled Afloat Riverboats Trust. Tel: 01452 410022.

Acknowledgements

Brian Collings designed and executed the front cover; David & Jennifer Alison and Keith Goss provided extra photographs as credited; the staff of the Local Studies section at Gloucester Library were particularly helpful in the provision of 6" OS mapping dating from the 1920s - grateful thanks to them all. Thanks also to Toby Bryant of Central Waterways Supplies, Jackie Pearson, Karen Tanguy and Cristina Negri and all her colleagues at STIGE.

Boating Directory

Waterways World

the *NUMBER ONE* inland waterways magazine

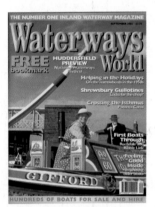

● **news** each month *Waterways World* reports all that is happening around the waterway system.

● **canal heritage** restoration reports, waterway history - the boats, people and companies that worked and built the canal system.

● **boat sales** more boats for sale every month than any other inland waterway magazine.

● **practical advice** for boat owners and aspiring boat owners - new and used narrowboat reviews, engine development, the latest equipment narrowboat fit-outs and much more.

● **enjoyment of the waterways** explore a different waterway each month with cruising reports, events, hire boat reviews, continental cruising.

Available from newsagents, boatyards and on subscription

Published by Waterways World Ltd, 151 Station Street, Burton-on-Trent, Staffs DE14 1BG   Telephone 01283 742970